The Leaders Praise *Write on Target*

Donna Stein and Floyd Kemske have written a very practical *how-to* for newcomers and non-writers, and a powerful *reminder* checklist for experienced practitioners. Wish I'd had this book when I first started out!

> **Katharine Barr**
> **President**
> **Katharine Barr & Associates**

Write on Target is not only a great introduction to copywriting for aspiring direct marketing creatives, it's a valuable refresher course for veterans. Read it, then keep it for inspiration. You'll find yourself going back to it again and again.

> **Jack Crumbley**
> **Partner**
> **Holland Mark Martin**

…deserves a place of honor in a DM copywriter's basic library—right there between Bob Stone's "bible" and that well-thumbed thesaurus.

> **Ginny Daly**
> **Daly Direct Marketing**

Here's a new book that's a jewel! You'll read with relish a sampling of the best direct marketing ever mailed. At the same time you'll enjoy a rare reminiscence of some of the medium's early stars.

> **Lu Corbett Daly**
> **Promotion Writer**

Every chapter is "right on target." They cover all aspects of copy creatively, completely, cogently and carefully. It's also cerebral for the authors explain the strategy and thinking that made the campaigns successful.

Readers will be glad it also covers cyberspace since this will be increasingly important in DM as we move into the next millennium. The examples are particularly helpful.

John Jay Daly
Chevy Chase, MD
Former Senior VP, Direct
Marketing Association,
Washington DC

As Director of the Center for Direct Marketing at Merrimack College, I see lots of direct marketing reference and instructional materials. This clear, useful, comprehensive and well-written copywriting guide was about the best I've read to date.

Leslie Dangel, Director
Center for Direct Marketing
Merrimack College

Write on Target is truly a cornerstone book—one you'll read, reread, and refer to often. I suggest that this superb book be in the personal professional libraries of creative and account service people working for both direct response and general advertising agencies, plus the clients they serve—particularly those who want better *results* from their advertising budgets.

Earl Hogan
Earl Hogan Direct Marketing

This comprehensive book on how to write for all the important direct marketing media is written by two professionals who have a track record of success. They share the inside thinking on how they go about writing those award-winning letters.

Here's a book that gives the proven principles of direct marketing writing…and most importantly *Write on Target* illustrates these techniques with a number of the classic letters of direct marketing plus a number of the new winners. An enjoyable read and one that will lead to greater results and profits for your direct marketing efforts…filled with the proven principles of direct marketing writing—illustrated with some of the classic letters of direct marketing plus a number of new winners.

Roland Kuniholm
President, Kuniholm Associates,
Inc., Reston, VA

Write on Target is an excellent handbook for all who want to improve their direct marketing copywriting knowledge and skills. Donna Baier Stein and her co-author Floyd Kemske are to be commended for providing their readers with one example after another of writing to specific markets and targeting for direct response, the end goal of every word you write in a field where sheer creativity is the magic element that separates "just-average" writers from the great ones.

I recommend this valuable manual for all who write on target!

Ed McLean
Ed McLean Creative Services

Donna Baier Stein and Floyd Kemske have crafted a true "how-to" manual for copywriters of tomorrow and today. For students considering a career in creative, *Write on Target* belongs at the top of the syllabus. Those already started in the business will discover a plethora of invaluable information, techniques and trade secrets. And for all the seasoned writers out there, this is the book we all said we were going to write. I, for one, am delighted that somebody finally did!

Erica Meyer
Epsilon Creative

When you are sitting there, on a tight deadline, facing a blank computer screen that must turn into informative, motivational copy, pick up a copy of *Write on Target*. It's filled with examples of how to turn features into benefits and on ways to motivate prospects to action.

I especially recommend that anyone responsible for creating a home page on the Internet's World Wide Web, or those unhappy with the response to their home pages, read *Write on Target*. The authors discuss and provide direct marketing examples that show how good, well-chosen words were never more powerful.

Thomas D. Patrick
President
Windstar Wildlife Institute

Write on Target—Stein and Kemske are a winning team with sound advice for everyone who writes—or who longs to write—words that move and motivate. Listen to them and you'll create stronger copy whether it's direct mail, print, broadcast, or digital.

Joan Throckmorton

Well-written, clear and concise, filled with timely and timeless examples of how to craft effective direct marketing copy.

Dave Novak
Program Director, Direct
    Response Marketing Program
Bentley College, Division of
    Continuing Education

One of the most readable, enjoyable, and *usable* books on direct response copywriting I've ever seen. It takes a great direct response copywriter to write a great book on direct response copy. Donna Stein's done it with *Write on Target.* If you're just starting out as a copywriter, this is the book you would want to read first.

Kate Petranech
Kate Petranech Advertising

Stein and Kemske have done a great job of combining their own theories on direct mail copywriting with a wonderful blend of information from yesterday's and today's most successful copywriters.

Roger S. Sakolove
Associate Creative Director and
    Senior Copywriter
Directech, Inc.

Donna Stein is one of the best direct response writers I know. What makes her writing so compelling is the fact that you always get the feeling that she's simply talking to you as a friend—not trying to sell you something—although, inevitably, she does a very good job at both!

Not surprisingly, *Write on Target* has that same wonderful quality. It's simple, direct, honest, sincere, easy to understand and very persuasive. You "get it" without feeling like you're plowing through a textbook. It masterfully combines the strategic and conceptual aspects of this challenging craft with practical how-to and proven techniques and formulas. Step by step, she helps you understand The Why, then supplements it with The How.

Any copywriter—and their client!—could benefit from the principles, tips, suggestions and observations included in this well-documented handbook.

Steven R. Tharler
Co-Founder and Partner
Tharler-Opper Marketing
Communications & Design

DONNA BAIER STEIN
FLOYD KEMSKE

Write On Target

The Direct Marketer's Copywriting Handbook

Foreword by Bob Stone

Printed on recyclable paper

NTC Business Books
a division of *NTC Publishing Group* • Lincolnwood, Illinois USA

To my father with whom I couldn't have lived without
catching his insistent and contagious love of direct marketing…

And to my mother who nurtured the love of words.

Library of Congress Cataloging-in-Publication Data

Stein, Donna Baier.
   Write on target: the direct marketer's copywriting handbook /
Donna Baier Stein, Floyd Kemske.
      p.   cm.
   Includes index.
   ISBN 0-8442-5914-4 (alk. paper)
   1. Sales letters—Handbooks, manuals, etc.   2. Advertising copy—
Handbooks, manuals, etc.   I. Kemske, Floyd, 1947-   . II. Title.
HF5730.S73   1997
653.8'1—dc20   96-32303
                                                               CIP

Published by NTC Business Books, a division of NTC Publishing Group
4255 West Touhy Avenue
Lincolnwood (Chicago), Illinois 60646-1975, U.S.A.

6 7 8 9 0 QB 9 8 7 6 5 4 3 2 1

CONTENTS

FOREWORD

"Response is the end goal of every word you write."

With these ten words Donna Baier Stein and Floyd Kemske set the stage for a most remarkable book.

Their focus throughout never deviates: <u>response is the end goal of every word you write</u>.

The structure of *Write on Target* provides a treasure trove of information for copywriters of the '90s and beyond. The authors tell you how and what to write whether your medium is mail, TV, radio, diskette, telephone, catalogs, print or the Internet.

Stein and Kemske, at home with all the electronic wonders, put them in their proper place. These are sophisticated tools to be used on command as the copywriter sees fit. Copy is king; the tools are the servants.

At a time in history when a computer program can become obsolete in a matter of months, it boggles the mind to realize that there is one "computer" that will never become obsolete—the human mind.

The mind is capable of taking an array of possibilities and molding them into a creative proposition so powerful that response becomes bountiful. In the final analysis, it's creativity that separates average writers from great writers.

Greatness is impossible without a keen understanding of human behavior. The authors of this book show how to generate positive action by understanding what motivates the consumer. This understanding is invaluable because, as Stein and Kemske point out, the difference between a well-written ad and a mediocre one can increase response exponentially.

Write on Target is replete with example after example of writing to specific markets. (That's where the tools come in.) The extra bonus in reading this book is that it is written by great copywriters. So it's easy to read and understand.

Take Chapter 11, "Copywriting for Online Media," for example. The author takes what is a terrifying subject to many—the mental leap into cyberspace—and removes all the fear and confusion. E-mail falls into step with direct mail. Online sites move into Internet malls where target audiences congregate. Complexities evaporate.

When you finish reading *Write on Target,* it is more than likely that you, too, will preach the Gospel—"Response is the end goal of every word you write!"

Bob Stone, Chairman Emeritus
Stone & Adler, Inc.

ACKNOWLEDGMENTS

As with many copywriting jobs, this book has felt the touch of many hands. In particular, I'd like to thank Peter Golden and Jonathan Evans for immense help and excellent writing. Jeff Laurie for his window on the online world. Axel Andersson for sharing his Axel Award-winning packages—that are not only well-written, but most importantly of all, *repeatedly pull a great response*. All the skillful direct marketing colleagues and friends cited in this book. And my "other" writing friends—Sally Brady, Beth Berg, Mary Mitchell, Alan Emmett, Rick Reynolds, Betsy Cox, Alex Johnson, Barbara Shapiro, Jan Brogan, Diane Bonavist and of course my multitalented co-author, Floyd Kemske. They *all* appreciate and honor the power of words.

And special thanks, of course, to Larry, Jonathan and Sarah, with love and gratitude always.

1

COPY
What It Is and What It Can Do

Never underestimate the power of words.

From tongue, pen, or computer screen…written or spoken in jest, anger, supplication, love…words entertain, stab, coax, restore. And even in this age of high technology and low attention span, words are one of your most vital marketing tools.

Words can make us **buy**. They tell us how sexy we'll look in that satin side-slit nightshirt. How successful and effective we'll be if we attend this time-management seminar. How satisfied we'll feel if we help preserve the Amazon's dwindling rain forests.

THE RIGHT WORDS

Nothing is more likely to make us buy than effective direct marketing copy—the words that speak directly to customers from catalogs, direct mail sales letters, telemarketing scripts, Web sites, and any number of other marketing vehicles that aim, above all else, to make customers respond to an offer in a predefined, measurable manner (filling out a coupon, for example, or phoning an 800 number). According to the Direct Marketing Association's *WEFA Economic Impact Study*, "U.S. sales revenue attributed to direct marketing [was] estimated to reach $1.1 trillion in 1995." This same study stated, "In 1995, 19.0 million workers [were] employed throughout the U.S. economy as a result of direct marketing activities."

Today, as direct marketing continues to grow exponentially and is integrated more and more into general advertising, the demand for well-written, response-boosting copy is increasing as well. Executives, managers, staff, and sales personnel from a wide spectrum of commercial and nonprofit arenas want to know how to write and evaluate an effective direct mail package or direct response space ad.

How do you find just the right words that will make your prospect buy?

Let's start with this premise: You have something you want to sell. It may be a product, a service, or a cause. It might be a subscription, a membership, or a corporate jet. It might be office supplies, dental work, or the idea that Columbia College or the Salvation Army is worth giving money to. It might be season tickets, computer software, or handcrafted furniture.

Whatever you are selling, you're going to have to ask yourself four questions before you even begin to use words:

---

1. What am I selling?
2. Who am I selling to?
3. Why am I selling this now?
4. What do I want my prospect to do?

The answers to these questions will determine what you write—whether your medium is mail, television, radio, diskette, telephone, kiosk, billboard, or the Internet. The medium you use will determine the specific components of your sales message, but these questions must be answered in order to effectively target your words. Today more than ever, advertising copy that isn't targeted to a specific market audience is simply ornamental. In *The One to One Future: Building Relationships One Customer at a Time* (New York: Currency/Doubleday, 1993), Don Peppers and Martha Rogers write:

> In the most fundamental transformation of commerce since the invention of the assembly line, information technology is driving businesses away from their one-size-fits-all struggle for mass brand recognition....

Already, too many advertising messages chase too little consumer attention....

Companies now have the computational power to remember every detail of a customer's transaction history. (It's about time. After all, customers have always been able to remember their interactions with companies.)....

By knowing more about an individual customer than the competitor, the 1:1 marketer can cater to that customer better, hence tapping a greater share of that customer's business....

For marketers and advertising professionals, this paradigm shift will mean a much greater challenge in personalized message delivery. For consumers, the shift may mean more messages that are useful, and fewer messages that we classify as "junk."

Messages that *are* useful, copy that *is* targeted, will be able to persuade...to sell.

THE MAIN DIFFERENCE BETWEEN DIRECT RESPONSE COPY AND ALL OTHER WRITING

Direct response copywriters are a singular breed because using words *to sell* is a singular undertaking. Copy begins with the same goal as fiction, journalism, even legal briefs: to get people's attention, and then hold it. Unlike a storyteller, a journalist, or a lawyer, however, the copywriter is not grabbing attention to entertain, report news, or argue a case. Good copy might do any or all of these things, but its principal aim is to sell. And unless that sale is made, the copy hasn't done its job.

A good copywriter has to be two people in one:
1. A skillful writer who can weave words in a way that seduces and sustains interest.
2. A salesperson who sticks his or her foot in the door, keeps it there despite difficulty, and won't leave without an order or strong expression of interest.

A good copywriter has to learn how to translate product features into customer benefits, motivate the reader to action, write with style, and keep it simple.

The worth of a great copywriter isn't subjective. That evaluation is determined by the numbers—the numbers of people who subscribe to the magazine, vote for the candidate, or buy the CD-ROMs. Unlike general advertising, direct marketing is *measurable* and *accountable*. Every package or ad you write will cost money and will bring in a number of results. The relation of those results to the costs will determine whether or not your copy is successful.

Top-notch direct marketing copywriters like Hank Burnett, Joan Throckmorton, Frank Johnson, Bill Jayme, Linda Wells, and others made their names not just because they wrote well, though some are true masters of the written word. They've become known because of the **response** they brought in. The 60 people who, back in 1968, invested $10,000 apiece in response to Hank Burnett's direct mail letter for the Admiral Richard E. Byrd Polar Center didn't do so just because Hank was a great writer but because he *wrote well to sell*. That classic letter persuaded 60 targeted recipients to join an expedition simply through words.

The aim of this book is to help you write to a specific market—whether you're a small business owner eager to write your own sales literature, an aspiring direct response copywriter, or a pro who wants to brush up on the basics in this new and challenging era of home pages and Web sites. We will examine two examples and begin by looking at how the Admiral Byrd letter successfully targeted *its* audience. The market for this unique transpolar expedition included upper-income travel-and-adventure–oriented prospects with the ability to invest $10,000 and 26 days. Recipients of the letter included Fortune 500 presidents and board chairmen, jet and turbojet aircraft owners, and boat owners older than 40.

The target audience is addressed from the letter's opening words. "As Chairman of the Admiral Richard E. Byrd Polar Center, it is my privilege to invite you" establishes a tone of intimacy between one successful person and another (Exhibit 1.1). The invitation to "become a member of an expedition which is destined to make both news and history" promises a benefit that's intriguing even to those who seem to have everything. And the candor of the second paragraph—"It will cost you $10,000 and about 26 days of your time. Frankly, you will endure some discomfort, and may even face some danger"—recognizes both the reader's wealth and bravery in a satisfying, manly way.

The letter is filled with other benefits that appeal to a well-heeled, proven, and adventurous group.

EXHIBIT 1-1   Admiral Richard E. Byrd Polar Center letter

```
                                                          Kirkland 7-3500
                            EDWARD C. BURSK
                             Soldiers Field
                        Boston, Massachusetts 02163

Editor
Harvard Business Review
                                  Please reply to me in care of:
                                  Transpolar Expedition
                                  Admiral Richard E. Byrd Polar Center
                                  18 Tremont Street
                                  Boston, Massachusetts 02108

                                                     September 3, 1968
Mr. R
            Ave.
Pelham, N.Y. 10803

Dear Mr. Archer:
```

As Chairman of the Admiral Richard E. Byrd Polar Center, it is my privilege to invite you to become a member of an expedition which is destined to make both news and history.

It will cost you $10,000 and about 26 days of your time. Frankly, you will endure some discomfort, and may even face some danger.

On the other hand, you will have the rare privilege of taking part in a mission of great significance for the United States and the entire world. A mission, incidentally, which has never before been attempted by man.

You will personally have the chance to help enrich mankind's fund of knowledge about two of the last earthly frontiers, the polar regions.

I am inviting you to join a distinguished group of 50 people who will fly around the world longitudinally, over both poles, on an expedition which will commemorate Admiral Richard E. Byrd's first Antarctic flight in 1929.

Among the highlights of this transpolar flight - the first commercial flight ever to cross both poles and touch down on all continents - will be stopovers at the American military/scientific bases at Thule, Greenland, and McMurdo Sound, Antarctica.

Because this expedition has the interest and support of much of the Free World, you and your fellow members will be honored guests (in many cases, even celebrities) at state and diplomatic receptions throughout the itinerary. You will have the opportunity to meet and talk with some of the world's important national leaders and public figures, such as Pope Paul VI, the Emperor of Japan, General Carlos Romulo, and many others who are already a part of history.

By agreeing to join this expedition, you will, in a sense, establish yourself in history too. For you will become a Founding Trustee of the new Admiral Richard E. Byrd Polar Center, sponsor of the expedition.

Your biography will be recorded in the Center's archives, available to future historians. The log, photographs and memorabilia of the expedition will be permanently displayed in the Center. And your name will be inscribed, with those of the other expedition members, on a bronze memorial tablet.

(continued)

EXHIBIT 1-1 Admiral Richard E. Byrd Polar Center letter *(continued)*

- 2 -

Before I continue with the details of the expedition, let me tell you
more about the Byrd Polar Center and the reasoning which led to its establishment this summer.

Located in Boston, home of the late Admiral and point of origin for each
of his seven expeditions, this nonprofit institution will house, catalog and
preserve the papers and records of both Admiral Byrd and other Arctic and
Antarctic explorers.

But the Center will have a more dynamic function than merely to enshrine
the past. It will be a vital, viable organization devoted to furthering
peaceful development of the polar regions, particularly Antarctica.

It will become, in effect, this country's headquarters for investigation
and research into the scientific and commercial development of the poles. The
Center will sponsor, support, initiate and conduct studies and expeditions.
It will furnish comprehensive data or technical assistance to the United
States, or to any university, institution, foundation, business organization
or private individual legitimately interested in polar development.

In other words, the Center has set for itself a course which the Admiral
before his death endorsed wholeheartedly. He foresaw that mankind would one
day benefit enormously from development of Antarctica's vast potential. And
he perceived that Antarctica's unique and diverse advantages and resources
might best be developed by private capital in a free enterprise context.

The Byrd Polar Center is dedicated to these objectives. And the essential purpose of this commemorative expedition is to dramatize the role that
private enterprise - and private citizens - can play in the opening of these
last frontiers.

At the same time, the expedition should help prove a few other important
points. It should demonstrate the feasibility of shrinking the world through
longitudinal navigation. It should also help blaze a trail for commercial air
travel over the South Pole. Presently, to fly from Chile to Australia, you
must go by way of Los Angeles, even though a straight line trans-Antarctic
route would be far shorter.

There is another factor I should mention, one which I think lends a certain urgency to the work of the Center. Development of the polar regions en-
joys a high official priority in the Soviet Union - higher, some believe, than
in the United States.

The Center's activities can provide a tangible, effective complement to
those of our own government, and over the long term, contribute meaningfully
to preservation of the Arctic and Antarctic regions for peaceful purposes.

These objectives, I think you will agree, are entirely valid. And important, for the future of humanity. It is for this reason that the inaugural
activity of the Byrd Polar Center will be an expedition of such scope and
magnitude.

The expedition will be led by Commander Fred G. Dustin, veteran of six
polar expeditions, advisor to Admiral Byrd and one of the intrepid group which

EXHIBIT 1-1   Admiral Richard E. Byrd Polar Center letter *(continued)*

- 3 -

spent the winter of 1934 in Little America on Byrd's Antarctic Expedition II. Commander Dustin is a member of the U.S. Antarctica Committee and President of the Byrd Polar Center.

Considered the ranking American authority on the polar regions, Fred Dustin is probably better qualified to lead this expedition - and brief members on virtually every aspect of the polar regions - than any man on earth. The Center and the expedition are fortunate to have Commander Dustin, as you will discover should you decide to participate.

The flight will be made in a specially outfitted, four-engine commercial jet with lounge-chair-and-table cabin configuration. A full flight crew of six will be headed by Captain Hal Neff, former pilot of Air Force One, the Presidential plane. Special clothing and equipment, such as Arctic survival gear, will be provided by the expedition and carried aboard the plane.

The expedition members will meet in Boston on the evening of November 7, 1968, for briefing and a reception and send-off party with the Governor of Massachusetts, Mayor of Boston, local officials and directors of the Byrd Polar Center. Next day, we will take off, head due north from Boston's Logan International Airport and follow this itinerary (as I have not yet visited all these places myself, I have drawn on the descriptions submitted to me by Commander Dustin and the other experienced people who have planned the expedition):

Thule, Greenland

Far above the Arctic Circle, past the chill reaches of Baffin Bay, lies desolate Thule, the northernmost U.S. air base. Almost 400 miles further north than the northern tip of Alaska, Thule was originally surveyed as a possible military site by Admiral Byrd and Commander Dustin. Here, in the deepening Arctic winter, you will get your first taste of the rigors of polar existence. You will have the chance to inspect the installations and meet the men for whom Arctic survival is a way of life.

North Pole

According to those who have crossed the North Pole, you will completely lose your day-night orientation. Sunrise and sunset occur within minutes of each other, a strange and unforgettable phenomenon. After Thule, you will cross the geographic North Pole, just as Admiral Byrd did in his pioneering trans-Arctic flight with Floyd Bennett in 1926. A memorial flag will be dropped.

Anchorage, Alaska

After crossing the pole, the plane will bank into a 90° left turn and head south, over the Arctic Ocean and Beaufort Sea, past Mt. McKinley, North America's highest peak, and on to Anchorage. There, you will meet the Governor and key officials.

Tokyo, Japan

The highlight of your stopover in Japan will be an opportunity to meet the Emperor and Premier. (Fishing: excursion to Hakone and Atami by bullet train; tea ceremony at private homes.)

EXHIBIT 1-1   Admiral Richard E. Byrd Polar Center letter *(continued)*

- 4 -

Manila, Philippines

General Carlos Romulo, the legendary patriot and statesman, an old friend
of Admiral Byrd, will give the expedition a warm welcome in Manila. (Folklore
performance; hunting for duck, deer, wild boar and a special species of water
buffalo; fishing for tuna and marlin.)

You will note that here and elsewhere we have prearranged a considerable
amount of hunting, fishing, and so on. These activities are optional. (Members of the expedition will be asked to indicate their preferences 30 days before the flights.) For those who do not want to participate in any of these
events, there will be sight-seeing, golf and many other things to do.

Darwin, Australia

Hard by the Timor Sea, tropical Darwin offers some of the world's most
superb beaches. You will have time not only to sample the sand and water
sports, but to see Australia's great outback. With its spectacular chasms,
canyons and gorges, the rarely visited outback is a scenic match for our own
West.

Sydney, Australia

You can look forward to an enthusiastic reception in Sydney by the Prime
Minister and government officials. For one thing, Australia is on particularly good terms with the United States. For another, Australia has traditionally been in the vanguard of nations involved in Antarctic exploration
and development. (Hunting for kangaroo, crocodile, buffalo, wild boar, duck,
and goose; or off-shore fishing for rifle fish, salmon, and giant grouper.)

Christchurch, New Zealand

This is our staging point for the flight of Antarctica, and it couldn't
be more appropriate. Most of the early expeditions departed from New Zealand,
and Admiral Byrd is still considered a national hero there. New Zealand is
Antarctica-conscious and its people take almost a proprietary interest in the
frozen continent. You will be something of a celebrity in New Zealand, and
can expect a thoroughly enjoyable visit while the expedition awaits favorable
weather reports from McMurdo Sound. (Deer hunting - where deer are so plenti-
ful that they pay a bounty; fishing for all of the great species of marlin -
in an area known for the greatest marlin fishing in the world - also Mako
shark.)

McMurdo Sound, Antarctica

I am told that only a total eclipse of the sun is comparable, in emotional
impact, to the first sight of Antarctica. Once experienced, neither can be
forgotten. If you prove to be like most who have seen Antarctica, you will
need somehow, someday, to return. And when you do, the emotional impact will
be just as profound. That is what the Antarctic veterans say.

For Antarctica exists well beyond the boundaries of the world you know.
You will see there a sun you have never seen, breathe air you have never
before breathed. You will see menacing white mountains towering for thousands

EXHIBIT 1-1   Admiral Richard E. Byrd Polar Center letter *(continued)*

- 5 -

of feet over a black ocean in which, with luck, you might survive for 45 seconds. You will see the awesome Ross Ice Shelf, as large as France, with its
50 to 200 foot ice cliffs cleaving the sea for 400 miles. You will see the
active volcano, Mt. Erebus, 13,000 feet of fire and ice.

And you will see the huts, so well preserved they seem to have been in-
habited only yesterday, which Shackleton used in 1908 and the ill-fated Scott
in 1911. Antarctica, apparently, is not subject to the passage of time as we
know it.

At McMurdo Base, you will meet the military men and scientists who inhabit this strange, alien territory. And you will inhabit it for a while too -
long enough to feel its bone-chilling cold, to hear its timeless silence, to
perceive, at the very edge of your composure, the terror of its mindless hostility to human beings.

While you are there, you will learn, as few men have ever had the opportunity to learn, about Antarctica. You will learn about survival, but
more important, about what men must accomplish to truly open this formidable
frontier.

South Pole

Admiral Byrd was the first man to fly over the South Pole. In all of
history, probably fewer than 200 men have crossed the pole, by air or otherwise. As a member of this expedition, you will join that select group.

Punta Arenas, Chile

From the South Pole, you will fly to Punta Arenas, on the tortuous Strait
of Magellan which separates continental South America from bleak Tierra del
Fuego. The visit here will be brief, but you should get some idea of the fla-
vor of this nearly forgotten outpost.

Rio de Janeiro, Brazil

This memorable stopover will include a diplomatic reception. You will
also have a chance to relax and sample the sights and sounds of fabulous Rio.
(Special plane to Belo Horizonte for hunting boar, duck, jaguar, panther,
water buffalo, crocodile and deer.)

Dakar, Senegal

You may never have expected to see Dakar, but you will on this expedition. (Tribal dancing; safari.)

Rome, Italy

No trip would be complete without a stop in Rome, where we will be received enthusiastically. During our stay there we will have a private audience with the Pope.

EXHIBIT 1-1 Admiral Richard E. Byrd Polar Center letter *(continued)*

- 6 -

<u>London, England</u>

From London, the expedition will fly back across the Atlantic and terminate with a debriefing, critique and farewell dinner in Boston, on December 3.

As mementos of the expedition, you will receive a leather-bound, personalized copy of the log book and a piece of the fabric from Admiral Byrd's original plane, mounted in crystal.

You will also be presented with a framed certificate from the Admiral Richard E. Byrd Polar Center, affirming your appointment as a Founding Trustee and expressing appreciation for your interest in, contributions to and efforts on behalf of the Center and its objectives. In the future, you will be kept fully advised of the plans and activities of the Center, and be invited to participate to whatever extent you wish. And of course, you will have life-long access to the Center's archives and services.

Most important, you will take back with you a once-in-a-lifetime experience. The day may come when journeys to and over the poles are commonplace. But today, the privilege is available to very few.

It is true, I think, that this privilege does carry responsibility with it. By the time you return, you will have received a comprehensive indoctrination course in the polar regions by the world's leading authorities. Your responsibility will be to make the most of the knowledge you will gain, to become an active advocate - perhaps even a disciple - of polar research and development.

It is a responsibility which, I trust, will weigh easily upon you. For once the polar air has been absorbed into your bloodstream, there is no cure. Like others who have been stricken, you will probably find yourself reading every word you can find on the North and South Poles. And, most likely, thinking about your next trip.

But first of all, you must decide about this trip. If you have a sense of adventure, a certain pioneering spirit, and if the prospect of taking part in a mission of worldwide significance and historical importance appeals to you, perhaps you should consider joining the expedition. It is doubtful that you will ever have another chance like this.

Obviously, you can't make a decision of this magnitude instantly. But a word of caution: reservations will be accepted in the order received - a total of only 60, including ten standbys. The departure date, remember, is November 8, 1968, so there is little time to waste.

The price of $10,000 includes food and beverage, all accommodations (the best available under all circumstances), transportation, special clothing, insurance, side excursions - virtually everything except your travel to and from Boston.

Money received will go into escrow at the United States Trust Company in Boston until the time of the flight. To the extent that revenues from the trip will exceed costs, the activities of the Polar Center will be accelerated.

EXHIBIT 1-1   Admiral Richard E. Byrd Polar Center letter *(continued)*

- 7 -

To reserve your place in the expedition, just drop me a note on your letterhead or personal stationery, with your deposit check for $2,500, made out to the United States Trust Company. Incidentally, if anything prevents your leaving as planned, you can send another in your place; otherwise, cancellations cannot be accepted later than 30 days before departure.

If you have further questions, please write to me in care of the Transpolar Expedition, Admiral Richard E. Byrd Polar Center, 18 Tremont Street, Boston, Massachusetts 02108.

I hope we may hear from you soon - and that we will welcome you to the expedition.

                              Sincerely yours,

                              Edward C. Bursk

                              Edward C. Bursk

ECB:EHK

P.S.: We have just made arrangements for a professional camera crew to accompany the flight, and as a result we will be able to provide you with a short film clip and sound tape of your experiences.

1. This market of people who have already accomplished great things might be persuaded by the chance to do something even bigger: "You will have the rare privilege of taking part in a mission of great significance for the United States and the entire world." And "You will personally have the chance to help enrich mankind's fund of knowledge...."

2. The targeted people are accustomed to being treated well: "You and your fellow members will be honored guests...". "You will have the opportunity to meet and talk with some of the world's important leaders and public figures...."

Many of this letter's techniques are still being imitated in the direct mail you receive or send today. The personal letterhead from Edward C. Bursk, then editor of the *Harvard Business Review*. The dated, personalized letter. The closing postscript offering one additional benefit for accepting: "We have just made arrangements for a professional camera crew to accompany the flight, and as a result we will be able to provide you with a short film clip and sound tape of your experiences."

The second example (Exhibit 1-2) is a promotion mailed by Nintendo to announce a new game, Donkey Kong Country™.

The **teaser** (the words used on the outer envelope or box of the mailing) is simple: "Enter the jungle...Nov. 21." But unlike the expedition offered by the Admiral Byrd Polar Center, this journey is designed to appeal to interactive-savvy kids. There's no letter inside the box, but a small, graphically exciting brochure reads, "Congratulations! You were chosen from a select list of Super NES® owners to receive this exclusive preview video....Not everyone will be so lucky. So, pop it into your VCR, hang on, and enjoy the ride!"

While copywriter Hank Burnett used words alone to woo his prospects on the Byrd polar expedition—"the chill reaches of Baffin Bay," "a sun you have never before seen," and "the menacing white mountains"—Nintendo recognized its target audience (video game enthusiasts) would prefer to *see* the ice-capped mountain peaks, shark-infested waters, and secret passage caves of Donkey Kong Island. So the mailing includes a free video on "The Making of Donkey Kong Country" and offers a free Donkey Kong Country Player's Guide.

Let's consider how this Nintendo mailing answers the four questions posed at the beginning of this chapter:

1. *What am I selling?* The copywriter responsible for this promotion had to know everything he or she could about this brand-new, yet-

EXHIBIT 1-2   Targeting an Interactive Generation

Box for Nintendo Mailing

Source: Donkey Kong Country™ © 1996 Nintendo.
Used courtesy of Nintendo.

(continued)

Brochure for Nintendo Mailing

to-be launched game. What was offered was fun, excitement, and a sense of being on the inside.

2. *Who am I selling to?* The target audience was owners of Super Nintendo systems and/or their children.

3. *Why am I selling this now?* The timing was based on an upcoming game launch date—November 21.

4. *What do I want my prospect to do?* The action desired from the prospect was purchase of the new game as soon as it was released. What's interesting about this carefully targeted mailing is how it could have been strengthened even more by including an early reservation form or other response device instead of just directing prospects to go to their nearest store.

While the seven-page Admiral Byrd letter and Nintendo video represent two extremes of the marketing media spectrum, they illustrate how vital it is for copywriters to know how to *write on target*—using both long-standing methods and new approaches more likely to succeed in a changing world.

A New Era of Advertising Copy

The look and sound of things is changing. With a generation weaned on MTV and sound bites, advertising has come into "a new era." This is what Steven R. Tharler, cofounder and partner of Tharler/Opper, recently noted in the New England Direct Marketing Association newsletter *Rollout*:

> There is an increasing number of people—especially those in their 20s and 30s—who *can* read, but who seem disinclined to do so. They are products of their times, subject to a series of cultural/technological "phenomena" that, gradually, are affecting us all.
>
> It's important to look at our new visually (vs. verbally) oriented society, because to be successful—as marketers, advertisers, communicators—we have to *be* in touch with the best ways to *get* in touch with our respective audiences.

Think of the new technologies that have developed in the past few years! As the Direct Marketing Association of Washington's Interactive Marketing Council Co-Chairs Mark Heller and Tony Cornish noted in a recent article in *Marketing AdVents*, 40 years ago, there were few computers and credit cards, no 800 numbers or ZIP codes. Direct marketing was simply a return-mail, check-with-order business. Now we have video promotions, CD-ROM catalogs, home shopping TV channels and infomercials, the self-segmenting marketplaces of the Internet, and so much more. Do you use the same copywriting techniques? Not always. New media demand new messages. In a September 1995 *Scientific American* article called "Digital Literacy," Richard A. Lanham stated that, "Multimedia will require equal facility in word, image, and sound."

But the basics still apply. All these new media are bringing us is better, more intimate access to our customers, our target audience. The skill of the copywriter in connecting with that audience must keep pace.

A mailing from New Market Forum (Exhibit 1-3) shows how a targeted mailing can successfully combine new media and old. Directed to a target audience of association leaders, this promotion announces "a powerful new tool for developing your association's strength" and offers "a complimentary copy of a valuable educational and reference CD-ROM to evaluate for potential distribution to your members to help them succeed in using the Internet." The accompanying CD is a "door-opener," designed to whet the prospect's interest and prompt an order. The targeted letter salutation reads, "Dear Association Leader."

The brochure targets its audience with the benefit-oriented headline, "Building a Stronger Organization through Understanding—Teach Your Membership How to Profit from the Internet." Inside the brochure, New Market Forum, which maintains information on more than 10,000 associations and chambers of commerce across the country and around the globe, offers to "customize this CD to fit your group's specific mission" and mentions other benefit programs like its Events Directory on the World Wide Web.

The CD-ROM arrived with all the accoutrements of a basic direct mail package: an outer envelope, a letter, a brochure, a response form. The time-tested techniques of writing those components remain essential even in today's technologically changing world.

Another recent mailing (Exhibit 1-4) that successfully targets a specific audience is a piece from *PC World* magazine that has been a multiyear **control** (the mailing that generates the best results).

EXHIBIT 1-3   New Market Forum Mailing

Intnl Interactive Communications Society
14657 SW Teal Boulevard Suite 119
Beaverton, OR 97007-6194

NewMarket Forum, Inc.

Dear Association Leader,

31 MILK STREET
BOSTON, MASSACHUSETTS
02109-5107

617-423-4373
FAX 617-423-4597

Enclosed is a powerful new tool for developing your association's strength.

We all look for the glue that can bind our organizations together. The kind of thing that will add strength to our membership, give us an edge in the industry, and help us all reach our financial and personal goals.

We think the enclosed *"Using the Internet for Profit"* CD is one of those important items. This isn't just a CD. This is a door-opener. Especially if your organization is like thousands of others that we talk with, organizations starved for information about the Internet. But, don't just learn about the Internet, learn how to use it for profit.

This CD is a practical, easy-to-understand guide that will lead you and your membership through the intricacies of the Internet and show you how to use it for fun, entertainment, and profit.

As the world embraces this new technology, your organization and each of your members will need to know more about the Internet in order to grow.

As a company that has built our entire business based on the Internet, we are true believers. As your partner, we are prepared to help you gain an understanding of the Internet so that you can compete in the new media world being created by the business leaders of today. That's why we've sent the enclosed CD for you to sample.

Our commitment to you runs deeper than just a promise.

We are so committed to helping your organization grow that we have made a special arrangement with Paul Earl, President of CD Solutions, to provide you with the following:

1. A complimentary copy of a valuable educational and reference CD-ROM to evaluate for potential distribution to your members to help them succeed in using the Internet.
2. An opportunity for your organization to have its own *"Using the Internet for Profit"* CD-ROM to reflect your branding and to include a greeting by your organization for remarketing to your membership, prospects, and the community-at-large.
3. Guest speakers to come to your organization for a *"How to Use the Internet for Profit"* presentation.

As a matter of fact, Paul Earl told me that he would personally present to your group as long as there were no scheduling conflicts.

You can see we are committed. We're committed to your success, your growth, and your presence on the Internet.

Sincerely,

Robert Scott
President

P.S. If you haven't yet completed our business listing information, please do so at this time. If there are upcoming events that you would like to list on The NewMarket Forum™, please contact us at sales1@newmkt.com. We look forward to being your Internet partner for many years to come.

The letter   *(continued)*

Other components

Source: Reprinted with permission of Berenson, Isham and Partners.

EXHIBIT 1-4 *PC World* Magazine Mailing

PC WORLD MAGAZINE
CORDIALLY WELCOMES YOU
AS A PROVISIONAL
SELECT SUBSCRIBER.
YOU ARE INVITED TO SAMPLE
A TRIAL ISSUE
WITHOUT COST OR OBLIGATION.

PLEASE RETURN THE ACCEPTANCE FORM
BY JANUARY 31, 1994.

Select Subscriber Privileges Include Special Introductory Savings,
Free Gifts, Free Instant Reference Cards Every Month,
Prestige Personal Service, And More.

Dear Select Nominee,

Welcome to the club!

You've already made the PC commitment, now collect the benefits — beginning with the free INSTANT REFERENCE CARD accompanying this invitation!

As the INSTANT REFERENCE CARD demonstrates, PC World delivers more than just words and pictures on a page. Through our Select Subscriber program, we've forged a unique partnership between our editors and an elite corps of PC-proficient managers. Obviously, not everyone qualifies as a Select Subscriber. But we think you do.

You've lived through the trials and triumphs of putting PCs to work, and you've got the knowledge to prove it. Windows 3.1 or NT? 486...Pentium...PowerPC...or Alpha? Now people ask <u>you</u> for advice. It hasn't been easy, but you've done it. <u>You've earned preferential treatment.</u>

By activating your trial Select subscription now, you'll be rewarded with a dazzling array of privileges and benefits designed to save you time and make you a more efficient, more productive leader.

Your INSTANT REFERENCE CARD is only the first of many advantages awaiting you as a Select Subscriber...

Return the acceptance form today and you'll immediately receive our
Windows 3.1 Instant Reference Mouse Pad and "PC World's Best Windows Tips"
as additional <u>free</u> gifts. We'll also rush you the current issue of PC World for
your examination.

Enjoy these benefits without obligation for a month. Then, to take full
advantage of your Select subscription, pay the invoice when it arrives. If you
decide not to continue, return the invoice marked "cancel."

PC World is tailor-made for you. As a Select Subscriber, you'll <u>save money</u> — 12 issues of PC World magazine at a special, introductory discount. <u>Buy PC systems with superior service and support</u> — refer to PC World's unique Service and Support Monitor before you

PC World *SELECT SUBSCRIBER PROGRAM* ▪ 501 Second Street ▪ San Francisco, CA 94107

The letter   *(continued)*

buy, and be eligible to win a hot new system every month. <u>Get free special reports on the multimedia revolution</u> — every quarter we'll keep you abreast of what's new and what's next in multimedia. <u>Enlarge your options</u> — Buyers' Guides to point you to the best products at the best prices.

<u>Work smart</u> — Instant Reference Cards every month to make you and your staff more productive on today's major applications. <u>Enjoy your status</u> — take advantage of prestige, personalized customer service. And each month, through PC World — <u>get the edge</u>.

In every issue, PC World brings you hot news, product previews, and authoritative reviews backed by our own testing laboratory.

You'll learn new ways to use your systems. New ways to use your software. New solutions to business problems. Plus... free programs and productivity tactics to further your success in today's competitive business world.

Will PC World make a difference? As a Select Subscriber, you'll use and enjoy a sumptuous menu of resources to fire your imagination, sharpen your instincts, and spark new strategies to meet the challenges you face.

Why not join us on a provisional basis and see for yourself?

Your name and address appear on the trial form enclosed. To activate your provisional Select subscription, complete and mail the form today.

<u>Send no money now</u>. Your first month is without obligation.

<u>Free Windows 3.1 Instant Reference Mouse Pad and "Best Windows Tips</u>." Two handy references to help you get the most from your software and Windows — *free just for returning the trial form!*

<u>Introductory Discount</u>. Your Select subscription rate is only $19.97. That's a savings of more than 57% off the newsstand rate of PC World magazine alone (and you get so much more — including 2 FREE GIFTS!).

<u>Your satisfaction guaranteed</u>. PC World must be all we say it is or your investment will be refunded in full.

May we look for your response by return mail? Hurry! The application period is limited. Beat the deadline!

Sincerely,

Heather Martin

Heather Martin
Vice President

P.S. The success of the PC World Select Subscriber Program is contingent upon sufficient enrollment. Whether you wish to accept or decline, would you extend us the courtesy of a reply by January 31, 1994.

WELCOME TO THE

PC WORLD
SELECT SUBSCRIBER PROGRAM

A Unique New Partnership
Between You and PC World

When you've worked your way to the top, you deserve special treatment. Which is why we created the PC World *Select Subscriber* Program for you. As a *Select Subscriber*, you'll enjoy individualized attention available to only an elite corps of PC-proficient managers.

We'll accord top priority to your questions…help you solve your most pressing problems…give you direct access to PC World's award-winning editorial team…help you find information without time-consuming delays…alert you to money-saving opportunities…reward you with free gifts…and more.

Your participation opens the door to convenience, flexibility, and access to information available only to the few.

■ SELECT SUBSCRIBER BENEFITS ■

1. PC WORLD

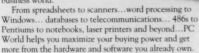

Every month, you'll join over 4,000,000 top managers who read PC World for product news, objective performance reviews, buyers' guides, and strategies and tactics to give you the edge in today's competitive business world.

From spreadsheets to scanners…word processing to Windows… databases to telecommunications… 486s to Pentiums to notebooks, laser printers and beyond…PC World helps you maximize your buying power and get more from the hardware and software you already own.

- Best mail order deals
- Low-cost laser printers
- Best Windows software
- Hundreds of tips for DOS, Windows and all major applications
- Portable computing advice
- CD-ROM, multimedia, and more!

Plus, in every issue, savvy "Here's How" columns —
Like *Help Line* for answers to your questions.
Star-Dot-Star where readers share their PC discoveries.
Spreadsheets to help you process and display information more effectively. *Word Processing* for power tips and tactics, and more.

2. Speed your work in Windows 3.1 — *free!*

Receive this exclusive Windows 3.1 Instant Reference Mouse Pad just for trying PC World!

FREE when you return the acceptance form! This handy Instant Reference Mouse Pad puts the most common Windows 3.1 mouse and keyboard commands literally at your fingertips! The mouse pad has a soft rubber base and a firm plastic surface that provides excellent, resistance-free traction for your mouse. Four-color printing makes instructions easy to read — and won't wear out. PC World's Instant Reference Mouse Pad is not for sale. It's available FREE only when you return the acceptance form. Do it now!

NOT SOLD IN STORES

Brochure   *(continued)*

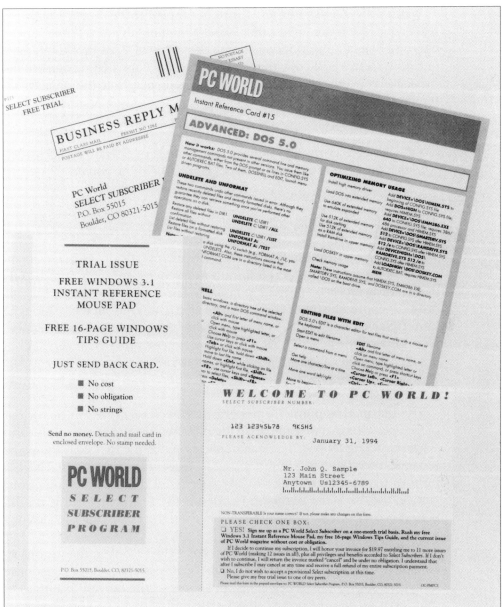

Source: Reprinted with permission of *PC World* Magazine.

Other components

Written by copywriter Jeff Laurie to appeal to *PC World*'s business readership, the letter invites the "Select Nominee" to join a flattering category of Select Subscribers. Echoing the Admiral Byrd invitation, page one of the letter is filled with benefit-promising copy that recognizes the particular concerns and needs of its target audience. Note the language on the first half of the page:

- "You've already made the PC commitment, now collect the benefits."

- "...an elite corps of PC-proficient managers. Obviously, not everyone qualifies as a Select Subscriber. But we think you do."

- "You've earned preferential treatment."

- "You'll be rewarded..."

The package also includes a **freemium** specifically targeted to *PC World*'s business audience: an Instant Reference Card with immediately usable information on current, popular PC programs. The simple but colorful brochure illustrates the **features** of the offer as membership-type **benefits**. Numbering the items highlights their quantity. Each item begins not with the actual name of the department, product, or service, but with a benefit headline—"Speed your work in Windows 3.1—*free!*," "Buy PC systems with superior service and support," and "Get the best products at the best prices...."

The L-shaped response form is effective because the tower on the left presents a billboard to summarize the offer, while the half-size reply form suggests incompletion. There's an implication that the two sides should be separate, thereby inducing the reader to tear off the reply form. This is a form of **involvement**—key to any successful direct marketing effort. Notice, too, how the numbered code on the response form is repositioned as a "Select Subscriber Number," thereby reinforcing the idea of a selectively targeted audience.

In the following chapters, we will take a closer look at the various elements of effective copywriting in other successful envelopes, response forms, letters, brochures, catalogs, and some of the newest examples of the electronic word. Copywriting for the end of the second millenium is a skill like any other—learned by imitation, practice, and a careful analysis of the results. The first step is to consider the target—the "you" at whom your words will aim.

2

WRITING TO A MARKET

"You"—what a fabulous word! Few words have its power and significance for the target of your direct marketing effort. The media or format makes no difference. The little extra effort it takes to unlock the dynamic selling power in that word—to find the real "you in you," to borrow from Gertrude Stein—is at the heart of effective copywriting.

The fundamental assumptions of direct response include:

1. An exhaustive effort will be made to refine the lists that best represent the audience to which your offer will be addressed.

2. The offer—or variations of it—will be given a thorough test or be fully proven through previous usage.

3. Compelling "visuals" and carefully chosen formats (e.g., the cover letter, brochure, "buck slip," "lift letter," response card, and other components of the direct mail package) will contribute to the total "pulling power" of the direct response ad.

All things being equal, however—an attractive offer, carefully selected lists, and attention-getting graphics—the copy platform is the bedrock on which your sales message rests. Your copy has to find and sell all those at whom you target your sales message.

GETTING TO KNOW "YOU"

A recent conversation with an expert in magazine subscription direct response brought this comment: "Yes, I read the stuff the marketing people send my way, but most of the time we just throw offers against the wall and see what sticks. No one has the time or budget to really do anything exhaustive."

In another instance, the copy chief of a medium-sized direct response agency said that his account managers "boil down the data in summary form," so he can gloss it in preparation for the writing process. His client contact is quite limited. Then again, whenever he did have time to work directly with a client (and, by inference, develop really solid buyer information), the results were invariably superior.

Day-to-day pressures and limited budgets can overwhelm the impulse to do research—to "get into the head" of the buyer and refine a strategy that brings exceptional response. Complacency can become a problem, too. It's not unusual for experienced copy practitioners to adopt an attitude of "when you've seen one, you've seen 'em all." The danger in this attitude is that it can quickly lead to formulaic writing and flat presentations. The compelling need to be "right on target" requires that we "scope out" a market and "psych" an audience sufficiently to gain the incremental response that can make all the difference. How we go about this process, and in doing so jump-start our creative juices, is what this chapter is all about. We'll begin with a brief look backward to see how research and demography first began to affect the process of creating winning direct response.

BEGINNING TO UNDERSTAND

In a very real sense, our ability to understand the collective psyche of our buying audiences started with just five digits: the ZIP code strings chosen by the U.S. Postal Service in 1963 as a means to more efficient mail delivery. Martin Baier developed the original ideas and programs that revolutionized the practice of direct marketing through the use of ZIP code analysis. In his work for Old American Insurance Company, he first proposed the idea of "sorting" ZIP strings as a new approach to defining homogeneous marketing targets. To quote from a *New York Times* article published in 1988 on the 25th anniversary of the introduction of codes: "In tracking transportation patterns down to the neighborhood level, the

Postal Service had accidentally identified economic cultural clusters of individuals who shared similar buying habits. A code was more than a post office address. It was a marketing unit."

Baier published an article in the *Harvard Business Review* in 1967 refining his ideas on the new approach, and direct marketing campaigns based on computer-sorted ZIP code strings began. By the 1980s, programs such as "VALS" (values and lifestyles) had supplemented code analysis as a way to understand the wants and needs of defined buying audiences.

Currently, census block data is lending further clarity to the targeting process, providing refined data on as few as 350 households, as compared to the average of 4,000 in a code area. When combined with opinion surveys, other market research (such as subscription and purchasing history), and the processing power of a supercomputer, the targeting ability of today's direct marketing managers is formidable.

Behind all the sophisticated database "massaging" that accompanies contemporary direct response practice, the raw power of code sorting is still at the very center of market analysis. Taken as a self-evident component of any research exercise, it's worth remembering that as recently as a generation ago, code analysis was revolutionary.

Exhibit 2-1   Mr. ZIP—An Early Sign of Segmentation

MR. ZIP

COPY CONTENT

But what about actual copy content of your mailer, infomercial, free-standing insert (fsi) in a Sunday paper, or file on an Internet home page? How can you add value to your copy component to create a strong "lever" to accompany the "fulcrum" represented by all the other components?

One of the first things you'll do is look at the demography behind the list to which your direct mail package will be distributed

A good list broker can give you detailed information on the consumers or business-to-business buyers to whom you'll be selling. Depending on the general characteristics, purchasing history, predisposition to buy, and specific needs of your audience—along with such other variables as seasonality or product and service availability—you should get sufficient information to begin to define your copy strategy.

Like the transformation of a graphic image on a computer screen, a rough composite of your audience should emerge as you review the demographics of your list. Self-evident characteristics such as geographic location, age, sex, income bracket, purchasing history, predisposition to respond to particular offers, and other quantitative information will give you a general idea of the "you" to whom you're selling.

More on Copy

Information from your list source is only the *beginning* of your research if you really want to "get into the head" of your prospect. All the research in the world won't make up for a misdirected offer, a weak headline, and poor body copy. "What's in it for me?" is still the reader's question every copywriter has to answer. And the timeless injunction to sell on the benefits, then explain the features still holds true. Telling the prospect how to use the product—or showing examples of satisfied customers—is still as powerful a selling tool as ever.

With today's sophisticated consumers, presenting correct information is one of the ground rules. Whether you're writing 100 words for a 30-second television commercial or 1,500 words for a direct mail letter, be sure that every product feature and reader benefit you present is 100 percent correct.

Remember—you aren't just attracting people's interest, establishing an identity, or creating a memory—you're trying to sell. And you can't sell anything to anyone if he or she doesn't have enough information to make a decision to buy. (More on benefits and features later in this chapter.)

One benefit that research holds for even the most intuitive writer is that a bounty of product and buyer knowledge can stimulate subconscious images and ideas that would never develop otherwise. If you're a member of the "sleep on it" school of creative ideas, research is almost a foolproof way to ensure that your dreams and waking intuitions will be richer and more fully realized.

Other Avenues

Although a limited budget and tight deadlines may seem to limit your research, other ways are available for developing a copy platform that puts you "right on target."

The next best place to look for information is with your client. Whether you're working in-house, for an agency or free-lance, you are likely to be working with and for a third party with valuable insights into your customer and the segment to which the customer belongs. Sophisticated clients will brief you, sure in the knowledge that their years of experience and volumes of ordering data are reliable indicators of how offers should be framed, copy platforms structured, and package components included.

But what if your client isn't Publishers' Clearing House or Lands' End? What if list demography is limited or nonexistent, as is often the case with in-house or membership lists? Gather the marketing information you need for a compelling presentation from salespeople, marketing managers, customer service representatives, route managers, association and institutional executives, and, of course, actual customers. All can contribute valuable intelligence regarding the selling environment, the copy style, and the points you'll need to highlight.

At the same time, the sophisticated segmenting techniques made possible by the supercomputer and fully relational database technology may give you the opportunity to design promotions and appeals targeted on a dozen or more segments of a single market.

Consider the challenge posed by a recent direct response fundraising appeal launched by Brown University as part of a capital campaign (Exhibit 2-2). Within the broad spectrum of the Brown community were current students, recent alumni, faculty, mature alumni, affluent alumni, women, minorities, and other segments of what otherwise might be construed as a relatively homogenous database. **In fact, 18 different appeals were written and mailed in what proved to be a successful attempt to maximize response from an otherwise well-defined audience!**

Exhibit 2-2   Response Form Variations

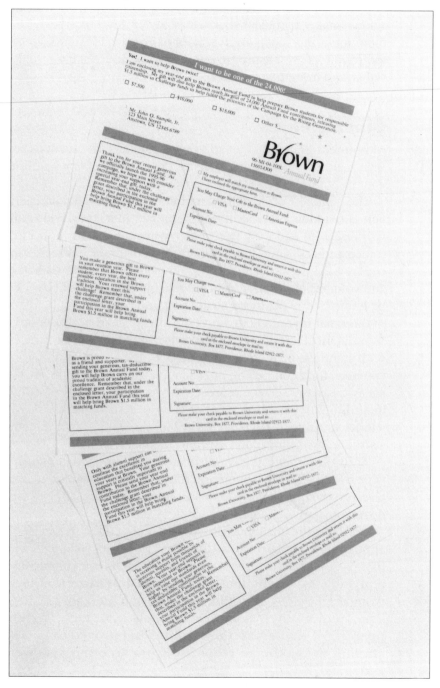

Source: Reprinted with permission of Brown University and Bachurski Associates, Inc.

Whether you're developing numerous variations on a theme or a single package, you need to proceed methodically. The goal is to develop a "composite" of sufficient richness and complexity for you to write with sufficient authority and expertise to command your audience to respond. What kind of information are you looking for?

Start with a review of mailers previously "dropped" (mailed) across current lists or ones like that with which you're working. If response information is available, or at the very least an indexed list of most successful to least successful packages is at hand, pay close attention to such key content as:

- Offer(s), teaser style, size and color(s), package components, unique selling proposition.

- Letter length, format, headlines, salutation/postscript, order of presentation, key copy points, corporate/product positioning, typeface, key underlining/bolding, italics, etc.

- Brochure design, order of presentation, format, use of graphics, key copy points, use of color, etc.

- Incentive components, including cents-off, free trials, and other special incentive/discount offers.

- Involvement techniques like paste-ons, cutouts, sweepstakes, etc.

No matter how simple or complex your package, it must be keyed to the culture and consciousness of the prospect; otherwise, response will be lower. Your situation isn't very different from the direct salesperson or telemarketer trying to pull a phone sale. How do they get the prospect's attention? And after they do, how do they convert buying interest into an order?

Gathering detailed market intelligence is always a good idea. Little nuggets of information often can stimulate selling phrases so powerful that the positive buyer response is almost a reflex.

CONTEXT, AFFILIATION, AND RELATION

Here's another way to picture your audience—one that will give your offer and presentation energy and attractiveness. Take a look at the heads and leads on two "financial education" promotions received in households and offices throughout greater Boston in the fall of 1995 (Exhibit 2-3).

Exhibit 2-3   Self-Mailers Promoting One Seminar to Two Different Markets

An educational seminar.

Northeastern University

UNIVERSITY COLLEGE

Northeastern University is an equal opportunity/affirmative action educational institution and employer.

Call (800) 370-3166 for reservations.

Presents

America's most popular financial education course.™

SUCCESSFUL MONEY MANAGEMENT SEMINAR

You will learn how to . . .

☑ Manage your money
☑ Reduce your taxes
☑ Save and invest
☑ Allocate your investments
☑ Create a plan to achieve your financial objectives
☑ Reduce insurance costs

There are literally thousands of ways
to achieve financial security.
Put into action those that will work best for you.

Complete Agenda Inside

A Conservative Approach to a Secure Retirement

This information-rich seminar introduces you to the concepts and practices that will help you spend your retirement comfortably and in control of your finances. Financial Strategies for Successful Retirement® will show you a conservative approach to wise money management and will help you identify lifestyle issues facing retirees.

You will learn how to get the most from your investments, Social Security and retirement plans. The course will also show you how to protect your hard-earned assets from erosion due to inflation and the possible cost of long-term health care.

Your registration fee includes a colorful, in-depth seminar workbook and a Retirement Planning Data Form that will help you develop a written inventory of your assets, income, Social Security and pension benefits.

The information you learn at Financial Strategies for Successful Retirement will pay dividends for the rest of your life. Call or send your registration form today.

What You Will Receive:

Informative Instruction

The four information-packed sessions are taught using easy-to-understand terms and interesting examples, in an enjoyable classroom setting.

Seminar Workbook

The colorful seminar workbook contains practical exercises and examples to help you learn and remember everything covered in the seminar. It is a valuable reference tool designed to help you reach your retirement goals.

Personal Financial Data Form and Instructional Tape

An audiotape will give you step-by-step instructions for developing a written summary of your finances. This valuable exercise will help you develop a written summary of your assets, income, Social Security and pension benefits.

Optional Planning Consultation

You are entitled to an optional one-on-one consultation after the conclusion of the seminar. This is your opportunity to ask specific questions regarding your financial future and goals.

Comprehensive Seminar Agenda

Session 1

Foundation for Successful Retirement
• Retirement planning is for everyone
• Retirement income: perception vs. reality
• Objectives of retirement planning
• The Success Triangle™
• Nine main reasons people fail to capitalize on their retirement years

• You can put your dollars to work with compound interest
• The impact of inflation on income
• Taxes and their impact on retirement planning
• The "Double Whammy" of Taxes and inflation
• Social Security

Session 2

Your Retirement Income
• Company retirement plans
• Lump-sum distributions
• Selecting pension benefit options
• IRAs
• Home equity
• Working after retirement

Putting Your Dollars to Work — Fixed-Income Securities
• Savings and cash reserves
• Tax-deferred annuities
• Corporate & Treasury bonds
• Municipal bonds — tax-free income
• Nine steps to retirement success
• Your personal retirement plan

Session 3

Putting Your Dollars to Work — Equity Investments
• Common stock
• Preferred stock
• Mutual funds
• Inflation-proofing income — systematic withdrawal programs

• Investing in mutual funds on a tax-deferred basis
• Direct participation programs
• Portfolio hedging with tangible assets
• Asset allocation

Session 4

Risk Management
• Medicare
• Long-term health care
• Life insurance at retirement
• The facts about disability insurance
Estate Planning
• Objectives of estate planning

• Understanding probate
• Advantages of joint tenancy
• Using trusts to reduce estate transfer costs
• Three ways to avoid estate shrinkage
• Charitable giving

Session 5

Everyone attending is entitled to a personal retirement planning consultation after the seminar — this is your opportunity to ask specific personal questions regarding your financial future.

Will You Be Ready For Retirement?

1. Should you take a lump sum or monthly payments from your company retirement plan?

2. How much of your Social Security benefits will be taxed?

3. Are your investment returns keeping ahead of taxes and inflation?

4. What is the best place for your existing IRA accounts?

5. How can you reduce or avoid estate taxes?

6. How should your investment allocation change after retirement?

7. Which monthly retirement option is really best for you and your spouse?

8. What should you do about your insurance?

This seminar will help you answer these and other questions, and achieve a financially secure retirement.

Complete registration information on back.

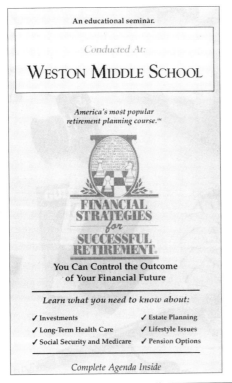

Variations in theme and copy points are minor. The same pitch and offer—learn how to build your wealth or plan for retirement—is restated in various ways. What's really intriguing is the way in which the marketer chose to approach the various audiences, using age as the main segmenting criterion in one instance (parents whose children attend a particular school), and affiliation with an academic institution in another. (Another mailing, not shown here, segmented according to income demography: that is, high earning power/net worth.)

Such sophisticated list segmentation, when based on affiliation, has particular implications for the copywriter. For the audience that affiliates around the university, the emphasis is on planning, with a supporting Q&A section speaking directly to "what, where, why and how" issues. The academically oriented angle is subtle. Prestige of affiliation becomes a pillar of the copy presentation, with an "insider's newsletter" feel to the piece. The other piece, advertising sessions at a middle school, is keyed to themes of "conservatism" and the "entitlement" of all attendees to receive a free, postseminar financial consultation. Both presentations feature a methodical, step-by-step learning process and emphasize educational materials, and both are reminiscent of the adult learning programs popular in so many upscale suburban communities.

Notice the almost total lack of emphasis on the name, background, and affiliation of the seminar presenter. The developer of these self-mailers is evidently a financial services vendor prospecting for clients and has consciously excluded almost all reference to the seminar presenter, knowing well that most upscale baby boomers have zero interest in being propositioned by one more stockbroker. This bit of knowledge—one that comes with the territory for anyone selling financial services—is a major factor in setting the tone of the whole promotion. It runs entirely counter to a widely followed approach in the boom years of the 1980s: Direct response packages featured the speaker as a guru. Digging out such nuggets and using them in ways both subtle and direct to enhance the impact of the copy platform is what good research is all about.

CULTURE AND COMPULSION

What handles can you use to gain insight into your market segment? Think about the values and predominant themes that express the culture surrounding the prospective customers.

General Business Markets

Managers of commercial and government enterprises, taking their cue from the problems faced by American manufacturers competing with Japanese producers, have become obsessed with "quality" and "customer satisfaction." These themes have become predominant factors in human resources development and even compensation plans with incentives.

In appealing to these buyers, show clearly that by responding to your offer they'll be subscribing to current best practices, and that in doing so the benefits they'll reap will be shared by the larger group. How can you gain insights such as this one? A short read of key trade publications representing the segment into which you're selling can provide the vital nuance and contextual detail that might be missing in a list profile or marketing plan.

Industry and Manufacturing

This market is concerned with catering to specific demand on one hand, and quick response on the other.

What are the implications for those who are selling direct to the harried management and engineering staffs on the plant floor? To begin with, the industrial prospect is intimately involved in maintaining and upgrading a "system." The offer must contribute to system enhancement or operating efficiency. It must also be easy enough to integrate so as not to disrupt the orderly execution of whatever process "adds value" to the system and the products it produces.

A Push-Pull Strategy

The following push-pull strategy is a good example of the way creative copy and careful market segmentation can work. Roger Sakolove, associate creative director of Lexington, Massachusetts-based Directech, relates the case of a vendor of network systems—the complex equipment used to link computers within an organization—that used a push-pull strategy to boost sales. The foundation of the computer equipment client's approach was to recognize the mindset of the two key buying constituencies within larger corporate information system departments. To quote Sakolove:

> The top tier was high-end health industry information executives with a broad view of what they need. The package was simple, comprised of a letter, reply card, and envelope, designed to look like

high-level business correspondence. It included a semi-testimonial from one of the product's users, but the endorsement letter never mentioned the vendor by name, instead simply talking about what they do. The offer was very targeted—a video that sketched out the full story of the installation at a nationally recognized health center. It was a good high level offer.

A completely different package went to the technical middle management audience; including an information-heavy brochure that pushed the urgency of making a decision. That kind of latitude is possible in the technical tier; users want the technical information that would be of less interest at the top.

Travel and Leisure

Within the last decade, huge volumes of business that previously flowed through travel agencies have been preempted by direct marketing organizations, including many subsidiaries of airlines and cruise lines. Delta Dream Vacations, for instance, are sold direct by catalog, as well as through traditional agency channels. The senior and adventure travel segments, the former comprising the majority of all travel business, the latter a relatively new but rapidly growing category, use direct mail to pull hundreds of millions of dollars of tour business annually.

The openings of two "sell" letters are presented here. One is directed at seniors, and the other is targeted at adventure travel prospects. Note the distinctive positioning in the two appeals, each sells tours directed toward carefully segmented audiences.

Dear Traveler,

I'm delighted to inform you that you're among a select group of seasoned travelers we've chosen to receive advance notice of 2 special, all-new European vacation opportunities.

Both offer exciting destinations, comfortable pacing, and great value. And like all our programs, they represent outstanding opportunities for personal growth and cultural enrichment. Once you learn more about them, I'm sure you'll agree one will make a perfect vacation for you next spring or fall!

Dear Adventure Traveler:

Have you ever dreamed of going on safari in East Africa?

Of spending days among the Masai people learning about a way of life still lived according to tribal custom and ancient tradition....

Of actually sitting up close to a mountain gorilla family in the wilds of Rwanda....

Of rising at dawn for a game drive among a herd of zebra stretching as far as the eye can see...or watching a pride of lions on the hunt...and sharing a sumptuous meal around a campfire beneath a sunset of soul-stirring beauty?

If you think such extraordinary adventures must remain as dreams and the time and expense needed to experience them will always elude you, then this announcement will come as especially good news!

Both appeals share a respect for value—a common theme in most travel marketing, due to the high dollar cost and the fact that travel is a discretionary purchase. But distinctions between the two audiences are clear: Where the first letter stresses that one is part of a select group and that comfort is a paramount concern, the other seeks immediately to wrap the reader in the dream, regardless of comfort issues. Indeed to see zebras, one must arise at dawn—but why not, for this special experience. Also note the introduction of the "time" issue—a serious concern for the upscale younger set, whose high disposable incomes are often gained at the cost of limited time due to heavy workloads.

Insights such as these come through conversation with tour directors and marketing managers, whose appreciation for nuance and attention to detail are finely honed. In the travel industry a dozen or more major competitors often are after the same travel dollar.

WHAT WE DREAM VERSUS WHAT WE KNOW

One of the most powerful tools of the direct response copywriter is the ability to interweave the *benefits* and the *features* of a product or service. Carefully managed imagery that propels the recipient into the "dream of possession" or the "marvel of experience" on the one hand, and the objective utility, value, or benefit of ownership and use, on the other, makes for powerful and compelling selling pieces.

You can achieve this power by using visual and verbal representations of products and services that correlate feature/benefit statements with a style consistent with the culture of the segment your package is targeting. For example, here is one travel vendor's checklist of features that buyers consistently rated as essential:

- Unique destination

- Varied experience

- Moderate price

- Value

- Complete

- Well managed

- Comfortable

- Enjoyable

- Contributory to self-development

Complementing this content guide, brochures carry documentary images and objective, descriptive information, including trip description, itinerary, pricing, departures. Everything looks and sounds great.

The accompanying "sell" letter takes a very different tack, using rich, evocative imagery and enthusiastic claims to draw the traveler into the "moment" of the trip.

In combination with strong headlining (often accompanied by preheads noting a key feature), a powerful opening, and a compelling limited offer in the postscript, such copy platforms can be formidable sales tools.

Not-for-profit

Dolores McDonough, a vice president at Washington, D.C.–based Bachurski Associates, relates what well may be one of the most carefully segmented development campaigns in recent memory—and a model for how to appeal to the broadest community of interest associated with an institution:

> "While reviewing the overall annual campaign of a prestigious Eastern university, we realized that when it came to 'hard dollar' fundraising (named gifts, special endowments, etc.), our client did just fine. It was with respect to the annual campaign that questions of efficiency arose. In fact, the exact same appeal was being sent to all 60,000 members of the university community!"

Bachurski Associates created a base letter for the general mailing, with content that was pretty much the same. *But then they fine-tuned it to appeal to different constituencies.* Key mentions were faculty, students, buildings, and grounds. The subtleties included language used with previous donors (upgrade), as opposed to those who had never given (importance of participation).

Further customization was directed at current parents ("The education your son or daughter is getting is very special") and past parents ("You must help to sustain the institution that gave your child such a great education!"). Some copy changes even focused on alumni who had attended, but not graduated, from the school! One part of the program included a lift letter from an alumnae fund chairman targeted to high-income alumnae stressing the tax value of capital gift giving. Another component included segmenting mailings along the size of past gifts.

While much of the more arcane segmenting was never tested, the overall impact of the campaign was to create a dramatic rise in both volume and size of donations.

PYRAMIDS HAVE BASES, TOO

An intriguing sidebar to the notion of segmenting not-for-profit audiences comes in an article published in *Fundraising Today*, a promotional newsletter of New Hampshire–based Brick Mill Studios. An unattributed article called "Are You Targeting the Right Portion of the Pyramid?" makes a point about big ticket donors being oversolicited, while fundraisers neglect to solicit small donors.

The secret to building volume and gaining upgrades from small donors is to give a premium to boost response. Asking for smaller, more manageable gifts also helps, as do carefully thought out renewal mailings and packages designed to increase gift size.

MARKET SEGMENTS

Ethnicity, gender, and class are the three timeless themes of consumer direct marketing. Those selling into the domestic U.S. market in the last decade have noted a phenomenon previously unseen since before World War I—the rise of ethnic and other market segments. Blacks and women, leading developing segments in the 1960s and 1970s, are now being followed by Latinos, Asians, Russians, and Caribbeans.

Columnists whose expertise is in ethnic, women's, and men's segments are always worth reading when they appear in direct response trade publications. But such segments are only one sector in an infinitely wider spectrum. Access all the previously mentioned resources (marketing and list managers, etc.) when researching these areas, but consider other sources as well.

Previous Packages

Don't be afraid to borrow from previous attempts. In fact, work on the assumption that a format, style, and offer that worked once will work again. Build on what's already proved successful. Modify copy points and headlines in some instances; repeat "what worked" in other instances. The touchstone of previous work is the "control" package that outpulled any other offer. Revising it may outpull any new innovation.

Surveys/Focus Groups

Someone spent long hours and paid hard dollars to gather this information. Take a close look at whatever is available.

Debriefs

"Turnover meetings," as they are sometimes called, invariably involve senior marketing managers and even executive officers. In such sessions, key background and strategic direction is provided, often including documentation like product literature and press kits, calls to field staff, quick video presentations, etc. This may be the one time that senior management will make its wishes clear regarding strategy, positioning, key copy points, special features/benefits, etc. A small tape recorder is handy at such events, along with a willingness to ask questions.

Personal Files

Everyone in the advertising business keeps a "book" and a supporting set of files. Keeping yours organized and accessible means it will be that much easier to reference for a special project.

Magazines

Chances are the list you'll be mailing across will in whole or part represent a subscription or membership list. Magazine and newspaper editors, along with organizational leadership, have an intimate relationship with their readers/members. So you might consider talking to an ad rep or editor or an executive director. Insights gained in this way can be illuminating.

Expositions and Trade Shows

No matter what market you're targeting, a show is often its purest focus. Walk the aisles of shows devoted to alternative medicine, seafood, home improvement, historic restoration, personal computers, money matters, and any of a hundred other topics and your insights into how buyers think—and what they're thinking about—will be vastly enhanced.

This goes doubly so in commercial and technical areas, where both vendors and attendees at a show illuminate whole galaxies of issues—from product features and application areas to buying interests and new trends.

Competitive Files

This is a rich resource that almost always informs the creative process. Marketing and sales managers always have them in one form or another. In them, you'll find material generated by your competitors, including direct response packages. If something's been mailed more than once, pay attention to it; it works!

Organizational Literature

Handbooks, press kits, and other literature published by unions (automotive, police, teachers, etc.), professional societies (doctors, lawyers, accountants, realtors, etc.), academic groups (engineers in particular), ethnic organizations (immigrant societies and fraternal groups) and business organizations (chamber of commerce, trade associations, etc.) can prove invaluable in learning about special markets. Find out about them, send for their materials, and talk to the people who run them.

Commercial Atlases, Maps, and Travel Guides

For a "Cook's tour" of a marketplace without ever leaving a library chair, open a U.S. commercial atlas. The wealth of data on income, ethnicity, population clusters, commercial centers, and more can be a revelation, leading to insights that can enrich copy platforms and enhance selling power.

Likewise, road maps are often rich in points of interest, both natural and historical, that can trigger rich imagery attractive to a local or regional population. Similarly, travel guides can provide explanations of local customs, holidays, and landmarks, all or some of which can influence the way you approach the writing process.

Internet and Web Sites

For those impossible-to-answer questions, research librarians worldwide share a special Internet site called "Stumpers." Otherwise, GOPHER and WAIS searches can often reveal Newsgroups whose members can provide all sorts of firsthand information on virtually any subject, product, or service. And Web sites, depending on your need and the power of your home or office computer, can deliver a wealth of visual background, which can really energize your copy.

Video

More and more material, from product demonstrations to travelogues, television "specials," and more is available on video.

Special Events

Manufacturers, distributors, retailers, institutions, and others like to party as much as any of us. New product introductions, award and incentive events, sales kickoffs, and other special occasions can prove invaluable as resources for learning about how products and services are sold.

The Designer or Concept Originator

In the age of corporate decision making and team product development, the image of "Gyro Gearloose" at work in an inventor's loft hardly describes the individual(s) who created the service or product you're promoting. There's no guarantee your source will understand the market into which you're selling, but his or her product and application knowledge may be exceptional, triggering fresh copy ideas that never would have occurred otherwise. Don't miss the chance to tap this special resource.

On the Job

It's commonplace for method-trained actors to literally "get under the skin" of the characters they portray by observing or even going on the job at a work site. Imagine the impetus your medical product copy will gain from actually seeing it used. The same with consumer and industrial products. Your client will often be glad to oblige (time and money allowing) when you make such requests.

Access the wealth of material available to you. Feed your brain until you get an intimate, accurate picture of the "you" you're trying to reach. In the next chapter, we'll explain one of the most time-honored direct marketing media in which your "you"-oriented sales message can appear.

3

ANATOMY OF A PACKAGE

Direct mail is only one component of today's complex marketing mix. As noted earlier, television, radio, video, telephone, and online advertising can and often will be incorporated in your direct marketing efforts to sell your product, service, or cause. The exciting thing that drives direct marketing today is selectivity—targeting your market with ever-increasing accuracy. And to date, direct mail offers *far* more selectivity than television, radio, or the Internet.

Let's say the New England Direct Marketing Association decides to send out a direct mail package to promote its two-day annual conference. It's going to acquire names of likely prospects: lists of members of the Boston Ad Club and Boston chapter of the Public Relations Society of America; subscribers to industry publications like *Direct, Direct Marketing, DM News, Target Marketing Magazine*, and *Who's Mailing What!*; and attendees at other related conferences and seminars. It will find the names of the authors of this book on several of those lists, indicating interest in or connection to direct marketing and targeting them as likely prospects. Then, the association will mail each of them a package to make its sales pitch for the conference. And, in all likelihood, they will respond. And that is what makes direct mail copy so effective—and so essential to understand in today's fast-changing marketplace; it asks for and gets a response.

Top copywriter and consultant Brian Christian Turley of Melrose, Massachusetts, has been a frequent contributor to *DM News* and other industry publications. His is a strong and wise voice in the current hustling for position of "integrated marketing," "relationship marketing," and "database marketing." He states:

> Direct mail has three important things going for it: **accuracy**, **privacy** and **intimacy**. The accuracy of pinpoint database management and delivery. The privacy of the mailbox, the office, or the home. The intimacy of a direct, personal appeal to an individual— not to an audience. And therein, when entrusted to competent, experienced professionals, are the keys to its effectiveness.
>
> Just as there are talented professionals who turn out great television, radio, and print, so there is a distinct, recognizable, and professional art to effective direct mail creativity. Every letter and printed piece is sweated over...written and re-written to make certain that virtually every word has a function in the proposition. It is part talent, part training, part experience, part failure and part success.

PACKAGE COMPONENTS

Let's take a look at the individual components of this powerhouse marketing tool. Many direct mail packages include:

- **An outer envelope, or carrier**
- **A response device or order form**
- **A letter**
- **A brochure**
- **A lift letter**
- **A buck slip, free premium, or other enclosure**
- **A postage-paid response envelope**

This 1994 mailing, an Axel Award winner, contains all of these elements (see Exhibit 3-1).

The list of elements that make up a mailing is far from hard and fast, however. A successful direct mail package may consist of as little as a postcard...or as much as a 3-D box. Sometimes, a mailing may begin its life in a 6×9 carrier envelope with a response form, four-page letter, and an

Exhibit 3-1   An Axel Award–Winning Complex Mailing

This Time-Life mailing and others indicated as Axel Award Winners throughout the book were provided by Axel Andersson, founder of the Axel Andersson Academy, Hamburg, Germany, a leading home-study school in Germany. Mr. Andersson, now based in Palm Harbor, Florida, is owner of the largest private Direct Mail Archive and Library in the U.S. He correctly believes that true excellence in direct mail lies not in creativity but longevity. The Axel Andersson Award of Excellence in Direct Mail is given to mailings that have been continuously mailed for three or more calendar years. Two hundred and fifty mailings have been named Axel Award Winners.

Source: Provided by Axel Andersson. Reprinted with permission of Time-Life, Inc.

11×17 color brochure. Subsequent testing may prove that a variation of the package in a #10 envelope with a two-page letter and no color brochure outpulls the original.

But long before you start strategizing and testing what mix will work best, it's important to understand the role and appearance of each direct mail package component and how these components relate to each other.

THE OUTER ENVELOPE

The outer envelope is your first, best chance to make your sale. To get your reader's attention and draw him or her inside. Like the cover of a book, its goal is to get you to open it up and see what's inside. But its task is tougher. Your direct mail package will arrive on your prospect's desk or kitchen counter with many other offers competing for time and attention. Not to mention the myriad other distractions your prospect faces. And unlike a book, your carrier envelope must get your prospect to open it and also to communicate back to it, *to respond*.

An outer envelope can:
a. Make a challenge.
b. Begin a story.
c. Ask a question.
d. Sound an alarm.
e. Flatter your reader.
f. Highlight a special offer or premium.

According to the Direct Marketing Association's (DMA) *1995/96 Statistical Fact Book*, the average consumer receives 21.31 pieces of mail per week. In 1994, the volume of third-class mail was 69.4 billion pieces. You face a tough task. How can you make your package stand out among the crowd (Exhibit 3-2)?

Never forget how easy it is to throw away a direct mail envelope unopened. You've probably done it yourself hundreds of times. And people are going to do it to your package unless you give them a strong enough reason not to!

Exhibit 3-2   Make Your Envelope Stand Out from the Crowd

Exhibit 3-3, from the DMA's *1994/95 Statistical Fact Book* helps to illustrate this point.

If all we had to do was get the recipient to open it, we'd certainly write **"Cash Inside! Open Immediately!"** on every envelope.

Don't. A prospect you immediately disappoint won't be receptive to anything you have to sell. First impressions count. The graphics and copy on your carrier will set the tone for what follows. And even here at the beginning, you can use the information your database gives you to *"write on target"*—pinpointing your exact audience of one. Exhibit 3-4 is an excellent example of an outer envelope advertising *National Geographic Traveler* magazine. According to Associate Creative Director Elizabeth Murphy, "This package beat a double postcard in both response and cost—a copywriter's dream. It shows how using an editorial premium and smart marketing can beat even a 'soft free-trial' postcard offer."

Exhibit 3-3 Why Consumers Open Direct Mail Envelopes

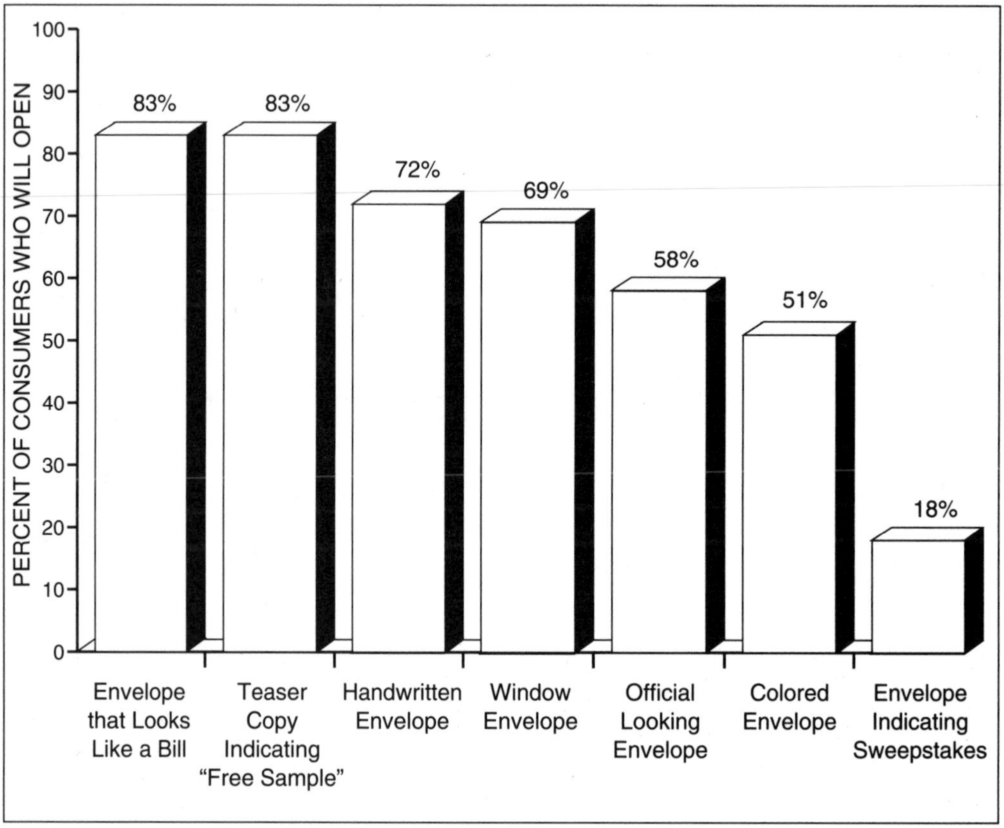
PERCENT OF CONSUMERS WHO WILL OPEN
100
90
80
70
60
50
40
30
20
10
0
83%
83%
72%
69%
58%
51%
18%
Envelope that Looks Like a Bill
Teaser Copy Indicating "Free Sample"
Handwritten Envelope
Window Envelope
Official Looking Envelope
Colored Envelope
Envelope Indicating Sweepstakes

Source: Adapted from *Journal of Direct Marketing*, 1993.

THE RESPONSE FORM

The response, or order form, is the second most important element in your package. This is the vehicle by which your reader becomes your buyer. Designed for action, the response form should ideally be able to stand alone as your sales message, without any accompanying letter or brochure.

Exhibit 3-4   Carrier Envelope from *National Geographic Traveler*

Source: Reprinted with permission of *National Geographic Traveler*.
Designer Jonathon Halling, copywriter Margaret Mayer.

This is where you state your offer clearly and simply. State it in a way that makes it easy for your reader to respond. A number of involvement devices can be used to encourage physical interaction with your prospect: tokens, stamps, punch-outs, puzzles, premiums. Any time you create an opportunity for interaction, even if it's just checking the ☐ YES! box, you're strengthening your prospect's relationship with your product or service.

A response form can:
a. Announce your offer and benefits.
b. Involve your reader.
c. Announce introductory savings, trial offers, or other special offers.
d. Offer easy payment methods.
e. Highlight a premium or other free gift.
f. Offer a money-back guarantee.

The complexity of the response form can range from a simple postage-paid card with checkoff box to a multipage application for an insurance policy. It may be a survey, an acceptance form for a trial subscription offer, or a catalog order form with credit card or billing option instructions and product/shipping selections.

Whatever copy it includes must be presented in a clear, straightforward manner. The response form must have your respondent's name and address—either on a mailing label or on the form itself, handwritten or personalized. You may want to ask for a phone number as well. The response form will clarify how much, if anything, the respondent is supposed to pay, and in what manner: cash, credit card, monthly payments, etc.

Exhibit 3-5 shows the response form used in a mailing for *National Geographic Traveler* magazine. Note its tear-off stub, highlighted 24 percent savings, bill me option, and free premium.

THE LETTER

Although the letter isn't as immediately related to the sale transaction as the response form, the direct mail letter is often the copywriter's favorite part of the package. Some copywriters believe you should start the letter by repeating the same teaser copy you put on the outer envelope—assuming that what got your prospect to open the package will get him or her to read it as well.

Exhibit 3-5   Response Form from *National Geographic Traveler*

Source: Reprinted with permission of *National Geographic Traveler*.

A letter can:
a. State your offer.
b. Provoke a response.
c. Tell a story.
d. Sound an alarm.
e. Hang out a carrot.

But how do you write a letter? That's a chapter in itself (for a detailed discussion see Chapter 6), but what's important is to remember the copywriter's two-fold goal: to get interest and action. Interest without action doesn't count.

The "operatic principle" of direct mail copywriting is A-I-D-A:

A Attract attention
I Incite interest
D Develop desire
A Acquire action

There are lots of other formulas for letter writing, too. Sometimes when you sit down to write a letter, you can follow a path trailblazed by a great copywriter. We'll take a look at some of those paths—like Star-Chain-Hook and Picture-Promise-Prove-Push—in Chapter 6. But the best advice for writing a really effective direct mail letter follows no formula at all: Write a simple, personal letter from one human being to another.

Always write your letter as though you are writing to one person. And like a good conversationalist, talk more about "you" than "me." Just as you enjoy talking to someone who remembers your personal interests, a good letter will let your reader know that he or she is recognized by the letter writer—as a new member, a lover of good books, a concerned conservationist.

Write your letter simply and comfortably. Two- to three-line paragraphs are easy to look at and read. Use subheads, indentations, underscoring, and handwriting, when appropriate. More on these details later.

For now, know that your letter is your best personal communication of your product or service benefits. Remember that your reader wants to know "What's in this for me?"

What about letter length? No rules apply. When asked how long his legs were, Abraham Lincoln is said to have replied, "Just long enough to reach the ground." So, too, your letter should be just long enough to tell your story and make your sale.

Exhibit 3-6 shows the two-page letter used to promote *National Geographic Traveler*. The letter "works" for, among other reasons, its use of paragraphs, bulleted listing, subhead, and postscript.

THE BROCHURE

Brochures are great places to whet your reader's desire. Let the language follow the tone of your letter, but use the brochure as a place to describe your product or service in even more detail. Show someone using your mower on a well-manicured lawn. Repeat the raves current subscribers give your cooking magazine. Show a picture of that handsome tote bag you're offering as a free gift for joining this environmental organization.

Exhibit 3-6   Letter from *National Geographic Traveler*

Traveler
1145 17th Street N.W.
Washington, D.C. 20036-4688 U.S.A.

Plan the perfect vacation with the travel magazine chosen "best" by the publishing industry for three years in a row!

Dear Friend,

Who else but the well-traveled experts at National Geographic could bring you a travel magazine that surpasses all others in making trip planning easier and more rewarding?

Every issue of NATIONAL GEOGRAPHIC TRAVELER is packed with the invaluable knowledge of globe-trotting writers and photographers...to give you a vacation guide you can rely on year-round.

Designed for "real people" (as one reader remarked), this award-winning magazine works for you whether your budget is slim or substantial. In fact, TRAVELER was named "Best Travel Magazine" for three years running by publishing-industry publications *Folio:* and *Magazine Week!*

Unforgettable photographs, detailed maps, exciting destinations, and a wealth of trip-planning ideas make it the most useful travel resource available today.

Subscribe to TRAVELER now and
receive our 10th-Anniversary
Scenic Drives Guide...absolutely FREE!

Accept this invitation to enjoy a year of TRAVELER magazine for just $17.95, and we'll send you a detailed guide to 50 scenic drives in the U.S. — one in every state! Created for TRAVELER's recent 10th-anniversary issue, this 16-page booklet maps out some of our country's most spectacular scenery. It's great for cross-country trips...or weekend excursions.

Then get ready to enjoy the world through six beautiful bimonthly issues of TRAVELER. Explore magnificent parklands, historic sites, fascinating cities, popular resorts, and quiet out-of-the-way places. Each destination is illustrated by stunning photography in National Geographic's grand tradition. (You'll even discover the professionals' secrets for making your own vacation photographs more exciting!)

Each year, TRAVELER takes you to dozens of vacation spots in the U.S. and Canada, as well as to overseas locales. Your

(continued)

itinerary will be unlimited — from gems off the beaten track to intriguing places that you've always longed to visit.

And TRAVELER gives you a wealth of practical details that can save you time and money! Turn to...

* *Photography* for expert tips on film, lenses, lighting, and photo composition
* *Value Vacations* for advice on smart spending and saving
* *Foods of the Region* for an introduction to exciting regional cuisines
* *Travel Wise* for important information like when to go and how to get to your destination...expert recommendations for selected hotels and restaurants...the best things to see and do...detailed maps of your vacation area...and listings of key phone numbers and addresses.

You'll find out what's going on in your neck of the woods with TRAVELER's exclusive *Highlights* calendar that lists festivals and other special events in the U.S. and Canada.

Subscribe today and receive your FREE bonus gift!

For a limited time, just $17.95 a year — 24% off the newsstand price — brings you six bimonthly issues of TRAVELER along with a FREE copy of our exclusive Scenic Drives Guide! To start your subscription and receive your bonus Guide, simply drop the enclosed Reservation Card into the mail. We'll be happy to bill you. Or enclose your payment, and we'll rush you the Guide.

Whether you're a travel lover or an armchair adventurer (or both), you'll enjoy the world-wise tips and savvy insights that NATIONAL GEOGRAPHIC TRAVELER has to offer. Mail your Reservation Card today, and you'll soon be on the road to incredible vacations!

Sincerely,

Michela English

Michela English
Senior Vice President

ME/sd

P.S. TRAVELER's Scenic Drives Guide details stateside adventures from 40-mile jaunts to 400-mile journeys. Don't delay... send for your FREE copy now!

Recycled Paper
Printed in U.S.A.

Source: Reprinted with permission of *National Geographic Traveler*.

A brochure can:
a. Present testimonials.
b. List product features.
c. Restate terms of offer.
d. Announce deadlines.
e. Show your product in action.

If you need to get more technical, the brochure is a place to do it. Include product specifications: the dimensions and capacity of the dishwasher, the system requirements of the software.

Always make sure your brochure invites action as well. Add on a handwritten line that says "Please send a gift to World Wildlife Fund today!" or include a starburst that reads "See the enclosed order form to reserve your Mozart Treasury now!"

And test. Sometimes that beautiful, four-color brochure your agency wants to create isn't even necessary. Smithsonian Institution Press offers book and audio products that beg for great graphics, but they've found on occasion that a package without a brochure outpulls one with a brochure. That's not always going to be true, but you have to test to find out what works. Exhibit 3-7 shows the *Traveler* brochure, one side of which imitates the magazine cover.

LIFT LETTERS, BUCK SLIPS, AND OTHER ENCLOSURES

Sometimes a short secondary letter, a "lift letter," is included. It might be a note from a celebrity or spokesperson, or might be labeled "Open this if you've decided not to take advantage of this risk-free offer."

The lift letter creates another opportunity to reiterate or reinforce the sales message. Its chief characteristic is that it is signed by someone other than the person who signs the main letter.

What does the lift letter say? The original lift letter, which appeared in a package from Greystone Press, began with a sentence or two to the effect that "Frankly, I'm puzzled…". The idea was that the offer of the product (books, in this case) was so good that the publisher (the main letter in the package was signed by the editor) could not understand why anybody would be willing to pass it up.

Exhibit 3-7   Brochure from *National Geographic Traveler*

NATIONAL GEOGRAPHIC

Traveler

SELECTED BY MAGAZINE WEEK AND FOLIO: AS "BEST TRAVEL MAGAZINE" FOR THREE YEARS IN A ROW

In Every Issue

Great vacation
ideas for travel in
the U.S., in Canada,
and abroad

Stunning color
photography and
tips on taking better
travel pictures

Handy, detailed maps

Perfect weekend
getaways

Travel planning advice:
how to get there,
what to see and
do, where to eat
and stay

Sparkling Trunk Bay, St. John,
U.S. Virgin Islands—a paradise
for beach lovers, snorkelers,
and sunseekers

(continued)

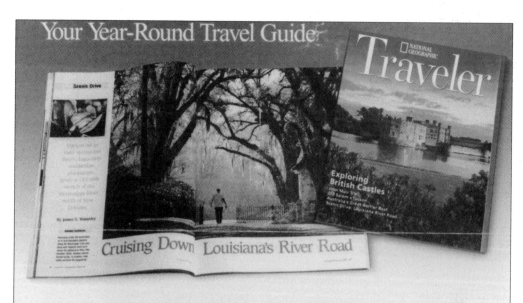

Pick Any Season, Pack Up, and Go!

Put more ease and pleasure into your vacations with NATIONAL GEOGRAPHIC TRAVELER! In each bimonthly issue you'll visit fascinating vacation spots in the U.S.A., in Canada, and abroad.

Journey to national parks, exciting cities, resorts, historic sites, and little-known places within easy reach of your budget and your home.

TRAVELER also offers you the practical travel information you need to plan the perfect trip. Turn to *Travel Wise*, a special section with tips on each TRAVELER getaway, for advice on where to eat and stay, what to see and do, and much more!

Check out *Weekends* for the best ideas for short jaunts. Get advice on shooting great pictures from National Geographic's experts in *Photography*. And consult *Traveling Easy* for ways to make your travels more enjoyable.

Brilliant photographs will dazzle you. TRAVELER will show you out-of-the-way places...insiders' secrets...the latest travel trends. And prompt you to enter *your* photos in TRAVELER's annual photography contest to win a dream vacation!

And share wonderful adventures like these:

❖ Tour Southwest British Columbia, a region of spectacular mountains and coastline steeped in rich history of the gold-rush days.

❖ Discover what's new and what's lasting in the city of jazz and Creole cooking — New Orleans.

❖ Explore Amsterdam, one of Europe's great commercial, intellectual, and artistic capitals.

It's all waiting for you in the pages of NATIONAL GEOGRAPHIC TRAVELER!

Respond now to receive a special introductory offer! A detailed guide of 50 great scenic drives in the U.S. is FREE with your paid subscription!

Only 17^{95}

for a full year of TRAVELER

NATIONAL GEOGRAPHIC SOCIETY

1145 17th Street N.W. Washington, D.C. 20036-4688

Copyright © 1994 National Geographic Society
♻ Recycled Paper

Save 24% off newsstand price!

Detailed area maps guide you to fascinating vacation sites.

Source: Reprinted with permission of *National Geographic Traveler.*

A lift letter can:

a. Present an additional benefit.
b. Argue against a negative response.
c. Provide authoritative confirmation.
d. Tell an inside story.
e. Repeat testimonials.
f. Give a gee-whiz fact or additional information.
g. Have a completely different voice and signature.

Exhibits 3-8 and 3-9 are examples of recent lift letters from the Quality Paperback Book Club and *Mid-Atlantic Country*.

OTHER ENCLOSURES

A buck slip can highlight a free premium (Exhibit 3-10). This separate slip might measure $3\frac{1}{2} \times 8\frac{1}{2}$ or $5\frac{1}{2} \times 8\frac{1}{2}$.

Another possibility is including a sheet of stickers, stamps, or personalized address labels. (Exhibit 3-11).

THE RESPONSE ENVELOPE

Unless your order form is a self-mailer, your package will need to include a business reply envelope. This has the advantage of encouraging cash payments and also gives your respondent a measure of privacy regarding his or her order. Don't forget that you can add a little sales sizzle even to your response envelope. A simulated rubber stamp indicating "Charter Subscription Enclosed. Handle Promptly" says the reader is a valued new subscriber. "Free Gift Offer—Return Immediately" reinforces the sale.

Now that you've taken a tour of a typical direct mail package, you still may be asking yourself, "How is learning about this ever going to help my *new* (read *electronic*) advertising efforts?" You'll find some specific advice on copywriting for the Internet later in this book, but for now remember this: **Everything you learn about the making of a successful direct mail package can prove just as beneficial on the electronic highway as it is on your postal carrier's route.**

Exhibit 3-8   Lift Letter from Quality Paperback Book Club (Axel Award Winner)

Dear Friend:

I know. It's hard to swallow. There's always a catch. "Sure," you're thinking. "Three books, three bucks. <u>Then</u> what?"

The answer? Nothing.

Really.

We're <u>so sure</u> that you're going to love being a QPB member...<u>so sure</u> you're going to eagerly await each issue of the <u>QPB Review</u>... and <u>so sure</u> you're going to be pleased with each issue's reading selection...that we're happy to make what -- admittedly -- is a pretty unbelievable offer. <u>Three quality books, of your choice, at a dollar each</u>, plus shipping and handling, with no obligation to buy more.

Look, if you never, ever, buy another book from QPB, you've taken advantage of the greatest book deal we know of. It's for real!

Join us -- today!

Cordially,

Tracy P. Brown

Tracy P. Brown
Editorial Director

Exhibit 3-9   Lift Letter from *Mid-Atlantic Country* Magazine

INSIDE:

A tantalizing offering

*and a few words from some
people who may be from your
neck of the woods . . .*

"The articles convey all the warmth and
hospitality that coincide with country living
and the country calendar is fantastic for
planning a country weekend."
> M. T. K.
> *Huntingdon Valley, Pennsylvania*

"MID-ATLANTIC COUNTRY is an
excellent magazine."
> T. M. S.
> *Clendenin, West Virginia*

"Have only been a subscriber for a short
time, but your magazine really fills the bill."
> D. N. E.
> *Voorhees, New Jersey*

"MID-ATLANTIC COUNTRY is one
really terrific magazine. I can hardly wait for
each new issue."
> L. K.
> *Landover, Maryland*

Take your mid-Atlantic neighbors' word for it. And take a
taste of MID-ATLANTIC COUNTRY free!

MID-ATLANTIC CRAB CAKES

1 pound Chesapeake Bay blue crab meat
½ cup diced sweet green pepper
½ cup diced sweet red pepper
1 tablespoon butter
⅓ cup tartar sauce
2 teaspoons Worcestershire sauce

2 teaspoons minced fresh parsley
1 egg
4 crumpled saltine crackers
Salt and pepper to taste

½ cup vegetable oil
⅓ cup butter

Pick over crab meat for bits of shell or cartilage. Saute peppers in 1 tablespoon butter until tender. Cool. Mix together all the ingredients with a fork. Do not overdo it; you want to retain the crab meat texture.

Mold mixture into about 16 flat patties approximately 2½ inches wide and ½-inch thick. If you wish, these may be made ahead and refrigerated a few hours.

In a large frying skillet, heat the butter and oil over medium heat. Fry cakes on each side until golden brown.

Serve at once with additional tartar sauce, roasted sweet corn ears, french fried potatoes, or on a bun with lettuce and tomato slices. 🍂

Yield: Serves 4.

MID-ATLANTIC COUNTRY caters to all your tastes...
These satisfied subscribers agree:

"Enjoy your magazine very much."
N. S. S.
Christiansburg, Virginia

"I always look forward to MID-ATLANTIC COUNTRY, and especially enjoyed "Historic Portsmouth" in the February issue."
Mrs. H. S. F., Jr.
Virginia Beach, Virginia

"...what an integral part MID-ATLANTIC COUNTRY has become in our summer travels. ...Keep sending us in exciting directions."
C. V. D.
Uniontown, Pennsylvania

"...to let you know how much I enjoy reading the interesting articles in your magazine. Your writers are simply terrific! They seem to know so much about the subjects of their stories. Keep up the good work!"
C. J. S.
Forestville, Maryland

Source: *Mid-Atlantic Country.*

Exhibit 3-10   Buck Slip from the Nature Conservancy

Source: Reprinted with permission of the Nature Conservancy.

The importance of benefits—telling your prospect what's in it for her or him. The necessity of accurate information and clear language. The absolute importance of the call to action!

We face an amazing world. And direct marketing is *the medium* for communicating in it. Thanks to technology, the possibilities—for targeting our markets and tailoring our messages—are endless. Today more than

**Exhibit 3-11   Personalized Labels Enclosure from African Wildlife
Foundation**

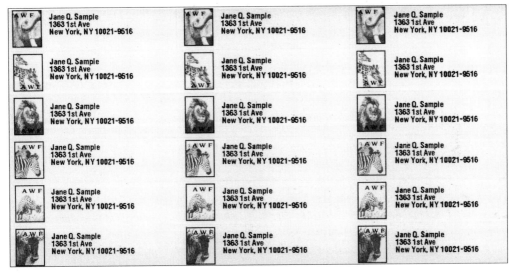

Source: Reprinted with permission of African Wildlife Foundation and Bachurski Associates, Inc.

ever, you can use copy to target whomever you specifically want to reach: current, lapsed, or prospective customers; high-dollar or low-dollar donors; expires or first-year subscribers. Whether in a direct mail package or on a computer screen, you can use words to profit from the information your own database gives you. And remember, *without* words, a wealth of database information is useless.

Remember, too, that your goal as a direct marketing copywriter is to *write on target.* Use the information your database gives you. And write targeted direct marketing copy that grows ever closer to real one-to-one communication.

4

THE ENVELOPE, PLEASE

How do you get your reader inside the carrier envelope? What verbal hook will get him or her to make a step toward what you have to offer? What **teaser copy**—the words that are sometimes used on a carrier envelope or front panel of a self-mailer—will grab your prospect's attention strongly enough to prompt a physical move to open the envelope?

You have only 3 to 5 seconds to get your recipients to open your mailer. Copy giant Bill Jayme solved that problem for a *Psychology Today* mailing with this classic teaser copy: Do You Still Close the Bathroom Door Even When No One's Home?

Most copywriters spend a great deal of time considering the words that will go on the outer envelope. In a *Direct Marketing* magazine article called "Get Your Envelope Opened by Hook or by Crook," well-known copywriter, consultant, and control-beater John Francis Tighe wrote, "An envelope's sole function in life is to get itself opened. If it fails in that function, the whole mailing fails.... I tell people I spend 90 percent of my time thinking about it.... I have no doubt that many a great control mailing, when it starts to fade, could be revived, resurrected, and re-launched in a second blaze of glory by re-packaging it in a sparkling new envelope."

SIZE AND SHAPE

Before we look at the words used, we will consider the physical appearance of the envelope itself. Carriers come in all sizes, paper stocks,

Exhibit 4-1 Westvaco Envelope Selector Guide

GUIDE TO STANDARD ENVELOPES BY SIZES

2¼ x 3½	1 Coin
2½ x 4¼	3 Coin
2⅞ x 5¼	5 Coin
3 x 4½	4 Coin
3 x 4⅞	4½ Coin
3⅛ x 5½	5½ Coin
3⅜ x 6	10 Clasp Interdepartment 6 Coin
3½ x 6½	7 Coin
3 9/16 x 6	6¼ Executive Style (Regular and Outlook)
3 9/16 x 7⅞	Executive (Data Card)
3⅝ x 4 11/16	4 Baronial
3½ x 6	6¼ Commercial & Official (Regular and Outlook) 6¼ Commercial & Official Self-Seal (Regular and Outlook) 6¼ Kost-Kut
3⅝ x 6½	6¾ Executive (Regular & Outlook) 6¾ Commercial & Official (Regular & Outlook) 6¾ Commercial & Official Self-Seal (Regular & Outlook) 6¾ Banker's Flap (Regular & Outlook) 6¾ Square Flap (Regular & Outlook) 6¾ Kost-Kut
3⅝ x 8⅝	8⅝ Commercial & Official Check (Regular & Outlook) 8⅝ Dubl-Vue Check 8⅝ Commercial & Official Self-Seal (Regular & Outlook) 8⅝ Kost-Kut
3¾ x 6¾	7 Executive Style (Regular & Outlook) 7 Commercial & Official (Regular & Outlook) 7 Commercial & Official Self-Seal (Regular & Outlook)

19

weights, and colors. There are seal and clasp envelopes, flat mailers, window envelopes, embossed envelopes, jumbo mailers, tubes, brown kraft envelopes, recycled paper envelopes, transparent plastic envelopes, and much, much more.

A guide to standard envelope sizes from Westvaco Envelope Division is shown in Exhibit 4-1.

3⅞ x 7½	7¾ Executive Style (Regular & Outlook) 7¾ Commercial & Official (Regular & Outlook) 7¾ Commercial & Official Self-Seal (Regular & Outlook) 7¾ Banker's Flap (Regular & Outlook) 7¾ Square Flap (Regular & Outlook) Monarch Executive (Regular & Outlook) Monarch Commercial & Official (Regular & Outlook) Monarch Commercial & Official Self-Seal (Regular & Outlook) 8 Glove 7¾ Kost Kut
3⅞ x 8⅞	9 Executive Style (Regular & Outlook) 9 Commercial & Official (Regular & Outlook) 9 Square Flap (Regular & Outlook) 9 Commercial & Official Self-Seal (Regular & Outlook) 9 Kost-Kut 9 Dubl-Vue Statement 9 Banker's Flap (Regular & Outlook) 9 Square Flap (Regular & Outlook)
4 x 6⅜	7 Glove 15 Clasp
4⅛ x 5⅛	5 Baronial
4⅛ x 9½	10 Executive (Regular & Outlook) 10 Commercial & Official (Regular & Outlook) 10 Commercial & Official Self-Seal (Regular & Outlook) 10 Self-Seal Business (Regular & Outlook) 10 Banker's Flap (Regular & Outlook) 10 Square Flap (Regular & Outlook) 10 Policy 10 Medical Claim Form
4⅜ x 5⅝	5½ Baronial (Invitation) A-2 Announcement
4½ x 9½	10½ Self-Seal Business (Regular & Outlook) 10½ Banker's Flap (Regular & Outlook) 10½ Square Flap (Regular & Outlook)

20

4½ x 10⅜	11 Executive Style (Regular & Outlook) 11 Commercial & Official (Regular & Outlook) 11 Banker's Flap (Regular & Outlook) 11 Square Flap (Regular & Outlook) 11 Policy 11 Clasp Interdepartment
4⅝ x 5¹³⁄₁₆	5¾ Baronial
4¾ x 6½	A-6 Announcement
4⅝ x 6¾	25 Clasp Interdepartment 1 Scarf
4¾ x 11	12 Commercial & Official (Regular & Outlook) 12 Banker's Flap (Regular & Outlook) 12 Square Flap (Regular & Outlook)
5 x 6	6 Baronial
5 x 7½	35 Clasp Interdepartment 3 Scarf
5 x 11	Safety Fold
5 x 11½	14 Commercial & Official (Regular & Outlook) 14 Banker's Flap (Regular & Outlook) 14 Square Flap (Regular & Outlook) Safety Fold 14 Policy 14 Clasp Interdepartment
5¼ x 7¼	A-7 Announcement
5½ x 7½	4¼ Scarf
5½ x 8⅛	5 Booklet A-8 Announcement
5½ x 8¼	50 Clasp Interdepartment 6 Scarf
5½ x 11½	Safety Fold
5¾ x 8⅞	6 Booklet

21

One standard is a #10 envelope ($4\frac{1}{8}$" × $9\frac{1}{2}$"); a #9 reply envelope ($3\frac{7}{8}$" × $8\frac{7}{8}$") fits easily inside. But an astonishing variety of sizes and shapes is available: the 6 × 9 is only somewhat larger than a #10 but looks a lot bigger and can often be used to give a more substantive, elegant, or formal touch. A 9 × 12 looks imposing and demands attention. Both the 6 × 9 and

6 x 9	55 Clasp Interdepartment 6½ Booklet 1 Catalog
6 x 9½	A-10 Announcement
6 x 12	16 Banker's Flap (Regular) Safety Fold
6¼ x 9⅝	7 Booklet
6½ x 9½	63 Clasp
	Interdepartment 1¾ Catalog Flat Mailer (w & w/o First Class border)
7 x 10	3 Catalog 68 Clasp Interdepartment
7½ x 10½	Flat Mailer (w & w/o First Class border) 75 Clasp Interdepartment 7½ Booklet 6 Catalog
8 x 11	80 Clasp Interdepartment
8¼ x 11¼	8 Catalog
8½ x 11½	83 Clasp Interdepartment
8¾ x 11¼	9¾ Catalog 87 Clasp Interdepartment
8¾ x 11½	9 Booklet
8¾ x 11⅜	Letter
9 x 12	Flat Mailer (w & w/o First Class border) 90 Clasp Interdepartment 9½ Booklet 10½ Catalog Rate-Mate

22

9¼ x 14½	94 Clasp Interdepartment
9½ x 11⅜	Letter
9½ x 12½	Flat Mailer (w & w/o First Class border) 93 Clasp Interdepartment 12½ Catalog
9½ x 12⅝	10 Booklet
10 x 12	95 Clasp Interdepartment
10 x 13	Flat Mailer (w & w/o First Class border) 97 Clasp Interdepartment 13 Booklet 13½ Catalog Rate-Mate
10 x 15	Flat Mailer (w & w/o First Class border) Legal 98 Clasp Interdepartment 15 Catalog
11½ x 14½	105 Clasp Interdepartment 14½ Catalog
12 x 15½	110 Clasp Interdepartment 15½ Catalog

23

Source: Reprinted with permission of Westvaco.

9 × 12 can be made with a panoramic window, which provides an additional opportunity for graphic appeals.

Like everything else, carrier size should match your message and overall creative concept. And, you should **test**. One successful survey mailing for the National Parks and Conservation Association started out as a 9 × 12 carrier with a four-page letter, two-page survey response form, premium buck slip, and reply envelope. After that became the control and new testing began, a revised version of the same package—same teaser copy, same letter, same response survey, same everything—was mailed in a #10 and outperformed the original (Exhibit 4-2).

Exhibit 4-2   National Parks and Conservation Association—Two Carrier Envelopes

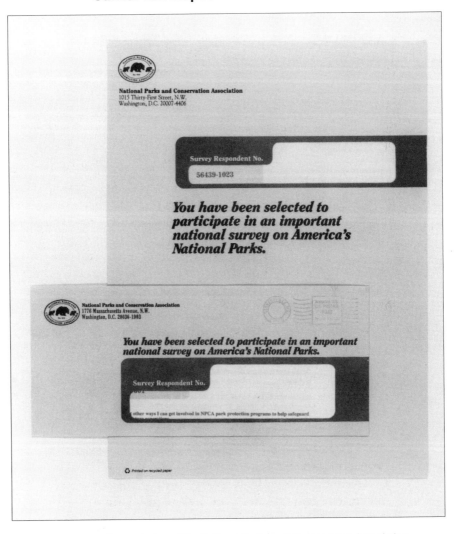

Source: Reprinted with permission of the National Parks and Conservation Association.

You can find or custom-design a carrier size and shape to fit just about any sales message. Anything that departs from the #10 window envelope is likely to get a little more attention when it arrives in a stack of #10 window envelopes, but anything that departs from the ordinary also will usually cost more. And if you want to use something *really* nonstandard (say, crescent shaped or triangular), be sure to check with the Postal Service first to see if it will go through the mails all right (Exhibit 4-3).

You may also ask your envelope supplier to create custom envelopes for your mailing—with special pull-tabs, die-cut windows, and more. Exhibit 4-4 shows a sample of custom-designed envelopes offered by Westvaco.

Exhibit 4-3   Postal Service Size Standards (Westvaco)

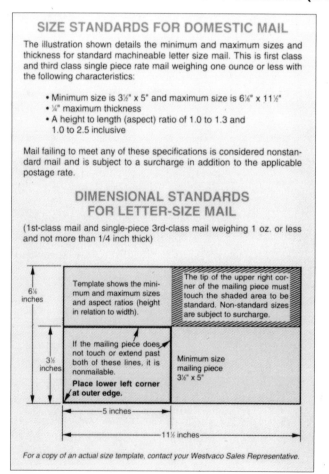

Source: Reprinted with permission of Westvaco.

Exhibit 4-4　Custom Envelopes (Westvaco)

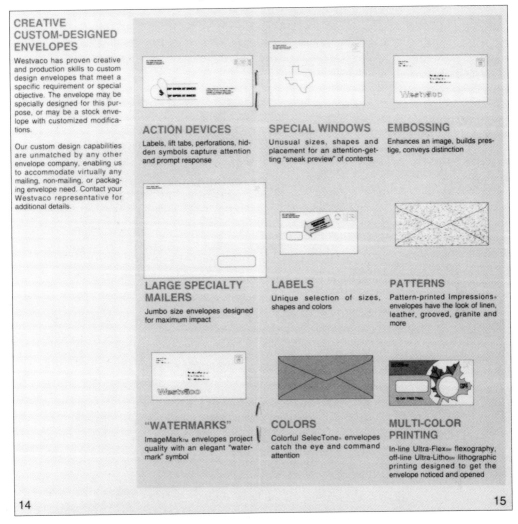

CREATIVE CUSTOM-DESIGNED ENVELOPES

Westvaco has proven creative and production skills to custom design envelopes that meet a specific requirement or special objective. The envelope may be specially designed for this purpose, or may be a stock envelope with customized modifications.

Our custom design capabilities are unmatched by any other envelope company, enabling us to accommodate virtually any mailing, non-mailing, or packaging envelope need. Contact your Westvaco representative for additional details.

ACTION DEVICES

Labels, lift tabs, perforations, hidden symbols capture attention and prompt response

SPECIAL WINDOWS

Unusual sizes, shapes and placement for an attention-getting "sneak preview" of contents

EMBOSSING

Enhances an image, builds prestige, conveys distinction

LARGE SPECIALTY MAILERS

Jumbo size envelopes designed for maximum impact

LABELS

Unique selection of sizes, shapes and colors

PATTERNS

Pattern-printed Impressions® envelopes have the look of linen, leather, grooved, granite and more

"WATERMARKS"

ImageMark™ envelopes project quality with an elegant "watermark" symbol

COLORS

Colorful SelecTone® envelopes catch the eye and command attention

MULTI-COLOR PRINTING

In-line Ultra-Flex℠ flexography, off-line Ultra-Litho℠ lithographic printing designed to get the envelope noticed and opened

14

15

Source: Reprinted with permission of Westvaco.

PERSONALIZATION

Moore Response Marketing Services is another leader in creating special envelope formats to strategically support their clients' objectives. The power of the Moore system enables them to incorporate special print techniques and customized information into the various pieces of the direct mail package (Exhibit 4-5).

Exhibit 4-5 Personalized Outer Envelope for *Worth* Magazine

82 Devonshire Street
R25A
Boston, MA 02109

BULK RATE
U.S. POSTAGE
PAID
WORTH
MAGAZINE

What the '90s say
to successful people like you
comes through loud and clear:

"DON' T EXPECT ANY SYMPATHY,
CARALE EDER!"

CARALE EDER
411 ACKLEY AVE
MT SHASTA, CA 96067-2614

FREE!

Maybe you need a friend!
To receive a FREE get
acquainted issue of WORTH—
the ultimate personal finance
magazine—a $3.00 value—
please return this label on
form enclosed!

(continued)

Source: Reprinted with permission of Moore Response Marketing Services and *Worth* Magazine.

Hugh Chewning of Chewning Direct Marketing said the following in *Cause and Effect,* Moore's quarterly newsletter for fundraising professionals:

Make Sure Your Mailing Envelope Is Doing What It's Supposed to Do

If there's one truism in direct marketing, it's that there is no "standard" direct mail package. From jumbos to self-mailers to the old standby #10 envelope package…from the "super-glitz" to the "quick and dirty"…who could possibly define the so-called "typical" direct mail package?

Yet, among the dizzying array of formats and sizes that turn up in our mailboxes on any given day, the basic components of a direct mail package have never changed…. The mailing envelope…is the first component the recipient will see in the mailbox. Because it is the first, in many ways it's the most important, so we need to take a good, hard look at what we need to accomplish when developing a mailing envelope.

The mailing envelope has two purposes:

1. To deliver what's inside it, and

2. To get opened.

When you think of the direct mail package as a door-to-door salesperson—because that's really what it is—the mailing envelope serves to "get a foot in the door." Your prospect is going to decide very quickly whether to look at your mailing or toss it aside—and they will base that decision in large part on what they see on that outer envelope.

You've probably heard about the three- or seven-second test. This is how long a prospect takes to make a decision about whether or not to open the package. Whether it's three or seven seconds is really not important. What is important, however, is creating an envelope that accomplishes its two objectives. Practically every mailing envelope has these common elements:

1 The corner card (or return address)

2. The type of postage (stamp, meter, bulk rate indicia, etc.)

3. Addressing

4. Teaser

5. Color

6. Paper stock

Which element is the most important?

Prospects typically look at their name on the envelope, and then their eyes move to the left. Next, their eyes move up to the corner card, then over to the right corner at the postage.

So if you've been wondering whether to put the teaser to the right or left of the addressing, you now have the answer. It's to the left.

Moving to the corner card, your first decision is whether or not to have one at all. If you've selected a very official approach, or you're mailing to people who haven't responded to previous efforts, then you may want to forego including a corner card identifying yourself.

When selecting how to handle the postage, remember that if you're going to mail your package first class, broadcast it by using multiple stamps and perhaps also adding to the envelope "FIRST CLASS MAIL."

The type of postage you select will also affect the "mood" of your envelope. For example, for an official look, a postage meter or even a pre-printed indicia may be more appropriate than a stamp.

Remember that whatever look you choose, make sure you carry the look not only on the envelope, but throughout the mailing. There's nothing worse than a hodgepodge approach that will look suspiciously like an inventory reduction mailing.

And when it comes to testing, always test new envelope graphics and teasers. It's one of the most cost-effective ways to keep a proven control "fresh." And it's an inexpensive test that can bring some pretty dramatic results.

And don't forget about the back side. Typically, as people open an envelope, they will spend more time looking at the back side than the front side. It's a great place to repeat a benefit.

THE ALL-IMPORTANT TEASER

You don't *always* have to put teaser copy on your envelope, and in fact, sometimes you'll definitely not want to. Lots of mailings go out with a simple RSVP, or blank (Exhibit 4-6).

Exhibit 4-6   Outer Envelope for Smithsonian Institution

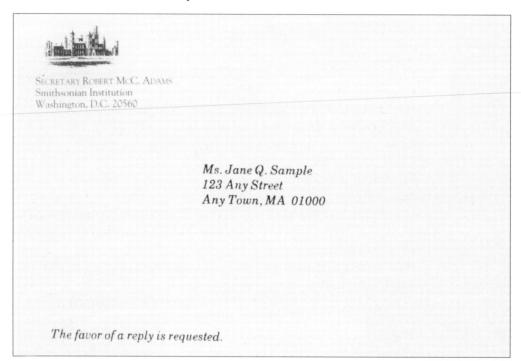

SECRETARY ROBERT McC. ADAMS
Smithsonian Institution
Washington, D.C. 20560

Ms. Jane Q. Sample
123 Any Street
Any Town, MA 01000

The favor of a reply is requested.

Source: Reprinted with permission of Bachurski Associates, Inc.

Especially with business-to-business mail, teasers can be deadly. Remember, with business-to-business mail, your package will often be prescreened by someone else before it reaches your main prospect. And teaser copy can alert a secretary that this is "advertising" and get your package tossed.

Let's say you are going to use a teaser. What should it say? Something that's going to get your prospect to want to know more. What's that? It depends on your offer and your audience. Notice how these examples do a good job of addressing a very specific audience of one:

Special Offer for Toyota Owners

An Important Notice for You as a Member of the American Diabetes Association

Zip Open Here for a Surprise Announcement about You and Your Birthday from *McCall's*

If you can, use "buzz" words like:

FREE

NEW

YOU

SAVE

ANNOUNCING

CHARTER

INTRODUCING

If you've got a strong offer—free trial issue, 3-months free membership, free bonus gift—try highlighting it in your teaser. But be careful—this can backfire. The Nature Conservancy tested a package offering 3-months free membership. The package that stated that offer on the envelope as well as on the response form didn't perform nearly as well as the control, which mentioned the 3-months free membership only in a small line of handwriting on the response form.

How do you know what's going to work? Again and always, you have to test.

If you are offering a free premium, you may want to show it through a second window on the carrier or on the reverse of the envelope.

Sometimes, when you're learning to write teaser copy, it helps to look at old-time print ads, like those written by copy great John Caples. Caples wrote that, "All messages have headlines. In TV, the headline is the start of the commercial. In radio, it's the first few words. In a letter, the first paragraph has a headline. Even a telemarketing script has a headline."

One of his first copywriting assignments was to write an ad for a correspondence course in piano playing. He wrote an ad with the headline: *"They laughed when I sat down at the piano—but when I started to play!"*

Other successful headlines for mail-order ads include: *"Do you make these mistakes in English?," "How a 'fool stunt' made me a star salesman,"* and *"How a strange accident saved me from baldness."*

As always, keep the word "benefits" emblazoned on your heart and head when writing teaser copy. Tell your prospect right away what's in it for him or her—or at least hint at something good, valuable, or necessary to come. Whether your teaser copy appeals to your prospect's curiosity or self-interest, it should sell the benefits. Clever copy doesn't always sell. And if you're going to be measuring the sales results of your advertising, write teaser copy that sells the benefits of buying the product or service you have to offer.

Here are some methods to try for creating teaser copy:

1. You may want to start with a question:
   - *"Database professionals only: May we send you a free, full-color, "Rules of Data Normalization" poster?"* or
   - *"Will you please do us a favor?"* (Just be sure never to ask a question your prospect can say No to!)

2. You may want to lead with your strongest benefits:
   - *"Attention Small Dish Owner: Tune in to exciting news that will make your TV viewing a whole lot easier, more convenient, and fun!"* or
   - *"A prescription to enhance your career…add to your knowledge…and benefit all pharmacists, pharmaceutical scientists, and students nationwide,"* or
   - *"Announcing our new audiobook club—so you can listen to the books you're too busy to stop and read!"*

3. You may want to use specific numbers:
   - *"Enjoy 63% savings on the #1 guide to satellite television,"* or
   - *"You can help save Cape Cod Hatteras National Seashore—plus 355,907 acres of National Park lands in North Carolina—but you must act quickly!"*

4. You may want to give news:
   - *"An Important Announcement for All Federal and Postal Employees…about the one book you must have before you retire from the government,"* or
   - *"Important: Your 1997 Annual Report Is Enclosed."*

5. You may want to tell the reader what to do:
   - *"Reserve your copy now!"* or
   - *"There's one simple thing you can do to save the rainforest—Adopt an Acre!"*

6. You may want to feature a low price or special savings offer:
   - *"R.S.V.P. for Big Charter Savings!"* or
   - *"Yours to Examine for 14 Days Free!"* or
   - *"Plus Free 'Life of Jesus' Gift Book. Details inside."*

7. You may want to make a challenge:
   - *"Unravel the mysteries of the DM universe if you dare…"*

8. You may want to quote an authority:
   - *"A special year-end message from the Secretary of the Smithsonian,"* or
   - *"Find out what surprising new predictions investment maverick Doug Casey is making about your investments."*

9. You may want to flatter your prospect:
   - *"Special VIP Privileges Reserved For:"* or
   - *"For You: An insider's guide to the good life,"* or
   - *"You have been selected to participate in an important national survey on America's National Parks."*

10. You may want to extend an invitation:
    - *"Your invitation to preview a timeless treasury of JAZZ PIANO,"* or
    - *"Here's your key to the city…and an invitation to enjoy Baltimore's best FREE!"*

11. You may want to imply urgency:
    - *"Advance Notice. Please Open Immediately,"*
    - *"Time-sensitive materials enclosed that require your prompt response."*

12. You may want to pique your reader's curiosity:
    - *"Intimate. Risky. Engaging. And only 8 cents a minute."*

13. You may want to offer a gift:
    - *"Two signed, limited-edition wilderness prints have been especially reserved for:"* or
    - *"A Free Gift of name-and-address labels especially for our friends…"*

14. You may want to begin a story:
    - *"They struggled, they knew hard times, but they worked hard and raised their family with love,"* or
    - *"You don't have to be human to know the pain of a broken home…"*

Remember, think about your audience. *Always write on target.* A renewal mailing for magazine subscribers, for instance, can assume a certain level of interest; write something based on the magazine's appeal:

- "Twelve more months of hard-hitting alien abduction stories!"
- "The only magazine that makes sense of building codes!"
- "We promise another year of award-winning product reviews!"

Or maybe the people you're writing to aren't previous buyers but are on a specially selected list of names. A mailing from *Writing for Money* had the teaser: "4 FREE Gifts for you…plus the Secret of Making Serious Money as a Freelance Writer. Details Inside!" This is a teaser obviously tailored to the recipient (presumably a free-lance writer), but it also illustrates the concept of not hiding your benefits when you write a carrier teaser (see Exhibit 4-7).

A mailing for a new science fiction publication came with the teaser: "The sun became a cinder. The stars themselves went dark. Earth had been abandoned but the robot was left behind to stand his lonely vigil in silence…(continued inside)." This teaser was printed in large, white type on a black carrier. Just below the teaser was a round hole in the carrier that revealed a vignette from the four-color brochure inside; it showed a robot looking skyward (see Exhibit 4-8).

A mailing from the Mystery Book Club had a cartoon that showed a woman reading a book and making a remark to a man sitting on the bench next to her. He was slumped over with a knife sticking out of his back. The caption said: "Honey, aren't you dying to know where Floyd Kemske finds all these great mysteries?" The teaser reinforced the joke: "Dying for a Good Mystery? FREE GIFT with membership!"

A carrier teaser for The Nature Conservancy was another clever appeal. The graphic was a black-crowned night heron chick, one of those birds that is so ugly it's cute. It wore an expression of panicked bewilderment. A teaser was written for this photo (Exhibit 4-9): "You don't have to be human to know the pain of a broken home…only to fix one. (Ten dollars will fill the bill.)"

Exhibit 4-7   *Writing for Money* Mailing

Source: Reprinted with permission of Blue Dolphin Communications, Inc., Sudbury, MA.

Exhibit 4-8 Sovereign Media Mailing

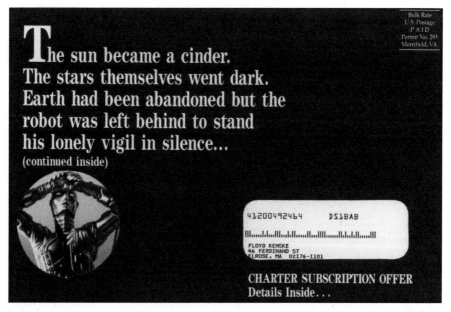

Source: Reprinted with permission of Sovereign Media and copywriter Denny Byrne.

Exhibit 4-9 Nature Conservancy Carrier

Source: Reprinted with permission of the Nature Conservancy.

Exhibit 4-10   *Home PC* Mailing

Source: Reprinted with permission of *Home PC* and copywriter Jeff Laurie.

Exhibit 4-10 shows the carrier for a successful launch package for *Home PC* written by copywriter Jeff Laurie. Laurie has done a lot of control mailings, and his work is an example of the good things that happen to clients when a writer brings a synthesis of *both* fine writing and sharp business acumen. This particular Laurie mailing uses high graphics, lots of color, and action to generate excitement and make promises (see Exhibit 4-10). Notice on the outer envelope how the "FREE" token is integrated into the "Wow!" headline, thereby accentuating both the message in the token and the headline on the envelope. The carrier immediately positions the magazine as being for the home. And the back of the envelope makes promises aimed at its target audience—nonprofessional computer users.

Another Laurie package is shown in Exhibit 4-11. This one is for *Fire Command*, the National Fire Protection Association's magazine for fire service leaders. The carrier basically tells a story using a dramatic picture of a fire and just one sentence: "Somebody's trapped inside." The next line of the teaser—"You're in command"—selectively targets the audience for the package (fire officers). Then the question—"What would you do?"—immediately involves the selected reader in a drama.

Exhibit 4-11   *Fire Command* Carrier

Source: Reprinted with permission of Jeff Laurie.

The effectiveness of your outer envelope can make or break your sale. When you're writing a package, start by writing the teaser to help clarify your thoughts about your offer, market, timeliness, and action desired from your prospect. Write down ideas for 5 to 10 teasers, maybe even more. Move phrases around, play with your ideas and various wordings of the offer. Then go on and write the rest of the package. As you're writing the letter, a completely new and great idea for teaser copy may come to you. Save it, pull it out, and add it to your list of teaser possibilities. Then let those ideas sit and go do something else. When you return, cast a fresh eye on the list and see which teaser stands out as your most powerful verbal weapon for attracting attention and action. Because, from your very first word on the carrier, you're aiming for **a response**.

5

THE RESPONSE FORM

Response is the end goal of every word you write. You don't mount a direct marketing campaign just to make people feel good about your company or to boost the image of your product (although it may well do both those things). After selecting your target audience, you're going to ask them to place an order, request more information, make an advance reservation, fill out a survey, indicate their preference, accept a trial issue, or take a shot at winning a million dollars in a sweepstakes. The communication between you and your prospect has to be two-way; otherwise, your copywriting efforts have failed.

Thus, the response form (the vehicle by which your prospect becomes your purchaser or lead) is an especially critical element of a direct mail package.

Comparing your direct mail package with a retail establishment, the brochure is your showroom, and the response is your live salesperson. It is that important. And, as in most retail situations, the customer's decision to buy is only tentative until somebody asks for the order. Your order form, as your salesperson, must be hard-working, effective, and easy to deal with. It should present your complete sales message as a stand-alone piece. Many people look at the order form first. They may glance at it and put it aside to fill out later minus the accompanying elements from the package.

Use everything you can to make your response form finalize the purchase decision. Include special guarantees, limited time offers, discounted savings. Create a sense of urgency about ordering your product or service now. And make it easy to do so.

First and foremost, a response form must do nothing to prevent responses. Think about how things can go wrong. What if the response form doesn't really look like a response form, and your recipients overlook it? What if your instructions on how to respond are too complicated for the average harried adult to understand? What if the response form is too big for the reply envelope, and your recipients assume they're not supposed to send it back? What if your response form is printed on dark paper and it's impossible for the recipient to fill out his or her name and address legibly?

A response form can get in the way of a response in dozens of ways. Too little space is left for fill-ins. The address where the completed form should be returned is missing. It's worth your time to think about them. After it's designed, fill it out yourself. Eliminate any obstacles to customer response.

What makes an effective response form? A lot has been written about response forms, but nearly everybody agrees on four basic points.

1. It must be easily identifiable as the response form.

2. It must be as clear and simple as possible.

3. It must include instructions to show the respondent what to do.

4. It must have a source code or otherwise show from what mailing campaign it came.

EASILY IDENTIFIABLE

A reliable percentage of your readers are going to go through the mailing to find the response form so they can read it first and see what's expected of them. Help them out. Make sure they can tell which piece is the response form (Exhibit 5-1).

Certain conventions help to identify the response form. It almost always has the recipient's name and address on it, either preprinted or pasted on as a mailing label. It almost always has check-boxes or something that shows the person is expected to interact with it.

But people are busy. They have a lot on their minds. If they can't tell instantly which piece in your mailing is the response form, you could lose them.

Exhibit 5-1 Response Form (Axel Award Winner)

Source: Provided by Axel Andersson. Reprinted with permission of the Smithsonian Institution.

Labeling

One way you can help identify it immediately is to label it. Give it a title. But don't title it "Response Form." Unless they write direct mail, they might not know what "response form" means. You could title it "Order Form," which is pretty clear, but doesn't that miss an opportunity to reinforce your sales message? At least call it an "Express Order Form" to let the reader know it will result in fast action.

Some different titles you might consider using on response forms for all kinds of mailings are shown in Exhibit 5-2.

Exhibit 5-2   Titles for Response Forms

- Savings Certificate
- Enrollment Form
- Membership Application
- Urgent Reply Form
- Acceptance
- RSVP Card
- Membership Invitation
- Discount Invitation
- Professional Savings Voucher
- Professional Courtesy Voucher
- Insurance Application
- Charter Enrollment
- Free Book Certificate
- Reservation Card
- Claim Ticket
- Preferred Subscriber Savings Certificate
- Free Trial Acceptance Form
- Confirmation Card
- Private Offer Savings Certificate
- Official Sweepstakes Entry Ticket
- No-Risk Trial Certificate
- Information Request Card
- Savings Coupon
- Free Copy Claim Ticket
- Complimentary Issue Reservation Card
- Collector's Subscription Certificate

- Rapid Renewal Form
- Free Issue Order Card
- Official Entry Certificate
- Free Issue Reservation Form
- Free Trial Acceptance Form
- Half-Price Reservation Card
- Free Issue Certificate
- Free Issue Claim Card
- Risk-Free Trial Card
- Free Gift Certificate
- 50% Discount Reservation Card
- Free Issue Invitation
- Free Trial Issue Order Form
- Trial Copy Reservation Card

The possibilities are endless. In lieu of a title for your form, you may want to headline some special benefit or premium you're offering:

- Free Trial Issue!
- Special Half-Price Offer
- 100% Money-Back Guarantee
- Free Sample
- Send No Money
- Limited Time Offer

Whatever copy you use on your reply form should mirror the tone of your letter and brochure. You may want to use RSVP to impart a sense of dignified fellowship to the transaction; this can work well for membership in a nonprofit or charitable association. The "Reply Memorandum" shown in Exhibit 5-3 was used in a mailing for World Wildlife Fund's Partners in Conservation, a group of high-dollar donors who pledge $1,000 or more.

"Urgent Reply Form" suggests fast action is required to take advantage of the offer before it goes away. "Savings Certificate" reminds the reader that this offer is being made at less than full price.

If you can, personalize your response form copy as much as possible. Say something like, "Free Issue/Free Gift Reservation Card For:" leading into the name of the recipient. Include personalized copy wherever you can. On renewal forms, for instance, you may want to include a variable paragraph with different messages to first-year members and multiyear members like these recently written for The Nature Conservancy:

(For first-year members)

Dear xxxxx:

Congratulations on your first year as a member of The Nature Conservancy. You have been instrumental in protecting the Last Great Places of the Earth. We look forward to working with you for another year. Please sign your membership card and carry it with you as a reminder of your very significant contribution to preserving our planet.

(signature)
John C. Sawhill, President and CEO

(Multiyear version)

Dear xxxx:

The Conservancy has especially important work to do this coming year. Will you please consider increasing your last year's level of support by just 25%? Your gift will be used to help fund programs to protect the Last Great Places of the Earth. Please sign your membership card right away to carry as a reminder of your significant contribution to preserving our planet.

(signature)
John C. Sawhill, President and CEO

Exhibit 5-3 Response Form for World Wildlife Fund High-Dollar Donors (Partners in Conservation)

```
                        Partners in Conservation
                          REPLY MEMORANDUM

        TO:      Kathryn Fuller

        FROM:


                 Mr. Lawrence V. Stein
                 7 Adams Street
                 Lexington, Massachusetts 02173
        -----------------------------------------------------------------
        Please renew my membership as a WWF Partner in Conservation.
        I have enclosed my tax-deductible renewal gift.  Use it to
        advance the ongoing efforts of World Wildlife Fund to save life
        on Earth.

            ☐ $1,000 Partner            ☐ $5,000 Leadership Partner

            ☐ $2,500 Sponsoring Partner ☐ $10,000 President's Circle

                ☐ I wish to pay in two installments.  My final
                    installment is due within three months.


                        2309681V    2038      PAF5B2

        Please make your check payable to World Wildlife Fund and return it with this Reply
        Memorandum in the envelope provided.  If you would prefer to make your contribution in the
        form of securities, please contact Rick Pavich at (202) 778-9520.
```

Source: Reprinted with permission of World Wildlife Fund.

Guarantee

Somewhere on your response form highlight whatever guarantee you can offer. This may include a refund for all unmailed issues of a subscription or the full subscription price, a free examination guarantee, a guarantee of postage and insurance to return a defective item, a guarantee of replacement, a third-party endorsement. Whatever your guarantee includes, describe it in clear, simple, and reassuring language. And if you have the chance, drive home one of your benefits again.

The guarantee offered by *The New York Review of Books* is (Exhibit 5-4):

My Risk-Free Guarantee: If I'm dissatisfied for any reason at any time during the course of my subscription, I'll notify you and get a complete refund of every penny I've paid toward my remaining issues. The free *Selections* is mine to keep forever—no matter what.

Exhibit 5-4 *New York Review of Books* **Response Form (Axel Award Winner)**

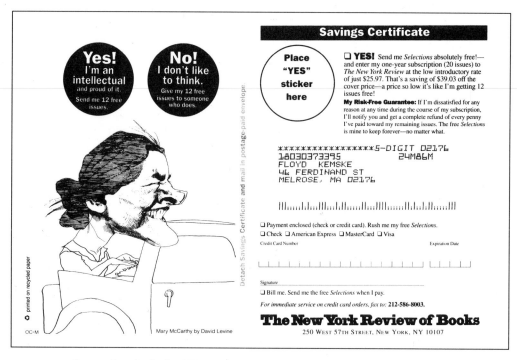

Source: Drawing by David Levine. Reprinted with permission from the *New York Review of Books*. Copyright 1963–96 Nyrev, Inc.

And from Quality Paperback Book Club:

Your Guarantee of Satisfaction: You may examine your introductory books for 10 days, free. If you are not satisfied, for any reason whatsoever, simply return the books and you will be under no further obligation.

Traditional wisdom has it that elaborately bordered response forms designed to look like certificates perform better than plain ones. Test for yourself.

Test an L-shaped format…a Reply-O device with the form enclosed in clear plastic on the front of your envelope…a perforated stub where the respondent can note their check number and date of order. Test pressure-sensitive stamps instead of check-off boxes or Yes/No/Maybe options. Test colored stock for your response envelope (some mailers swear by this).

CLARITY AND SIMPLICITY

One of the reasons the response form has to be clear and simple is that it is a contract. When the recipient returns it, something is expected of him or her, and he or she has a right to expect something in return—a promised premium, a membership kit, magazines, whatever. If the recipient expects something that is not delivered, you have an unhappy customer on your hands. It is an article of faith in modern business that an unhappy customer is worse than no customer at all.

The best way to prevent unhappy customers is to make sure all customers understand what to expect from you and exactly what they are obligating themselves for. This means clarifying payment terms, delivery times, return policies, guarantees, and all the other terms of the sale. The better the customer understands the terms of sale, the less possibility there is for disappointment.

Exhibit 5-5 is an interesting format for a reply form, but the terms it offers are somewhat confusing. Here's the copy:

( ) Yes, I want the rewards and recognition of being a published writer. I want one of your professional writers to work with me and share the secrets of being a published writer. Please enroll me in:

( ) Writing and Selling Short Stories

( ) Writing and Selling Nonfiction Articles

The problem is that nowhere in the offer does it state whether the registration fee is for one or both of the course choices. The two payment plans are explained on the back. Given the wording, you could reasonably check off both ( ) Writing and Selling Short Stories and ( ) Writing and Selling Nonfiction Articles. Maybe Writer's Digest School intended for registrants to get both courses for one fee. If not, this mailing could create unhappy customers.

That tiny 7-point type to the left of the mailing label reads as follows:

I understand that, upon payment of the registration fee, I may review the course materials in my home for 10 days without obligation. If I decide not to continue as a student, I may return the course

Exhibit 5-5   Response Form from *Writer's Digest* School

Enroll Before

October 31

to save $50!

**It's easy to enroll
in Writer's Digest School.**

- Fill out, detach and return the enrollment application below.
- Or, to receive your course materials even faster, just call toll-free
  1-800-759-0963 and use your VISA or MasterCard to enroll.
- And if you enroll within the next 30 days, you'll receive our
  "Pulitzer Prize Winner (in training)" T-shirt, absolutely FREE.

*Don't delay—
the price goes
up november 1st!*

Note: Your tuition may be tax deductible.
Check with your local tax authority.

SAVE THIS PORTION FOR YOUR RECORDS.
Registration 73-10-04591
Your signed enrollment form signifies that you have read, understood and agree
to the terms of enrollment and payment.
This application is subject to the approval of the professional staff of Writer's
Digest School.

Enrollment Application - Writer's Digest School

☐ **Yes,** I want the rewards and recognition of being a
published writer. I want one of your professional
writers to work with me and share the secrets of being a
published writer. Please enroll me in:

☐ Writing and Selling Short Stories

☐ Writing and Selling Nonfiction Articles

Signature _____ Date _____
(Your parent or guardian must sign if you are under 18 years of age.)

( ) _____ ( ) _____
Phone (day)   Phone (eve)

I understand that, upon payment of the registration fee, I
may examine my course materials in my home for 10
days without obligation. If I decide not to continue as a
student, I may return the course materials in good condition within 10 days and receive a full refund. If I
decide to continue, I will receive all the materials and
services listed on this Enrollment Application, for which
I will pay the registration fee and tuition fees in accordance with the payment plan I've chosen. I understand
that I have up to 24 months from the date on this enrollment application to complete my course. I have also
read and understand the options I may use, including
contacting the State Board of Proprietary School
Registration, should I have a question or a problem
with the school or course.

AAAWG1H4

FLOYD KEMSKE
46 FERDINAND ST
MELROSE MA 02176-1101

☐ **Yes!** I am enrolling within 30 days. Send my Free T-shirt.*
(Check one) ____ Large ____ X-Large
*Please return t-shirt with course materials if you decide the course is not for you.

IMPORTANT Please turn over to choose your payment plan.

Enrollment and Refund Agreement

10 day free examination. Upon payment of the registration fee, you
may examine your course materials with no obligation for 10 days. If
you decide not to continue, simply return your course materials in good
condition within 10 days and you will receive a full refund.
Reinstatement: The enrollment term allows plenty of time for you to
complete the course at your own pace. If, however, you are unable to
finish in the allotted time, you may extend your enrollment for an additional 12 months by paying a reinstatement fee of $75.
Early Withdrawal/Tuition Protection Plan: If circumstances force
you to withdraw from the course, let us know in writing before the 24
month completion deadline. We'll calculate the amount of tuition you
owe, or the amount of refund due you, according to the following
schedule. Of course, any tuition payments you've already made will be

credited to your account and deducted from your obligation—only the
balance will be owed.

If you withdraw	Your Obligation is
•After the 10-day examination period, but before you've submitted any assignments	$25
•After the Introductory Assignment	$47
•After submitting Sections One or Two	$137
•After submitting Section Three	$249

*Note: Postage and handling, interest paid, late payment charges,
and reinstatement fees are non-refundable. Cancellation requests
received after the 24 month completion deadline cannot be honored.*

Choose the payment plan that is best for you

☐ **Plan A:** Enclose $29 now ($25 registration fee plus $4
postage and handling). Then pay your tuition in 12 consecutive
monthly payments of $20 each. Payments are due on the 16th
of the month and start the month after you receive your course
materials. A $3 late fee is due with each late payment received
after the 15th of the month. Total course cost under Plan A is
$265, which includes registration fee, tuition ($224), and
finance charges of $16.

☐ **Plan B:** Enclose $253 (full tuition of $249 plus $4 postage
and handling) and save all finance charges. Your fees are completely refundable if you return materials within 10 days.
You can pay for your registration fee, postage, and tuition by
check or money order or with VISA or Mastercard. (Checks in
U.S. dollars or equivalent payable to Writer's Digest School.
Canadian students please add an additional $7 upon registra-
tion for international postage and handling.)

☐ Check enclosed   ☐ Money order enclosed

Please fill out for credit card payment

☐ VISA   ☐ MasterCard

Card# _____ Exp. Date _____

Signature _____

Amount charged:
☐ $29 - $25 Registration Fee plus $4 postage and handling

☐ $253 - $249 Registration Fee and Tuition plus $4 postage and han-
dling

Hassle-Free Payment Option: Many WDS students on Plan A choose
the convenience of having their monthly payments charged to their
credit card.

Truth-In-Lending Disclosure

Writer's Digest School is happy to offer students a convenient, easy
plan for paying their tuition on a monthly basis. In accordance with
Federal law, the details of the tuition installment plan (Plan A) are
illustrated below. The specifics and language of these disclosures are
mandated by law. (Postage and handling not included.)

	Reg Price (after Oct. 31)	Sale Price
Course cash price	$209	$249
Cash down payment (registration fee)	$35	$25
Unpaid balance of cash price	$264	$224
Amount financed	$264	$224
FINANCE CHARGE	$18	$16
Deferred payment price	$282	$240
Total Price	$317	$265

The finance charge on the unpaid balance of the cash price is comput-
ed at approximately 12.9% ANNUAL PERCENTAGE RATE. The
deferred payment price shall be payable in twelve consecutive monthly installments of $20, beginning with the month following the receipt
of your course materials (if you requested a payment coupon booklet,
it will arrive separately from your course materials). The total payment will be $240.
If either the specifics or the language of these disclosures is not perfectly clear to you, please write:
    Writer's Digest School
    Attn: Stephenie Steele
    1507 Dana Avenue
    Cincinnati, OH 45207-1005
Or call us toll-free in the continental U.S. at 1-800-759-0963 (outside
the U.S., dial 513-531-2690 ext 332).

Your Satisfaction is Our Concern
We're dedicated to your satisfaction. We know you'll find the course
stimulating and helpful, but if you should ever have a question or
problem about the school or course don't hesitate to give us a call,
toll-free, at 1-800-759-0963 or drop a line to Ms. Stephenie Steele,
F&W Publications, 1507 Dana Avenue, Cincinnati, OH 45207. If, after
contacting us, you still have questions you may contact Goldeam
Gibbs, Executive Director, State Board of Proprietary School
Registration, 35 East Gay Street, Suite 403, Columbus, Ohio 43266-
0591, (614)466-2752.

Source: Reprinted with permission of *Writer's Digest* School.

materials in good condition within 10 days and receive a full refund. If I decide to continue, I will receive all the materials and services listed on this Enrollment Application, for which I will pay the registration fee and tuition fees in accordance with the payment plan I've chosen. I understand that I have up to 24 months from the date on this enrollment application to complete my course. I have also read and understand the options I may use, including contacting the State Board of Proprietary School Registration, should I ever have a question or a problem with the school or course.

( ) Yes! I am enrolling within 30 days. Send my Free T-shirt.*
(Check one)   _____ Large   _____ X-Large
*Please return T-shirt with course materials if you decide the course is not for you.

This reply form has several problems. In addition to the confusing and long-winded copy, "the materials and services listed on this Enrollment Application" are nowhere to be found on the Enrollment Application. And the request to "Please return T-shirt with course materials if you decide the course is not for you" seems both petty and unhygienic.

Not that it's ever easy to write clear copy about a complicated offer. Offering two payment plans for two courses and several prorated opportunities to cancel, plus a promise on behalf of the State Board of Proprietary School Registration, is hard to reduce to something simple.

Is it possible to state a complicated offer clearly? Let's say you offer a 1-year magazine subscription (12 issues). You want to give the first issue free, provide two books as a premium immediately, send another book when it has been published later in the year, and remind the prospect that there is a special annual issue that's very important. Here's how *Consumer Reports* handled just such an offer Exhibit 5-6:

Please detach and mail this form today to accept our complimentary bonus offer.

( ) YES! Send my complimentary issue of *Consumer Reports* and my two free books: the *1994 Buying Guide* and *How to Clean Practically Anything*. If I decide to subscribe, I'll pay $22 and receive 11 more issues including the famous April Auto issue, plus the *1995 Buying Guide* (when published). Otherwise, I'll return your invoice marked "cancel," owe nothing, and keep my complimentary issue and two free books.

It's remarkably clear here what you are getting, what you have to pay for it, and what your options are.

Exhibit 5-6   Response Form from *Consumer Reports* (Axel Award Winner)

Source: Reprinted with permission of *Consumer Reports*.

Let's look at the *Consumer Reports* offer as a model for how to make a response form clear. What is it about this copy that makes it clear?

For one thing, it's short. The offer/guarantee is only 66 words (by contrast, the long paragraph in the Writer's Digest School offer is 139 words). The paragraph also uses short sentences and short words within those sentences.

Second, it has only one conditional (i.e., if you do this, that happens). Look again at the Writer's Digest School copy, which achieves the dubious feat of turning one conditional into two: "if I decide not to continue…" and "if I decide to continue…" Also, it's not a very good sales strategy to make the customer's first choice that of not buying.

Third, note that the verbs in the *Consumer Reports* offer are all simple and active: send, decide, receive, return, keep. Compare this to the Writer's

Digest School offer, in which the first verb is "understand," followed by: may review, continue, and may return.

If you want to write clear, simple copy in your offer, follow these guidelines:

- Keep everything as short as possible:
  -paragraphs with the fewest number of sentences
  -sentences with the fewest number of words
  -words with the fewest number of syllables.

- Minimize the number of conditionals (i.e., if you do this, that happens).

- Use active verbs.

Another aid to clarity and simplicity is the personal touch. People can always understand better when the transaction relates to them personally. This is why so many direct mail response forms have a first-person point of view: "Yes! Start my subscription now. I enclose my check for 12 issues." Put your customer in the copy. Make the response form his or her own story.

But personalized goes beyond just putting the customer in. You can put yourself (or your client) in as well. Show the customer that there is a person or a small group of people behind the mailing. Don't just say "100% Guarantee." Say "OUR 100% Guarantee" or, better yet, "MY 100% Guarantee" signed by the owner of the company. Stern's Nursery used to offer a personal guarantee from its president:

> To insure your gardening pleasure, I offer my personal assurance of satisfaction. If you have ever been disappointed at any time with anything you ever bought from Stern's Nurseries, please write to me personally, and I will do my best to see that you are completely satisfied.*

Or mention someone involved with the organization by name in your acceptance copy. The response form for Rail-to-Trails Conservancy accompanied a letter signed by the conservancy's president, David Burwell, as shown in Exhibit 5-7:

---

* Reprinted from Ed McLean's monograph on direct marketing—*The Basics of Copy.*

Exhibit 5-7   Response Form from Appeal Mailing for Rails-to-Trails Conservancy

The Cowboy Trail Is Only The Beginning!

Count me in, David! I want to see more successes like the Cowboy Trail, so that our dream of a network of rail-trails can become a reality. Please use my special gift *right away* to help develop rail-trails all around the country before they're sold out from under us. **Enclosed is my gift of:**

( )$20   ( )$25   ( )$30

A gift of this amount or more will reserve your copy of RTC's 1995 calendar.

02458784 A4F2AL

Please make your check payable to Rails-to-Trails Conservancy and return it with this form in the enclosed postage-paid envelope, or mail it to Rails-to-Trails Conservancy, 1400 16th Street, NW, Suite 300, Washington, DC 20036. All gifts to Rails-to-Trails Conservancy are tax-deductible.

Mr. J
        St
Buffalo, NY 14201-2020

❑ My employer's matching gift application is enclosed.

❑ Please send me information on including Rails-to-Trails Conservancy in my will.

Source: Reprinted with permission of Rail-to-Trails Conservancy.

❑ Count me in, David! I want to see more successes like the Cowboy Trail, so that our dream of a network of rail-trails can become a reality. Please use my special gift *right away* to help develop rail-trails all around the country before they're sold out from under us. Enclosed is my gift of:

In this copy, the customer and the mailer end up in the copy together. Note that this is "*our* dream of a network of rail-trails." (Also note the urgency in "before they're sold out from under us." This is a major theme of the accompanying letter.)

It is the personalizing aspect that inspires so many direct mailers to use script copy made to resemble handwriting on the response form. The same mailings for Rails-to-Trails Conservancy, for example, had a "handwritten" note with a circle around the choice of the $25 contribution: "A gift of this amount or more will reserve your copy of RTC's 1995 calendar." Lots of testing has been done on string-asks (variable dollar amounts for contributions) and price offers. Again, go to the experts to tell you what works and test for yourself.

But when you write the words on your response form, look for places you can shorten your sentences and your words, and look for ways to personalize it by putting the customer in the copy.

INSTRUCTIONS

One of the reasons experienced direct mailers advise you to give instructions on your response form is to guide (push!) people to the desired outcome—ordering or inquiring.

An involvement technique assists the ordering process by getting the customer to perform a physical action. The simplest one is the check-box:

☐ **Yes! Sign me up.**

Did you ever wonder why so many direct mail response forms have a box to check off, even when the only choice is yes? It's because checking the box is involvement, and involvement inspires action. Sophisticated and well-heeled direct mailers go far beyond the check-box to inspire involvement. Exhibit 5-8 is a good example. From Fidelity Investments and designed by Dwight Ingram, this form features four separate peel-off stickers, each of them bearing the logo of a magazine being offered complimentary to anyone opening a new Fidelity Plus℠ Brokerage Account.

Exhibit 5-8   Response Form from Fidelity

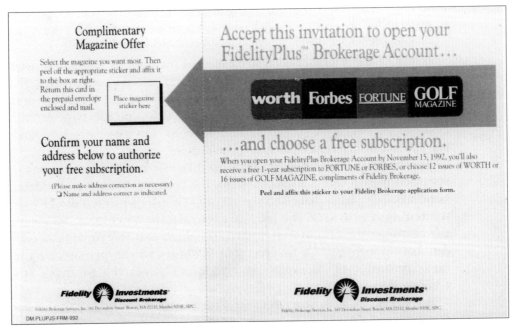

Source: Reprinted with permission of Fidelity Investments®.

This list of instructions from various response forms, in addition to suggesting several different involvement techniques, exemplifies clear, simple instructions:

- Place "YES" sticker here.

- Scratch off the gold foil to learn what your annual price will be for a full year. Will it be $36? $30? $24? $15?

- Paste stamp below to get a sample copy of *PC WORLD* plus a FREE Mouse Pad with Windows tips.

- Indicate by number the 4 books you want:

- Bend on cut, peel sticker, and place below.

- Detach here and place in envelope with our address showing through the window.

- Keep this portion for your tax records.

- Please detach and keep the bookmark above as our way of saying thank you for your support.

A check-box may well be the best involvement technique at your disposal for a given mailing, but before you simply write out your response form copy with one, think about the alternatives: stamps, tokens, punchout pieces, and tear-off items. Will one of these work well with your sales message?

If one of these higher-level involvement techniques will work, then take care to explain to the customers how to do it. Don't take anything for granted. Tell the customer how to use your involvement technique and how to make the purchase. And if you can combine the two instructions—e.g., "Put the yes token in the pocket to activate your savings and start your subscription"—so much the better.

Another part of your response form that may require instructions is checking the name and address. Usually the customer's name and address is printed on a label pasted to the response form or printed directly on the response form itself. The tendency is to assume it's correct, but giving the customer the opportunity to make changes not only provides an additional opportunity for involvement, it allows you to personalize the message again: "Is your name and address correct? Please make any changes in this space."

Is it necessary to instruct the customer to mail the response form back to you? Yes! And, you can use it as yet another opportunity to pump up

Exhibit 5-9 Response Form from Quality Paperback Book Club (Axel Award Winner)

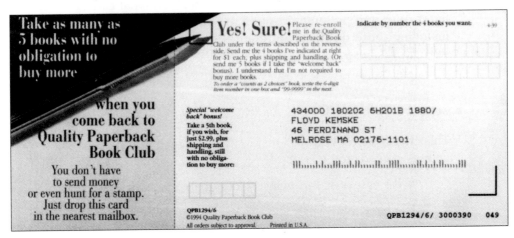

Source: Reprinted with permission of Quality Paperback Book Club.

your sales message: "Fill out and return this form in the postage-free envelope today!" or "Check the box and return this form within the next ten days to guarantee your savings!"

Exhibit 5-9 has this instruction printed on the tear-off stub of the response form for Quality Paperback Book Club: "You don't have to send money or even hunt for a stamp. Just drop this card in the nearest mailbox."

SOURCE CODE

Experienced direct mailers advise using source codes because making the sale, while it may be the most important goal, is not the only goal of a direct mail campaign. Any direct mail campaign worth the effort has a goal of acquiring new customers or enhancing an existing customer relationship. Coding may well be beyond your responsibilities as a writer in any given project, but you should be aware of its use in testing. The mailing label may have a code that identifies what list the name came from, and the mailer also can add a code to the response form to identify the mailing package.

In your own direct mail collection, you can find response forms bearing cryptic little devices like "ASPCD3A" or W•OC•11B" in a lower corner.

These signals are usually small enough that they don't attract the attention of the customer. But when the form comes back, if the code has been designed properly, such an identifier can tell you what carrier envelope, letter, offer, and premium inspired the customer to respond. Mixing and matching these elements and then testing each configuration tells you what works best.

CHECKLIST FOR RESPONSE FORMS

This checklist will help you make sure your response form has all the elements it needs to be effective:

☐ Is the response form clearly identifiable as the response form?

☐ Is it easy to fill out?

☐ Has it been tested for ease of use?

☐ Does it use its title and instructions as opportunities to reinforce the sales message?

☐ Does it restate any premiums, discounts, or special aspects of the offer?

☐ Does it state the offer clearly and simply?

☐ Does it include the return address (reply envelopes can get lost)?

☐ Does it provide a telephone and fax number for customers who want to buy by phone?

☐ Does it give the customer the opportunity to correct name and address information?

☐ Does it have an involvement technique?

- Check-box
- Punch-out item
- Tear-off stub
- Sticker
- Stamp
- Token

☐ Does it have clear instructions for using the form and the involvement technique?

☐ Does it collect credit card information (where appropriate)?

☐ Does it collect a signature for credit orders, insurance applications, etc.?

☐ Does it state all charges?

☐ Does it explain policies for return of merchandise and claims against the guarantee?

☐ Does it explain delivery time?

☐ Does it have a code to identify testing variables?

☐ Does the form look important?

☐ Does it prominently announce any deadline date?

☐ Are the choices offered the reader kept to a minimum?

6

THE LETTER

Dear Promising Writer,
And how do I know you are a promising writer?
I know that you are interested in writing. But to be honest...

The letter—your best opportunity for one-to-one, personal communication with your prospect or customer. Some copywriters believe you should start your letter by repeating the same teaser copy you put on the outer envelope—assuming that what got them to open the package will get them to read it as well. That's what the example above from Writer's Digest School does.

Remember, a letter can:

- Tell a story

- Sound an alarm

- Hang out a carrot

- State your offer

- Provoke a response

But how do you write a letter? What's important is to remember your two-fold goal mentioned earlier: to get interest and action. The first without the second doesn't count.

LETTER-WRITING FORMULAS

When you sit down to write your letter, you can sometimes follow paths great copywriters before you have trailblazed. We mentioned the "operatic principle" of direct mail copywriting—or A-I-D-A—earlier.

Attention

Interest

Desire

Action

There are other formulas as well:

Picture

Promise

Prove

Push

Attributed to Henry Hoke, Sr., this formula encourages you to:

Create a *picture* early in your letter to grab the reader's attention.

Describe the features and benefits of your product (*promise*).

Back up benefit claims with *proof* in the form of testimonials, endorsements, etc.

Push your readers to take action.

Another formula, created by Frank Dignan, is

Star

Chain

Hook

The idea here is to:

Attract attention by making your opening paragraph shine like a beacon of the heavens (*star*).

Follow this opening with a carefully sequenced flow of facts, features, and benefits, i.e. the *chain* that pulls your reader through to the end.

Conclude with a call to action (*hook*).

In *Successful Direct Marketing Methods* (Lincolnwood, IL: NTC Publishing Group, 1994), Bob Stone offers these letter-writing guidelines.

1. Promise your most important benefit in your headline or first paragraph.

2. Immediately enlarge on your most important benefit.

3. Tell the reader specifically what he or she is going to get.

4. Back up your statements with proof or endorsements.

5. Tell the reader what he or she might lose by not taking action.

6. Rephrase your prominent benefits in your closing offer.

7. Incite action—Now.

Of course, the point of learning any system of rules is to achieve a level of expertise that allows you to bend or break the rules on occasion. That's what Frank Johnson did in this quirky, sophisticated letter for the Nature Conservancy, a long-time control mailing for the organization (Exhibit 6-1).

This letter begins, "That bug-eyed bird on our envelope who's ogling you with such a bad temper has a point. He's a native American sandhill crane, and you may be sitting on top of one of his nesting sites." Not a word about benefits in there!

Or consider this great letter for Sotheby's (Exhibit 6-2).

This mailing beat the initial concept test by more than 50% on pure creative. The entire program increased net profitability by 181%. It also won a Direct Marketing Association Gold Mailbox Award and Gold Echo.

There was no carrier teaser, no exciting visual elements, no brochure, no big offer, no above-the-salutation copy...and the product cost $195. So what produced the breakthrough? Look at how the letter began:

Dear Collector,

When archaeologist Howard Carter first opened King Tut's tomb in Egypt, he knocked only a small hole in the barrier and then peered through.

Exhibit 6-1   Frank Johnson Letter for the Nature Conservancy

Donna Cherel
Director of Membership

1815 North Lynn Street
Arlington, Virginia 22209

Dear Investor,

The bug-eyed bird on our envelope who's ogling you with such a bad temper has a point. He's a native American sandhill crane and you may be sitting on top of one of his nesting sites.

As he sees it, every time our human species has drained a marsh, and plowed it or built a city on it, since 1492 or so -- there went the neighborhood. It's enough to make you both edgy.

So give us $10 for his nest egg, and we'll see that a nice, soggy spot -- just the kind he and his mate need to fashion a nest and put an egg in -- is reserved for the two of them, undisturbed, for keeps. Only $10. (Watch those crane come in to land, just once, and you're paid back. Catches at your throat.) Then the cranes can relax and so can you. A bit.

How will we reserve that incubator with your $10?
Not by campaigning or picketing or suing.

<u>We'll just BUY the nesting ground.</u>

That's the unique, expensive, and <u>effective</u> way The Nature Conservancy goes about its nonprofit business. We're as dead serious about hanging on to nature's balance as are the more visible and vocal conservation groups. But our thing is to let money do our talking.

We buy a whopping lot of land: starting with 60 acres of New York's Mianus River Gorge in 1955 (now 555 acres), we have protected more than 6.9 million acres -- an area about the size of Connecticut and Rhode Island. These lands dot the nation from coast to coast and from Canada deep into the Caribbean -- more than 10,000 protection actions securing lands ranging in size from a quarter of an acre to hundreds of square miles.

All of it is prime real estate, if you're a crane or a bass or a sweet pepperbush or a redwood. Or a toad or a turtle. And a lot of it's nice for

(over, please)

Recycled Paper

(continued)

Exhibit 6-1   Frank Johnson Letter for the Nature Conservancy *(continued)*

-2-

people, too -- lovely deserts, mountainsides, prairies, islands. (Islands! We own 90 percent of huge Santa Cruz Island, off the California shore, and tiny Dome Island in Lake George, and most of the Virginia Barrier Islands, and dozens more.)

So besides being after your $10, we invite you to see a sample of our lands. We have 59 chapters in 50 states. Check your phone book. Our field offices will guide you and yours to a nearby preserve where you're most welcome to walk along one of its paths, sit on one of the log benches, look about, and say to the youngster we hope will be with you, "This will be here, as is, for your grandchildren." Nice feeling.

We do ask that you don't bother the natives. For example, there's a sign in one preserve that says "Rattlesnakes, Scorpions, Black Bear, Poison Oak/ARE PROTECTED/DO NOT HARM OR DISTURB." For $10, you're privileged not to disturb a bear or stroke a poison oak. A bargain.

Bargains in diverse real estate are what we look for and find. But not just any real estate. We've been working for years to create a huge, always up-to-date inventory of the rarest animals, plants, and natural places in each of the United States. Set up with state governments, these "State Natural Heritage Programs" identify what's rare and what's threatened in each state: birds, butterflies, orchids, marshes, river systems, swamps, forests ... and crane's nests.

Then we try to protect those places that desperately need protection and preservation. We think big. For instance, the Richard King Mellon Foundation gave us the largest single grant ever for private conservation: $25,000,000 to launch the National Wetlands Conservation Project, which ultimately enabled us to save more than 20 major aquatic systems embracing well over 400,000 acres. Northern prairie potholes, remote desert oases, teeming marshlands, bird-rich coastlands, pristine lakes, rivers that crisscross the nation ...

And we continue to protect wetlands. In Florida, we recently secured more than 22,000 acres -- the heart of the Pinhook Swamp. Not only is this swamp a vital natural link and wildlife corridor between the fabled Okefenokee Swamp to the north and the Osceloa National Forest to the south, but it also happens to be home to the sandhill crane.

But we don't just shovel cash at the problems. We buy some lands, trade for others, get leases and easements, ask to be mentioned in wills.

Exhibit 6-1   Frank Johnson Letter for the Nature Conservancy *(continued)*

-3-

Then we give or, preferably, sell much of what we buy to states, universities, other conservation groups -- any responsible organization that can care for and protect the land from anyone. Unless the "anyone" builds nests or eats acorns.

That cash flow replenishes our revolving fund, every dime of which is plowed into the unpaved and as yet unplowed. All this activity generates a lot of fascinating true stories, and lovely photos. These we put into a small (40 pages) but elegant, sprightly, and ad-free magazine, our report to our 700,000 members every other month: Nature Conservancy magazine.

Here you may find that the land you and the rest of us have just protected is harboring a four-lined skink, or a spicebush, or boreal chickadees, or kit foxes. You've a lot to learn and see that's most intriguing, as you'll discover.

The Nature Conservancy magazine also describes well-led tours of our various perserves, tells you what we're doing in your state, and shows you how you can help.

And as you use the complimentary sandhill crane bookmark, you'll be reminded of your personal commitment to the preservation cause.

Now, you may think it's disproportionate to brag about how we're raising millions for our projects and then ask you for only $10. Who needs you?

We need you, very much! Those hardheaded foundations, corporations, and individuals who give us money or property must be convinced that our ranks include a lot of intelligent, concerned, articulate citizens: people who know that the natural world and all it harbors needs our help.

Yes, we need you and your ear and your voice -- and your $10 ($10 times 700,000 members helps protect a lot of acres). Please join us today. It's easy: Get a pen. Check and initial the "membership application" form that your hand is touching. Within about six weeks of receiving your contribution, you will receive your membership card and the first issue of the magazine. Enclose a check for $10 in the return envelope. (Send more, if you can spare it.) NOTE that it's tax-deductible. Mail the form. Go.

(over, please)

Exhibit 6-1 Frank Johnson Letter for the Nature Conservancy *(continued)*

-4-

Thank you, and welcome, fellow investor in nest eggs. For your fanfare, listen for the wondrous stentorian call of that sandhill crane.*

Sincerely,

Donna Cherel

Donna Cherel
Director of Membership

* We borrowed his picture from Country Journal magazine, where he illustrated an article about the International Crane Foundation of Baraboo, Wisconsin. The photo is by brave Cary Wolinsky. And we don't actually know if the crane is as upset as he looks. Maybe he's smiling. Certainly he will be if, after he leaves the Foundation, his first motel stop has been reserved with your $10.

DC/sgr

Source: Reprinted with permission of the Nature Conservancy.

Exhibit 6-2   Letter from Sotheby's

NEXT MONTH AT
SOTHEBY'S

Dear Collector:

When archaeologist Howard Carter first opened King Tut's tomb
in Egypt, he knocked only a small hole in the barrier and then
peered through.

Leaning over his shoulder was Lord Carnovan, his sponsor.
After a while, Carnovan asked impatiently, "What do you see?"

Another pause. Then Carter answered in a hushed voice, "I
see things. Wonderful things."

Every year tens of thousands of "wonderful things" pass
through the doors of Sotheby's offices in London, New York,
Monaco, Geneva and Hong Kong. The treasures of the world —
beautiful paintings, precious jewels, exquisite furnishings,
rare antiquities, ancient porcelains and pottery, and
magnificent sculpture ... some of the world's most
extraordinary art.

The unique and sometimes eccentric collections of celebrities
and royalty, rare objects and paintings that have been hidden
from public view for decades and even centuries, the best, the
finest, the most beautiful ... all these "wonderful things"
come to Sotheby's.

And, here the world's treasures are sold at auctions so
important that collectors wait by telephones in Tokyo, Riyadh
and Paris to participate in the bidding ... so crucial to the
world of art that sales may be reported on the front pages of
the major newspapers.

            You are cordially invited to share it all,
            this world of wonderful things, as a
            Charter Member of NEXT MONTH AT SOTHEBY'S.

When you become a Charter Member, each month you will
receive a unique and highly valued auction catalogue selected
especially for NEXT MONTH AT SOTHEBY'S members from among the
dozens of auctions held by Sotheby's all over the world.

You will receive the same auction catalogues that are
treasured by the world's leading collectors and carefully
retained as invaluable references. Each catalogue is
devoted to a special topic — perhaps Old Master Paintings ...
English Furniture and Decorations ... Jewelry ... Russian
Works of Art, Icons and Objects of Vertu ... Chinese
Ceramics, Jade, Works of Art and Furniture ... Oriental
Rugs and Carpets ... Antiquities ... Contemporary Art ...

1334 YORK AVENUE AT 72ND STREET, NEW YORK, NY 10021

(continued)

Exhibit 6-2   Letter from Sotheby's *(continued)*

Impressionist Paintings, Drawings and Sculpture ... and more.
Truly the "wonderful things" of the world.

You'll see why Pietra-Dura tabletops from the 17th and 18th
centuries are worth up to 50,000 Pounds Sterling — the patterns and
colors are remarkable! You'll wonder anew at the incomparable
skill of Chinese jade carvers. You'll discover new Old Masters
like Bouman, Van Delen and De Keyser, who have the same gifts for
light and life as their more famous brethren.

At times, descriptions can include fascinating history — in
discussing two Roman spoons, readers recently learned about the
mystery of the Kerynia Treasure. Another description of a rare
Egyptian wood sculpture included tantalizing information about how
women were treated in ancient Egypt.

You'll get full bibliographies when significant — a detailed
reading list if you ever want to learn more.

> Beautiful — yes! Intriguing and educational
> as well. And more: These auction catalogues
> are an invaluable way to stay in touch with
> the world of art, to keep up with values, spot
> trends and discover new treasures while
> exploring new areas of collecting.

These books are so different from what we ordinarily call
"catalogues" that they should not really have the same name. These
are catalogues prized for both content and presentation. Printed
on heavy, fine paper with laminated covers (sometimes hardcover),
filled with wonderful photography often in full color. Art books
to treasure just for themselves.

In the past, Sotheby's sold Van Gogh's Irises for a price that
set new standards in the art world. Sotheby's also auctioned the
jewels of both the Duchess of Windsor and Clare Boothe Luce, and
the collections of Andy Warhol and Elton John. As a Charter
Subscriber, the catalogs for these sales could have been part of
your subscription!

<u>As a Charter Member you'll receive even more, as well</u>!

·As a Charter Member of NEXT MONTH AT SOTHEBY'S, you participate
fully in the world of "wonderful things". Your Charter Membership
also brings you ...

... a subscription to <u>Sotheby's Newsletter,</u> the insider's guide
that keeps you up-to-date with the art market with 9 issues a year.
In our Newsletter, you'll find schedules of the sales and special
events coming up all over the world. You'll read behind-the-scenes
articles. And, you'll see color photographs of special objects
coming up for sale.

... a subscription to <u>Sotheby's Post-Auction Reports,</u> mailed

Exhibit 6-2   Letter from Sotheby's *(continued)*

approximately 3 weeks after every Sotheby's auction. The reports provide item-by-item actual sales prices.

... free estimates of what your objects might bring at auction. Our experts, who are among the world's most experienced, will examine photographs of your fine art and antiques.

... absentee bid forms which enable you to bid either by mail or telephone at any of our auctions. (By the way, although we are noted for the valuable items we handle, many of our pieces sell at surprisingly affordable prices.)

All these extras plus 12 carefully selected auction catalogues for our more exciting sales (shipped one each month) are yours as a Charter Member of NEXT MONTH AT SOTHEBY'S.

Purchased separately, the auction catalogues alone would cost well over $300. But as a Charter Member, you receive the 12 catalogues plus all the extras described above for only $195. An extraordinary price, I'm sure you'll agree — and, as a Charter Member, you are assured that you will always be offered the lowest possible subscription rates.

Plus a very special Free Gift for a prompt reply to our invitation: <u>100 Years of Collecting in America</u>, a 240-page book valued at $35.00!

An oversize art book, this is a marvelous history of Sotheby Parke Bernet that illuminates collecting and collectors with wonderful stories ... and includes dozens of full color photographs showing some of the finest works of art sold in the United States. This is a book to enjoy again and again ... and to treasure. It's yours free just for replying within 15 days.

A rare opportunity to share a very special world of "wonderful things" at a substantial savings plus a handsome free gift — can we offer more? Don't hesitate. Fill out the enclosed Charter Member R.S.V.P. Card right now. Say "yes" today.

Sincerely,

David L. Ganz

David L. Ganz
Director of Subscriptions

P.S.   This is a no-risk invitation — your Charter Membership is absolutely guaranteed. You must be completely satisfied at all times. If not, just let us know and we'll issue a prompt refund for the unexpired portion of your subscription. There's no reason to pause — please mail your R.S.V.P. Card right now.

Source: Reprinted with permission of Pat Farley, David Shephard, and Sotheby's.

Leaning over his shoulder was Lord Carnovan, his sponsor. After a while, Carnovan asked impatiently: "What do you see?"

Another pause. Then Carter answered in a hushed voice, "I see things. Wonderful things."

Every year tens of thousands of "wonderful things" pass through the doors of Sotheby's offices in London, New York, Monaco, Geneva, and Hong Kong. The treasures of the world....

What follows is an invitation to share the world of wonderful things as a Charter Member of *Next Month at Sotheby's*.

Here's what writer Pat Farley said about why she chose to begin the letter this way:

Why did I use a story? Because the motivation to buy was a desire to move up into more elite circles, something impossible to say directly. My solution was to subtly create that elite world.

Why did I choose this story? Not only did King Tut create the mood extraordinarily well, it also solved a serious writing problem. Membership in *Next Month at Sotheby's* was a vehicle for mailing 12 catalogs, chosen at random and covering an enormous range of subject areas. A member could receive catalogues on Faberge eggs, vintage cars, antiquities, antiques, great art, ethnic art, collectibles, coins, guns, sculpture, and more. As a writer, the idea of having to use 14 adjectives every time I mentioned the catalogues was a nightmare. But with the story setting up the entire promotion, I could use "wonderful things" throughout.

You'll learn more from Pat Farley on how, when, and why to tell a story later in this chapter.

Successful packages are being mailed that follow all the rules. Other successes break them. But as with all the other elements of your direct mail package, there are three absolutes to initially guide you:

1. Know your objective.

2. Know your prospects.

3. Know your product or service.

Know Your Objective

Knowing your objective means being aware of what you want your prospects to do. Do you want them to:

- Buy your product?

- Petition their Congressman?

- Join your organization?

- Request more information?

- Request a sales call?

Whatever your objective, let it serve as the touchstone for everything you say in your sales letter.

Here's an example of how the objective of a mailing can determine the treatment of the letter. One decision a mailer must make is whether to do a one-step or two-step mailing. In a one-step mailing, the goal is to complete the sale in one transaction. An example would be a mailing promoting the sale of a certain type of software. Such a package might include a letter and brochure explaining the features and benefits of the software, along with a reply card offering several payment options. If the software meets your needs, you buy it, and the transaction is completed.

A two-step mailing might be used by a stockbroker as a prospecting tool. Initially, a simple letter might be sent highlighting in a general way the benefits of using the stockbroker's services. A reply card would likely be included—not to complete a purchase, as in the case of the software mailing, but to allow prospects to request more information. Those responding to the initial mailing could be sent brochures on the specific investment vehicles in which they expressed an interest. The broker might then follow up the second mailing with a phone call to each prospect. The sale requires two mailings instead of one—hence, the reference to a "two-step" mailing.

How does this relate to writing an effective sales letter? Remember, with a one-step package, any response other than a purchase is considered a failure. Therefore, your letter and supporting materials must be powerful enough to stimulate prospects to take action. That means making your letter long enough to thoroughly explain all of the benefits of your product or service, as well as anticipate and counter the most likely objections.

Two-step mailings require less commitment from prospects, at least initially. The first step is often used as a lead-generating tool, setting the stage for a more intensive selling effort later. The aim is to be compelling yet brief—to sketch the benefits of the seller's product or service without delving into details that might deter prospects from responding. Exhibit 6-3 is an example of just such a lead-generation letter prepared by George Wojtkiewicz of GHW Associates for Litle & Company, who provide innovative credit-card processing services to companies selling through direct marketing. This mailing was one of a series designed to generate qualified prospects for Litle's sales force. According to Wojtkiewicz, the strategy was based on:

1. Creation of a database of select prospects.

2. Once a month lead generation mailings offering free information on topics related to Litle's innovative credit card processing services.

3. Pre-qualifying direct mail/800 number responses.

4. Telemarketing follow-up/qualification.

5. Tracking of lead status and results.

For creative, a straightforward 1-page letter, attached reply card, No. 9 Business Reply Envelope (BRE) and No. 10 envelope was used. The letters aimed at pre-qualifying response by asking for key information such as numerical ranges of credit card transactions, line of business, and so on. This lead generation program averaged about 12%—500% better than the original projection of a 2% average response rate!

KNOW YOUR PROSPECTS

You can't do an effective selling job if you don't know to whom you're selling. Part of your preparation for every letter-writing assignment should be to develop a profile of your ideal prospect. The profile should have as much detail as possible. Social and cultural circumstances, educational level, income, hobbies, sex, marital status, and many other factors should be considered.

For instance, if your target audience is CEOs at Fortune 500 corporations, your letter will be radically different from one aimed at midwestern housewives or Hispanic small business owners. The look, the sophistication of the language, the assumed knowledge, and most importantly the benefits you stress—everything will depend on your target audience.

Exhibit 6-3   Lead-Generation Letter for Litle & Co.

54 Stiles Road, Salem, NH 03079-4833 • Tel: 603/893-9333 • Fax: 603/894-5357

Dear Mr. Sample:

You are invited to receive a complimentary copy of a new report outlining techniques proven to be effective against credit card fraud.

This free executive briefing, called "<u>Shielding Your Direct Marketing Business from Credit Card Fraud</u>", will be mailed to you promptly. Simply complete and return the form below.

Mail and telephone credit card fraud is estimated to cost direct marketing companies nearly <u>$3,000,000 every week</u> -- directly impacting profits and customer service... plus adding to administrative costs -- and frustrations -- of dealing with credit card abuses and chargebacks.

That's why this informative guide will be very helpful to you <u>now</u> -- especially if you want to be sure your company is taking full advantage of the most effective credit card fraud precautions available to you.

You'll receive a helpful update on how to prevent credit card fraud... details on ten highly effective fraud prevention strategies... encompassing the newest innovations as well as time-proven fraud detection methods... including specific fraud prevention techniques to use with MasterCard, VISA, AMEX, and Discover Card.

You'll also benefit from an informative discussion of Address Verification Services (AVS) -- one of the most effective defenses against fraud.

For your complimentary copy of this useful report, simply verify your name, title and address on the form below -- then return it in the enclosed postage-paid envelope.

Sincerely,

Thomas J. Litle
Chairman

P.S. You can save time by FAXING the request form to 603-894-5357, or by calling us at 1-800-788-6010.

Complimentary Executive Briefing

"Shielding Your Direct Marketing Company from Credit Card Fraud"

☐ Please send me a complimentary copy of your new guide, Shielding Your Direct Marketing Company from Credit Card Fraud. I understand there is no cost or obligation connected with this request.

Telephone No. (   )

Mr. John Q. Sample
President
ABC Company
123 Main Street
P.O. Box 123
Salem, NH 12345

54 Stiles Road, Salem, NH 03079-4833

Please note any corrections to your name and address. Please provide your title if not included.

Well-known copywriter Herschell Gordon Lewis likens the process of getting inside a prospect's head to the way an actor immerses himself in a character. Says Lewis, "I've written many a package as a woman…a member of an ethnic or religious or political or philosophical group to which I don't belong or subscribe."

The June 1993 *Target Marketing* carried an article by Denison Hatch, the title of which, "Selling Steak with a Hot Potato," nicely sums up the appeal of Lewis's mailing for Omaha Steaks (so successful that it has been used as a control for more than 10 years). Lewis's letter displays keen insight into the nature of his typical reader: "I believe you're someone who travels well, eats in fine restaurants—and appreciates the difference between dinner at a four-star restaurant and a sandwich on the run." Lewis simultaneously accomplishes two important goals with this copy: He flatters his prospects, while effectively conveying his understanding of their needs and preferences. Lewis continues the fine dining motif: "You know, of course, it isn't unusual to pay a day's wages for a steak dinner.… I'm writing to invite you to have those same gourmet steaks—steaks you never on earth could get at any supermarket, steaks most restaurants can't even buy because there just aren't enough of them to go around." The implication: if you buy Omaha Steaks, you'll get a better meal than you would in most restaurants—at a lower cost. What steak-lover could resist that kind of offer!

Databases can help you get to know your prospects more thoroughly. In an article called "Versionalize," which appeared in the April 1993 issue of *Target Marketing*, copywriter Luther Brock, Ph.D., (known as "The Letter Doctor") examined how to handle a hypothetical case where database marketing allowed the identification of three distinct subgroups of prospects for a book on collection techniques.

Brock's strategy was to develop three different versions of the sales letter (and envelope) while keeping a lid on costs by using the same brochure in all three cases. A letter, he reasoned, has two features that make "versionalizing" it both desirable and feasible. First, it is the most personal part of the mailing, containing all the "you" copy by which the copywriter seeks to establish a level of intimacy with prospects. Second, the sales letter is typically one of the simplest, and therefore least costly, pieces in the mailing to produce. A brochure, on the other hand, has a less personal tone. Moreover, brochures are often lavish, four-color affairs with lots of graphics. Versionalizing such documents is more complex and costly.

The first version of the sales letter might go to collection managers. For these people, the prime concern is keeping their jobs. So their letter would explain how the book would enable them to maximize collections and thereby earn the praise of their supervisors.

The second audience might be small business owners. This subgroup has one basic concern: the bottom line. For them, Brock suggests an opening along these lines: "The better your collections, the more money you make. Here's how to get far more of your customers to catch up on payments fast!"

The third subgroup might be professionals—doctors, lawyers, architects, accountants, and the like. They are probably not involved directly in the collections process, so Brock suggests beginning their letter this way: "Here's the quick and easy way to help your assistant collect more accounts."

By using three different letter treatments with the same brochure, the mailer can respond effectively to three target subgroups with related yet distinct needs.

KNOWING YOUR PRODUCT

In order to make a sale, you must first make a connection between a prospect's needs and how your product or service meets those needs. That requires having a firm grasp on the features and benefits of what you are selling, and the difference between the two.

Features are qualities inherent in the product itself. Benefits, on the other hand, are statements of ways in which the product's features will help the prospect. Here are some of a computer's features, with their accompanying benefits.

FEATURES	BENEFITS
Pentium microprocessor	Faster processor lets you work faster, have more time for leisure.
1-gigabyte hard drive	Holds more program and data files, giving you more power and flexibility.
19" monitor	Easier to see what's on each page, and saves time normally spent toggling back and forth with smaller screens.

Features are cold and impersonal; benefits are warm and inviting. While prospects usually have some interest in features, benefits make the sale.

An effective sales letter interweaves features with benefits so that prospects get a healthy dose of both.

Remember, your prospect wants to know "What's in it for me?"

WRITING YOUR LETTER

Rules You Can Break

After you've translated the features of your product or service into benefits for your prospect or customer, you're ready to begin writing.

A good direct mail letter, like a good personal letter, is written in an intimate, friendly style and uses simple, everyday language. The conventions of standard written English are too formal and stuffy for direct mail copy. So what you've learned in school about what's right and wrong doesn't apply. Some of those rules have no place in direct mail:

- You can and should use contractions like "don't," "can't," and "aren't."

- You can start a sentence with "and," "but," "or," or "so."

- You can use sentence fragments.

- You can refer to yourself in the first person ("I") and your reader in the second person ("you").

In a direct mail letter, the object is to write the way you would talk to someone. Remember that point and you're halfway home.

Types of Leads

In *Profitable Direct Marketing* (Lincolnwood, IL: NTC Publishing Group, 1992), Jim Kobs identifies six ways of writing the opening or lead of a sales letter:

1. The offer lead

2. The flattery lead

3. The benefit lead

4. The timeliness lead

5. The narrative lead

6. The question or curiosity lead

The *offer lead* is a good one to use any time you have a particularly strong offer. A magazine publisher offering a free 3-month trial subscription might highlight that fact with the lead, "A FREE three-month subscription to the country's most respected health and fitness magazine can be yours—no strings attached."

The *flattery lead* is another favorite of direct marketers. Back in the 60s, *Newsweek* did a phenomenally successful mailing using the now well-known Ed McLean lead, "If the list upon which I found your name is any indication...." Lewis's letter for Omaha Steaks, discussed earlier in this chapter, also exemplifies the flattery lead. It begins with a heading just above the salutation: "A Private Message To a Very Special Person." After addressing the prospect with "Dear Friend," the first sentence continues, "This private invitation is going out to just a handful of people, yourself included."

The *benefit lead* is also popular because it is direct and to the point. The letter in a mailing selling tax preparation software might begin with this revelation: "Doing your taxes with our software is so quick and easy, you'll actually look forward to it!"

The *timeliness lead* can be effective if there is something about your offer that is precedent-setting or fulfills a need created by current circumstances. Here's an example of the former: "Never before available on compact disc—the complete works of Beethoven arranged for the piano." And as for the need related to current circumstances, consider this plea for a letter selling subscriptions to an investment newsletter: "Find out why the stock market is teetering on the brink of a massive selloff of 1929 proportions—and what you can do to avoid it."

The *narrative lead* is one of the hardest to create because the copywriter must develop a story that draws prospects in and serves as a platform for the selling statements that occur later. A fine example of this lead comes from what has been called, "the most successful advertisement in the history of the world": the 18-year control mailing for the *Wall Street Journal*. Written by Martin Conroy, the now-famous "two young men" letter begins, "On a beautiful late spring afternoon, twenty-five years ago, two young men graduated from the same college. They were very much alike, these two young men. Both had been better than average students..." And on it goes. Denny Hatch, editor of *Target Marketing*, has estimated that Conroy's letter (Exhibit 6-4) is directly responsible for bringing in $1 billion in revenues to Dow Jones & Co.

One other type of lead is the *question or curiosity lead*. An investment newsletter package began this way: "This man was rated the #1

Exhibit 6-4   Letter from the *Wall Street Journal*

THE WALL STREET JOURNAL.

World Financial Center, 200 Liberty Street, New York, NY 10281

Dear Reader:

On a beautiful late spring afternoon, twenty-five years ago, two young men graduated from the same college. They were very much alike, these two young men. Both had been better than average students, both were personable and both—as young college graduates are—were filled with ambitious dreams for the future.

Recently, these men returned to their college for their 25th reunion.

They were still very much alike. Both were happily married. Both had three children. And both, it turned out, had gone to work for the same Midwestern manufacturing company after graduation, and were still there.

But there was a difference. One of the men was manager of a small department of that company. The other was its president.

What Made The Difference

Have you ever wondered, as I have, what makes this kind of difference in people's lives? It isn't a native intelligence or talent or dedication. It isn't that one person wants success and the other doesn't.

The difference lies in what each person knows and how he or she makes use of that knowledge.

And that is why I am writing to you and to people like you about The Wall Street Journal. For that is the whole purpose of The Journal: to give its readers knowledge—knowledge that they can use in business.

A Publication Unlike Any Other

You see, The Wall Street Journal is a unique publication. It's the country's only national business daily. Each business day, it is put together by the world's largest staff of business-news experts.

Each business day, The Journal's pages include a broad range of information of interest and significance to business-minded people, no matter where it comes from. Not just stocks and finance, but anything and everything in the whole, fast-moving world of business. . . .The Wall Street Journal gives you all the business news you need—when you need it.

Knowledge Is Power

Right now, I am looking at page one of The Journal, the best-read front page in America. It combines all the important news of the day with in-depth feature reporting. Every phase of business news is covered. I see articles on new taxes, inflation, business forecasts, gas prices, politics. I see major stories from Washington, Berlin, Tokyo, the Middle East. I see item after item that can affect you, your job, your future.

(over, please)

(continued)

Exhibit 6-4   Letter from the *Wall Street Journal* (continued)

And there is page after page inside The Journal, filled with fascinating and significant information that's useful to you. The Marketplace section gives you insights into how consumers are thinking and spending. How companies compete for market share. There is daily coverage of law, technology, media and marketing. Plus daily features on the challenges of managing smaller companies.

The Journal is also the single best source for news and statistics about your money. In the Money & Investing section there are helpful charts, easy-to-scan market quotations, plus "Abreast of the Market," "Heard on the Street" and "Your Money Matters," three of America's most influential and carefully read investment columns.

If you have never read The Wall Street Journal, you cannot imagine how useful it can be to you.

A Money-Saving Subscription

Put our statements to the proof by subscribing for the next 13 weeks for just $44. This is among the shortest subscription terms we offer—and a perfect way to get acquainted with The Journal.

Or you may prefer to take advantage of our better buy—one year for $149. You save over $40 off the cover price of The Journal.

Simply fill out the enclosed order card and mail it in the postage-paid envelope provided. And here's The Journal's guarantee: should The Journal not measure up to your expectations, you may cancel this arrangement at any point and receive a refund for the undelivered portion of your subscription.

If you feel as we do that this is a fair and reasonable proposition, then you will want to find out without delay if The Wall Street Journal can do for you what it is doing for millions of readers. So please mail the enclosed order card now, and we will start serving you immediately.

About those two college classmates I mention at the beginning of this letter: they were graduated from college together and together got started in the business world. So what made their lives in business different?

Knowledge. Useful knowledge. And its application.

An Investment In Success

I cannot promise you that success will be instantly yours if you start reading The Wall Street Journal. But I can guarantee that you will find The Journal always interesting, always reliable, and always useful.

Sincerely,

Peter R. Kann
Publisher

PRK: id
Encs.

P.S. It's important to note that The Journal's subscription price may be tax deductible. Ask your tax advisor.

stock market analyst in 1994. He didn't buy a single stock the whole year. Yet he made enormous—almost obscene—profits." The same copy was used for both the envelope teaser and the letter lead. It's hard to imagine anyone even moderately interested in the stock market who could read that copy without feeling compelled to read further and find out how this apparent financial miracle was performed.

LETTER GUIDELINES

Structural Guidelines

- Make your letter long enough to tell your story.

- State some version of your main benefit near the beginning—don't wait until the end of the letter. Consider the use of a Johnson Box (copy positioned above the salutation) or some other attention-getting technique (Exhibit 6-5).

See art msp. 119A

- Make your letter visually accessible. Use short sentences, short paragraphs, and space between each paragraph to break up the flow of copy. Indent the first line of each paragraph.

- A nonproportional typewriter font, in which every letter is the same width, is the standard for direct mail letters. (This may be changing. In March 1993, *Target Marketing* reported the results of a 50,000-piece test mailing where half of the letters were set in Courier and half in Times Roman. The response rates were virtually identical. However, personalizing remains easier with nonproportional fonts because it's easier to predict how the characters will fill the space needed for the personalized information.)

- Use a postscript (PS). Tests show that it's one of the best-read parts of the letter.

- Consider using "handwritten" marginal notes, underlining, boldface type, or a second color to add emphasis.

- Choose a typeface from 10 to 12 points in size. Choose leading (the space between the lines of type) that is at least two points larger than your typeface. Generally, increasing leading increases readability.

Exhibit 6-5   Letter from *Smithsonian* Mailing (Axel Award Winner)

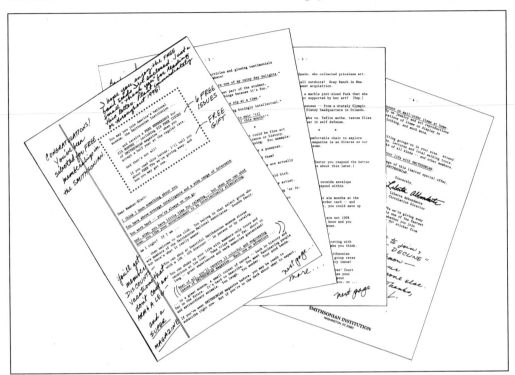

Source: Reprinted with permission of *Smithsonian* Magazine.

- Make the text flush left, with a ragged right margin, rather than justified.

- Center certain lines or subheads for emphasis.

- Use bulleted lists with hanging indents.

- Use ALL CAPS sparingly. It's difficult to read when used for long passages.

Content Guidelines

- Your writing style should be simple, personal, and friendly—as if you were writing to someone you know and like. People want to feel as if they're more than a face in the crowd.

- Develop supporting "arguments" that "prove" your benefit claims. Supporting arguments can be in the form of testimonials, independent test results, or a solid guarantee. Each, in its own way, helps to substantiate the claims you make about the product.

- Consider substituting specific claims for general ones. A good example of specificity comes from the headline of a direct response ad for binoculars. Rather than settle for something bland and general like "The power and clarity of these binoculars will astonish you," the company took a more unconventional approach with this intriguing lead: "You can look the sparrow straight in the eye from 250 feet, and you can see it blink."

- Don't write down to your prospects or be clever just to show off—both are common shortcomings of copywriters. To counteract this tendency, meditate for a while on your offer and your prospects before you begin writing. Try to focus on some likeable quality in your target audience, and approach the task of writing the letter with a friendly, open, and respectful attitude.

- Stress basic benefits. People are strongly drawn to products that help them feel better, richer, smarter, more attractive, or more important, as well as products that save time, money, or effort. On the negative side of the ledger, you will make sales by convincing prospects that your product will help them avoid pain, guilt, criticism, effort, or loss of reputation or wealth. Financial services in particular are often sold by making prospects feel guilty if they don't buy. "I should" buy life insurance to protect my family in case something happens to me. "I should" open a retirement account and have some long-term investments so that my spouse and I can live comfortably in our later years.

- With most mailings, personalization is a plus when used in moderation. Overuse of the prospect's name can work against you, however. Original methods of personalization are especially effective. *Advertising Age* recently did a successful mailing featuring a cartoon personalized with each prospect's name. The offer included an 8" × 10" limited edition of the cartoon suitable for framing with each paid subscription.

- Certain words have been proven to work well in direct mail. Use them wherever appropriate. The list includes "free," "no obligation," "you," "guaranteed," "now," "limited time," and "sale."

- Ask for the order, and don't let those who reject your offer off the hook. Spell out what they are giving up or what dire consequences will occur if they fail to respond.

- Use deadlines to add urgency and bonuses to reward quick action. Here's an example of urgency: In a fund-raising letter to people committed to eliminating the federal budget deficit, copywriter John Griswold wrote, "At our present rate of deficit spending we soon will not even be able to cover the interest payments on this rapidly growing debt. When that happens America will go bankrupt and everything you've worked and saved for will be wiped out."

- Watch your warm-up. Sometimes a copywriter can be like an old locomotive leaving the station at the head of a long train—it takes a while to build up steam. Similarly, it often takes a few paragraphs to begin turning out powerful copy. Because it's a common occurrence, be on guard. Try this simple test. Eliminate the first two or three paragraphs of your letter and see if it improves.

- Sweat the details. Don't use "art works" when "works of art" would be more elegant, "precious stones" when "precious gems" would fit better, and "yellow" when it would be more effective to say "golden." Remember that part of your job as a copywriter is to "romance" the product.

- Don't be satisfied with the first draft, or the second or third, for that matter. Revise and fine-tune relentlessly until you really feel you've got it right.

- Beware of writing letters by committee. One person, the main copywriter, should always review final copy to make sure it flows. Having too many editors can result in a hodgepodge of insertions and corrections.

Make no mistake: the letter is one of the most important copy elements in your marketing message. This is where you pull out all the stops with the most compelling persuasive writing you can muster. It's where the battle for your reader's mind (and pocketbook) is often won or lost.

THE STORY LETTER

Exhibit 6-6, written by award-winning copywriter Pat Farley, tells how, when, and why to write a story letter.

Exhibit 6-6   "Tell Me a Story" by Pat Farley

"Tell me a story"…isn't that an irresistibly appealing request? In your mind's eye, you see an adorable child cuddling a teddy bear and looking up at you with big, round eyes. In a way, that child is still alive in all of us.

Everyone loves to hear stories and every writer loves to create them. Back when I was first starting out in direct marketing, I read Bill Jayme's famous Smithsonian letter that began, "On a small island in the New Hebrides, you are worshipped." And I was hooked!

Since then, I've learned how to sell with stories myself, with considerable success, primarily because I also learned WHEN to tell stories…WHAT stories to tell…WHY to tell stories…WHERE to tell stories…and HOW MANY stories to tell.

You see, it's not just a matter of telling a tale. There are crucial strategic decisions involved. Because a great direct marketing story succeeds because it serves several purposes and observes many rules, I'm going to start with the rules and strategy. Then we'll have some fun looking at a variety of stories and figuring out which rules they follow.

First of all, WHAT IS a story?

Stories in direct marketing copy are a lot of things. A story can have classic form and take several paragraphs to tell. Or, like Jayme's Smithsonian package, it can be an intriguing statement followed by a short explanation. A story can be a series of adjectives that creates an emotion and sets a scene, or even a cartoon.

Probably the easiest explanation is that a story is any emotion-evoking dramatization, whatever form it takes.

WHEN do you tell a story?

All stories are emotional, so it's only appropriate to use this approach when emotion is a part of what will sell the product. It's dangerous to use stories when selling professionals, scholars, or any market that might resent having, as they'd say, "their strings pulled."

(continued)

Exhibit 6-6 "Tell Me a Story" by Pat Farley *(continued)*

It's also tricky to use stories in business-to-business—executives don't like to believe they've made purchasing decisions on emotional grounds. However, one of the all-time greatest business subscription mailings starts by telling a story of two college graduates with equal abilities. And I've used cartoons to dramatize the need for a business reference book. You can do it, but be careful.

With any product to any market, DO NOT use a story when it stresses one aspect of the product so strongly that you can't do justice to the rest.

And finally, DO NOT use a story when it has no appeal to a portion of the market. In this case, multiple stories are NOT the solution. Multiples are effective when you need a variety of situations to hit all segments of your marketplace but ALL the stories you use must have some impact on everyone you're addressing.

WHY do you tell a story?

This isn't a stupid client question—you never tell stories just because you like that kind of writing. Every time you use a story, you should always have a very good reason for doing so. What are the reasons?

- One reason is that story is the perfect solution when your primary benefit can't be stated outright. Sometimes, there just isn't a simple, direct, powerful way to state the benefit. The solution is to illustrate it with a story.

  At other times, the real reason people will buy your product is something that would insult them if you stated it outright— for example, you can't say, "Buy because you feel inferior and want people to admire you." But you can say, THEY LAUGHED WHEN I SAT DOWN AT THE PIANO!

- Another reason to use a story is when your primary benefit is best sold by a demonstration. When stated directly, does the benefit sound like "advertising-ese"? For instance, suppose your benefit is, "This Civil War documentary makes you feel like you're living the war." That sounds so hokey, you

Exhibit 6-6   "Tell Me a Story" by Pat Farley *(continued)*

can just imagine prospects responding, "That's just a lot of BS." But putting the reader there through a story PROVES your point before you make it!

- The third reason: Use a story when your sales presentation will have more impact if you get the product and the prospect on the same side. Establishing a strong, emotional link between the product and the prospect can be a powerful way to sell. A line like "You've got a RIGHT to know what's going on behind closed doors in Washington!" evokes a powerful reaction to a specific market. "You're damn right I do," they respond—and from that point on, they're with you.

- Finally, choose the story approach when emotion is what ultimately will drive prospects to act. This is what most fundraising is all about. The starving child, the sad puppy, the desperate dolphin—bring these situations to life and 99% of your job is done.

So long as we're talking about Why to use stories, let's look at the WHY NOTS:

- DO NOT use a story when you don't have a good one. Never force a story into your work.

- DO NOT use a story when you have a great offer. Stories are so appealing, the offer will be lost.

Now we come to WHAT STORY?

Where do you find your story or stories?

- A story can show how great the product is if it comes from the product, especially when the product is videos, books, or magazines. Nonprofit is also a rich source of wonderful tales—Jayme found the New Hebrides story in an issue of *Smithsonian* Magazine.

- Be careful when selecting a story from "outside." Use only stories that are perfect for the product and your objectives. I used a possibly apocryphal story well known to archaeology buffs to sell Sotheby's because it fit my goals perfectly.

Exhibit 6-6   "Tell Me a Story" by Pat Farley *(continued)*

But I've always avoided using any "outside" story to sell a book or magazine—in such cases, it's natural for the prospect to believe the story came from the product...and you'd be overselling the product.

- The right story can also be a matter of dramatizing and/or personalizing the situation by creating your own story.

WHERE do you put your story or stories?

Stories don't have to always be the lead of the letter. They work in many different places, sometimes all at once.

Put a story on the envelope when it's the most powerful device you have to get the envelope opened. For a mailing to sell a video series on war in the skies, I found a marvelous story in one of the videos. It was powerful, absolutely true, relatively unknown, and perfectly illustrated the main concept behind the series, so I began it right on the envelope to pull the reader inside.

Consider putting the story above the salutation in the letter: In this position, it works as an emotional set-up of the selling message, evoking the appropriate emotion needed to START selling.

A story works as the lead when it pulls the reader in with you AND it transitions smoothly into your product presentation OR it presents the primary benefit.

I've written packages where I weave stories throughout the body of the letter. With certain types of products and readers, it's the best way to keep the prospect reading, but it only works when the stories are an integral part of what you're selling. That warplane video package I mentioned is a good example—our series was different from the competition because it had a much more intimate slant. I proved this by telling the tale after tale that put the reader into the planes.

Stories even work in lifts. A great story will enable you to sell the prospect from an entirely different angle and/or totally personalize a key benefit.

Exhibit 6-6 *"Tell Me a Story" by Pat Farley (continued)*

HOW MANY stories do you use?

If you rely on one story, it must be tremendously powerful and appeal to the entire market. You're putting all your eggs in one basket...but when you have the right story, standing alone makes it even stronger.

When you're personalizing or dramatizing a situation, you're setting things up to move right into selling in a very intimate way, and one story is usually more credible.

If you use several stories, they have to be extremely brief. Choose multiple stories and sequence them to build intensity and excitement.

Or use several stories when you must cast a wide net because the market is too diverse to capture with a single story.

I hope I've also helped you recognize there's a time and a place to tell stories. And even that little one with the teddy bear and sleepy eyes isn't imploring you to tell any old story, but the right one. At bedtime. In bed. Plan what you're going to do with cold precision and marketing savvy, THEN let creativity fly! It's great fun!

Source: Reprinted with permission of Pat Farley.

7

BROCHURES

While the sales letter carries the primary burden of persuading prospects to buy, the brochure plays an important complementary role in many direct mail packages. In fact, prospects sometimes reach for the brochure first because of its eye-catching color and design.

How do you know whether or not to include a brochure in your direct mail package? As a general rule, use a brochure when you are selling products that are colorful or visually impressive. Collectibles, fine foods, colorful magazines, sports equipment, and consumer electronics are examples of products that tend to sell better with a brochure.

The relationship of the sales letter to the brochure can be summed up with the adage: "The letter sells, the brochure tells."

Like most adages, it oversimplifies. Although the brochure has a less "salesy" tone than the letter and includes purely factual information that you would never dream of putting in a sales letter, it must still be written and designed with your sales objectives firmly in mind. In addition, whereas the emphasis in the sales letter is almost entirely on copy, graphic elements (pictures, drawings, charts, tables, etc.) often play an important role in the brochure. Any discussion of brochures must therefore include some guidelines on how to handle graphics.

THE IMPACT OF WORDS *AND* PICTURES

Remember the old saying about a picture being worth a thousand words? Well, in brochures, self-mailers, catalogs and other direct mail media, you get to double the impact of your sales message by using words *and* pictures.

Just think of the possibilities: four-, or even five-color work, unusual folds, pop-up devices, die cuts, scratch-off spots. A brochure can be anything!

It can include:

- Photos

- Charts

- Tables

- Diagrams

- Maps

- Line Drawings

- Clip Art

- Comparison charts

- Product samples, like tipped-in swatches or article excerpts

And a brochure can be almost any shape. Selling real estate? You can design a brochure with a pop-up house in it. Season tickets to football? Design it to have a stadium seating plan on one side. Leather goods? Design one to look like a wallet. The choices in size, shape, paper stock, and colors are virtually unlimited. The only limitations you face are your budget and your imagination. You can use spot color, tints, blocks or screens to highlight certain areas of your brochures—heads or subheads, bulleted listings of upcoming issues, or starbursts announcing introductory savings.

A brochure can be anything, and the ability to include it in your package is one of the most important benefits of direct mail as an advertising medium. No other kind of advertising gives you such an easy opportunity to append detailed information to your sales message. This is the kind of information that helps your prospect make, and justify, a purchasing decision: "Gee, look at this, honey. It has four-wheel independent suspension, 16 megabytes of RAM, and an automatic ice maker!"

However, sometimes a mailing can be more successful without a brochure than with one, especially if what you're selling is so well known your audience doesn't need to see it. Hank Burnett's classic letter for the Admiral Richard E. Byrd Polar Center sold a round-the-world trip using only verbal pictures! It's imperative that you test for yourself.

But unless what you're selling really doesn't need to be illustrated in any way, or you're doing a lead-generation mailing and trying to qualify customers, you may well need a brochure. Seeing people actually using your product or service or happily enjoying the benefits of it can be a powerful motivator.

We will now examine the elements of an effective sales brochure.

THE BROCHURE COVER

The front cover is the first thing your prospects will see. Far too many brochures have only a product name and company logo on the front cover. The other common mistake is to use an attention-getting photograph with no text. You want prospects to read your brochure, so give them some incentive by putting a strong selling message on the front of it.

One option is to restate in slightly different terms the key benefit mentioned in the envelope teaser. In fact, the principles of writing envelope teaser copy provide a good model for writing cover copy for brochures. Whether it's getting prospects to open the envelope or open the brochure, the challenge is the same: motivating people to read what's on the inside. That motivation comes from powerful, **benefit-oriented** copy that speaks directly to readers' wants and needs.

If a picture, drawing, or other graphic would enhance the cover copy, use it. However, don't settle for the obvious choice. Consider, for example, a mailing aimed at selling postage metering and weighing equipment to small business owners. One option would be to have a picture of a happy business owner using the equipment with a headline like, "Process your mail in half the time with our postage meter and scale—at a surprisingly low cost."

Free-lance designer Ted Kikoler, who specializes in direct mail and has designed many successful packages, prefers a different approach. Kikoler sometimes likes to use graphics that get prospects to vividly experience the pain of not having the product described in the brochure. Using this approach, you might feature a picture of a frustrated owner, equipped only with stamps and an inadequate scale, struggling to process a mountain of mail. The headline might read: "Spending too much time weighing and stamping your mail?"

Body Copy

There are two main considerations in organizing body copy:

1. Important information should be given priority. For instance, the key benefits of your product or service should be positioned at or near the beginning. Don't worry about repeating benefit information provided in the sales letter—it's important; expose the reader to it more than once. Less important information about sizes, colors, technical specifications, and the like can go near the end, after the more basic issues have been addressed.

2. Think of the brochure as telling a logical and persuasive story, with a beginning, middle, and end. The structure of the story should be determined by what your prospects need to know to bring them to the next stage in the buying process.

In *The Copywriter's Handbook*, Bob Bly mentions some individuals who had a business that involved buying books from publishers and re-selling them to corporations. Because this business is not well under-stood by most people (including the business's prospects, corporate librarians), the brochure began by explaining in a general way what the service was and why corporate librarians might find it useful. Other, more conventional businesses may not require preparing the reader in this way.

After you've introduced the product and presented key information about its benefits and features, tell the rest of the story. Here are some areas Bly suggests you consider:

- How it works—a description of how the product works and what it can do. Service firms might use this area to describe their methodology for working with clients.

- Types of applications—this section describes the specific uses and markets for which the product or service was designed.

- Test results, client list, testimonials, and other ways of verifying the usefulness of the product or service.

- Product availability—models, sizes, materials of construction, options, accessories, etc. Include any charts, graphs, formulas, or other guidelines that might aid the reader in product selection.

- Prices, fees, and terms—information on what the product or service costs. Include prices for accessories, various models and sizes, quantity discounts, and shipping and handling.

- Technical requirements—for example, how much hard disk space, RAM, and what type of microprocessor are necessary to run a particular type of software.

- Q & A—answers to frequently asked questions about the product or service not covered in other sections. Remember that your mailing is your "salesperson on paper." Anticipate what your prospects need to know before they'll buy.

- Company description—a brief biography of the company, designed to give the reader confidence that the product is backed by a solid, reputable organization. A photo of the company headquarters is often an effective way to reassure prospects that they're not dealing with a fly-by-night operation. Service firms may also want to include biographies and photos of key individuals in the company.

- Support—information on delivery, installation, training, maintenance, service, and guarantees.*

You may be afraid of making your brochure too long if you include all this information. Understand, though, that your best prospects are hungry for information. Think about your own experiences with ordering merchandise by mail. Did you read every last scrap of copy to make sure that the product or service in question was something that would really serve your needs? Most people do when they're seriously considering a direct mail purchase.

THE IMPORTANCE OF MAKING THE SALE

Regardless of how the rest of your brochure is structured, there's only one way to end it: Repeat the offer at the end of the brochure and include a call to action. You want the reader to respond to your offer. Refer prospects to your 800 number, reply card, or other response mechanism. It's worth repeating your offer and response information on every single piece in the mailing. Be relentless. It pays.

Remember, a brochure should be able to stand completely on its own. It should have enough information for your customer to place an order from it, including your address and telephone number. Pieces in a kit can easily get separated, and some prospects could end up with nothing on hand but your brochure. Also, if a prospect uses the response form to

*Bob Bly, *The Copywriter's Handbook* (New York: Henry Holt and Company, 1990), pp. 174-179.

place an order, with a brochure that stands on its own, your new customer can circulate your pitch to other people.

MESSAGE AND MOOD

A brochure's text and graphics must fit with the rest of the pieces in the mailing package. A direct mail package should establish a mood, one that's in keeping with the sales message. The brochure should reflect that mood If you are doing a somber and serious package, for example, don't do a frivolous novelty item as your brochure. If your sales message encourages the buyer to flout convention, don't offer a staid brochure. If you're trying to sell on the basis of beauty, do a beautiful brochure, and so on.

Look at the somber brochure from the U.S. Holocaust Memorial Museum (Exhibit 7-1). From a control package created by Lautman & Company, this brochure was mailed to promote membership in the museum. There is no headline on the front of the brochure, beyond the museum's identification. The rest of the front is taken up with a wartime photo of a young woman wearing a numbered card on a string about her neck and a Star of David patch sewn onto the front of her coat.

Inside, the brochure leads (or "tracks") the reader from the cover to a page spread that describes the Museum's Identity Card Project, whereby each museum visitor receives an identity card representing a Holocaust victim and then learns the fate of his or her "companion" at the end of the visit.

It next tracks to a spread giving a fairly detailed description of the Museum and showing photos of some of the exhibits. A subhead reads "Our special mission: To educate the living and remember the dead."

The fully opened interior sheet shows plans of the Museum's second, third, and fourth floors, with photo vignettes and highlights showing points of interest in exhibits. This page has a boxed message that draws your eye:

> The soul of the United States Holocaust Memorial Museum is our Permanent Exhibition, which covers 40,000 square feet on three floors. Our challenge is to tell the entire story of the Holocaust inside this building. To transport our visitors 50 years back in time, a continent away, and introduce them to a world where ordinary lives are shattered by unspeakable evil.
>
> This extraordinary "Living Memorial" will ensure that Americans in every generation to come will remember the Holocaust as a catastrophic failure of humanity and a dire warning about the fragility

Exhibit 7-1   Brochure from the U.S. Holocaust Memorial Museum

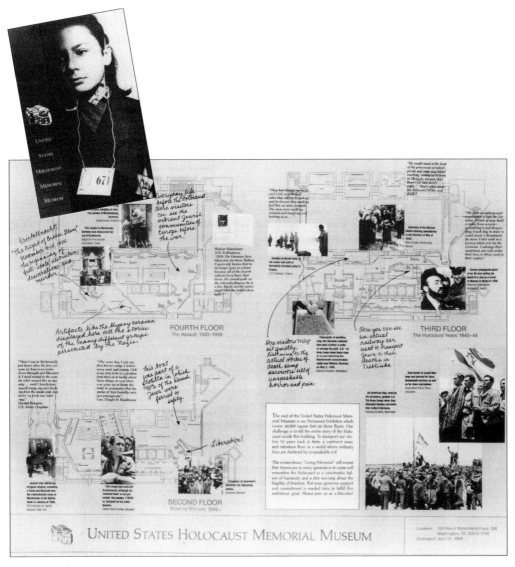

Source: Reprinted with permission of the U.S. Holocaust Memorial Museum and Lautman & Co. Photo by Jan Lukas.

of freedom. But your generous support and commitment is needed today to fulfill this ambitious goal. Please join us as a Member!

At the opposite end of the spectrum is a brochure from an affinity card mailing for *Outside* magazine, written by free-lancer Donal Gordon.

The package offers hotel, car, and travel discounts for the price of the magazine and includes a barrel-folded brochure (Exhibit 7-2).

Note that the cover of the brochure reproduces a real cover of the magazine, even down to the scanning code. Inside, active-verb, benefit-oriented, photo-enhanced headlines lead the reader on:

Go to the places you long to go to!

Do the things you yearn to do!

Meet the people you most want to meet!

All this—and so much more—in the magazine that's your personal passport to adventure!

Exhibit 7-2   Barrel-Folded Brochure from *Outside* Magazine (Axel Award Winner)

Source: Provided by Axel Andersson. Reprinted with permission of *Outside* Magazine, copywriter Donal Gordon, and Ron Bortz.

A consistent selling message is fundamentally important. The same message should be emphasized in the brochure, in the letter, and on the carrier. Don't fall into the trap of thinking the brochure gives you the room to develop a whole new sales message. A mixed sales message is by definition a watered-down sales message. If you want to use more than one sales message, do more than one mailing package, or target more than one audience.

Exhibit 7-3 shows a brochure that targets a specific audience. Written to promote the new Key Master Maps for Windows 95 and written only to current users of the software, this brochure does not waste a lot of space selling detailed information and trip-planning capabilities of the program (it assumes the recipient already recognizes the benefits of a map database). Instead, it highlights the fact that this is a new release and sells a newer, better version with headlines like this:

"All New Road & Highway Data!"
"Just look at all these new features."

It then presents a point-by-point summary of a better-performing, more comprehensive, easier-to-use package. This is the strongest sales message they can present to current users.

DON'T FORGET THE SKIMMERS

A large percentage of your prospects won't read your brochure from cover to cover. These are the skimmers—people who give the material a quick scan to see if it warrants deeper involvement. How many skimmers there are in your group of prospects will depend in part on your target audience.

You should design your brochure so that even a casual reader can get the essentials of your message. You do that by (1) breaking up your text with headlines and subheadings and by (2) using graphics.

Breaking up text with heads and subheads accomplishes two distinct goals. First, it makes reading the brochure a less intimidating task. No one likes to read endless blocks of solid text. It gives readers regular breaks and provides text in small easily digestible portions. Second, when worded properly, headlines and subheads function like an outline, leading skimmers through the brochure and communicating the gist of your story. There's even a chance of converting some skimmers to full-text readers if your headings are compelling enough. How do you make them compelling? By not being afraid to make them long enough to actually say something. Consider how much more compelling it is to say, "Use IRAs to

Exhibit 7-3   Brochure Targeted to a Specific Audience

Source: Reprinted with permission of Softkey International, Inc.

accumulate interest, dividends, and capital gains tax-deferred" than simply "IRAs."

Graphics is the second way to reach skimmers. By nature skimmers often shun words in favor of visual ways of processing information. You can accommodate this preference by illustrating your key points with photographs or drawings. Statistics show that captions have twice the readership of body copy, so supercharge your visuals with informative captions. Here, too, it pays not to skimp—make your captions long enough to be informative.

Sometimes it's desirable to include background information in your brochure that won't fit naturally into the body copy. To solve this problem, present your background material in a sidebar. Sidebars are ruled boxes set off to the side of the main text. They are perfect for checklists, specifications, and other "dense" information that tends to bog readers down. Again, the idea is to make detailed information available to those who want it while offering an abbreviated yet meaningful version of the story for those who don't.

TRACKING

Tracking is that knack brochures have for telling a story by the way they are folded. You look at the front panel of the brochure, and you get part of the story. You open the first fold, and you get more. You open the next and you get more, and so on. A brochure with good tracking will take you by the hand, lead you along, and take you to the punch line, which asks for the order.

An example of excellent tracking is a small four-color brochure for membership in the National Audubon Society. (See Exhibit 7-4.)

The cover is a close-up of a loon, swimming in the water away from you. There is only one word on it: "Discover..." When you open the first flap, you have another, much wider photo of a loon swimming farther away from you with the words "the world of AUDUBON..." Opening to the next side reveals the inside of the brochure, with some beautiful four-color nature photos and a listing of the benefits of Audubon membership. It's a simple brochure. The effectiveness of its tracking increases its impact an order of magnitude. It might be even more effective if it had a clearer ask.

A brochure with good tracking is fun to read. One with good tracking that matches the sales message and leads the prospect right to an order form is unbeatable.

Exhibit 7-4   Tracking a Brochure

Source: Reprinted with permission of the National Audubon Society.

MAKE YOUR BROCHURE A "KEEPER"

Ideally, you want prospects to read your brochure and then buy your product. But regardless of whether or not they buy, the best outcome is for them to keep your brochure for future reference. Even if your original prospect doesn't buy, someone else may see the brochure and make a purchase as a result. The longer the brochure is kept on hand, the better the chances of this kind of "delayed-reaction sale."

Prospects generally keep a brochure for one reason: it contains information they consider useful. The information may be about the product itself or general information that the prospect values. For instance, a brochure on a resort location might contain a detailed map of the area or a calendar of events for the upcoming busy season. A brochure for a commercial printer might include a list of the "Ten Most Costly Mistakes Made by Commercial Printing Clients."

It helps to put yourself in your prospects' position. What would they like to know? What helpful information could you provide that your typical reader might refer to repeatedly for an extended period of time? Put that in your brochure.

SUMMARY AND CHECKLIST

Summary

A winning direct mail brochure:

- features a strong selling message on the front cover.

- persuasively lays out the product's benefits and features, preferably near the beginning.

- has a well-organized sales story that thoroughly answers a prospect's most likely questions.

- uses photographs, drawings, charts, tables, and other graphics to support the sales story, not just for atmosphere.

- is as long as it has to be to tell the sales story properly.

- restates the offer and call to action at the end.

- uses headings, subheads, captions, sidebars, and other devices to allow skimmers to get the gist of the sales story.

- includes useful information that tempts readers to keep it on hand for ongoing reference.

A Checklist for Brochures

☐ Does your copy include information to answer a customer's questions about your product or service?

–Benefits
–Specifications
–Diagrams
–Feature lists
–Comparison charts with other products
–Performance data
–Product samples

☐ Have you included case studies and/or testimonials?

☐ Have you included photos of your testimonial givers?

☐ Is your product shown in action?

☐ Do you ask for the order?

☐ Do you include your company name, address, and phone number?

☐ Is your brochure sized to fit in your carrier envelope?

☐ Is spot color used sparingly?

☐ Does the brochure track logically, telling a story, and leading your reader through to the ask?

8

CATALOG COPY

Catalogs aren't new. An English gardener named William Lucas issued one as early as 1667, and Thomas Jefferson was reported to be a mail-order buyer of gardening products from a broadside catalog published in 1771 in colonial America by William Prince. The first guarantee of customer satisfaction may have been the one that appeared in a catalog published by Ben Franklin in 1744. That guarantee read:

> Those persons who live remote, by sending their orders and money to said B. Franklin, may depend on the same justice as if present.*

Mail-order catalogs really took off during the post-Civil War era. In 1872, Aaron Montgomery Ward produced on a single illustrated sheet of paper a price list offering savings of 40% to rural farmers. Twelve years later, that single sheet of prices had been expanded to a 240-page catalog containing 10,000 items.

And of course, another early catalog came from Richard Warren Sears, a telegraph operator from North Redwood, Minnesota, who had a shipment of undeliverable gold-filled watches. Cleverly recognizing that the best target audience for those watches would be other railroad agents like himself, he mailed in his offer to a specific market segment, and by 1897 had expanded that single offer into a catalog of more than 750 pages with 6,000 items (Exhibit 8-1).

*Much of this information came originally from the 1982 *Fact Book* of the Direct Marketing Association.

Exhibit 8-1 A Page from the Old Sears Catalog

You can see what's become of this early historical trend by looking at the proliferation of catalogs that appear on any given day in your own mailbox.

Here's how the 1994/95 Direct Marketing Association's *Statistical Fact Book* describes the catalog copywriter's job: "When you're through reading what the catalog copywriter wrote, you feel you have found a solution, or captured a dream, as well as touched a product or smelled a fragrance."

Working with few words, in very little space, catalog copywriters not only have to convey a specific description of the product being sold (like measurements, material, speed, and so on), they also have to woo the reader with the **benefits** he or she will derive from a purchase. And copywriters can't oversell, because the catalog merchandiser doesn't want too many returned items.

Photographs and/or illustrations will probably accompany their words, but catalog copywriters still must keep in mind their primary aim: to make the sale. Here especially, nothing beats simplicity. The catalog copywriter will want to use short, to the point, and powerful headlines and product blurbs. And he or she will want to spend plenty of time and attention developing an easy to read, easy to complete order form (Exhibit 8-2).

One thing that helps the writer is that catalogs are, almost by definition, targeted marketing vehicles. Just think of the "niche" catalogs that are among the thousands being published now: R.C. Steele's catalog of dog and cat products with everything from gem-studded collars to rawhide bones and play mice to bark inhibitors. Smith & Noble's *Windoware* with roman shades, cornices, and blinds. Rejuvenation Lamp & Fixture Company with reproduction lighting. There are catalogs from the Popcorn Factory, Wolferman's English Muffins, even one featuring only Hershey's chocolate products.

The writer's job, of course, is to understand the target market the catalog is aimed at, whether it's buyers of romantic lingerie from Victoria's Secret or buyers of outdoor wear from L.L. Bean. *As writer, you have to think like your consumer.* What would your prospective consumer most like to know about this particular product? Its durability? Its easy care? Its figure-enhancing style?

Usually, a catalog copywriter will be part of a team developing both copy and layout. They may also decide which product goes where and how much space it will be given in the layout. According to a Gallup Study, the reader may spend as little as 3.6 seconds on a page and probably no more than 6.8 seconds! (*Fact Book*, 1982.)

Exhibit 8-2   Order Form from the *Feelgood Catalog*

FOLD ↓

FOLD ↓ For credit card orders and customer service:
Order Toll Free: 1-800-997-6789
Hours: M-F 8-6, Sat. 10-3 (MST)

Fax Orders 24-Hours: 1-800-966-6387

The Feelgood Catalog™ Order Form

Name and address of person placing order:

Name _____

Address _____

City _____ State _____ Zip _____

Day Phone ( )_____ Eve. Phone ( ) _____

Gift Order or Ship to Name and Address:

Name _____

Address _____

City _____ State _____ Zip _____

Day Phone ( )_____ Eve. Phone ( ) _____

Qty.	Item no.	Size	R/L	Description *Specify size and color when necessary*	Price (ea)	Total
2	AF100	M	-	*Active-Fit Back Support (36 inch waist-black)*	$59.95	$119.90

METHOD OF PAYMENT:

_____ - _____ - _____ - _____
Card number, expiration date and signature (required for credit card orders)

☐ VISA ☐ MasterCard ☐ ☐

_____ - _____
Exp Date

Signature _____

Print name as it appears on credit card.

Check or Money Order #:_____
(Payable to The Feelgood Catalog) U.S. Funds Only

Current name, address and phone number must be pre-printed on checks. Sorry, no COD's accepted.

Merchandise Subtotal	
Colorado Res. Add 3.8% Tax	
Shipping & Handling Charge SEE CHART	
Total Enclosed	

31-Day Money Back Trial Guarantee
100% Customer Satisfaction
Guaranteed!

Help someone Feelgood!
Gift Certificates available for any
amount over $10.00

‑ ‑ ‑ FOLD ↓ To fit order form in envelope, please tear off at perforation and fold where indicated. FOLD ↓ ‑ ‑ ‑

**Phone Orders:
800-977-6789**

Fax Orders: 800-966-6387

Local: 303-790-7249 Fax: 303-790-1045

Our 100% Satisfaction Guarantee

You are assured complete satisfaction with your purchase from The Feelgood Catalog. If for any reason you are not completely satisfied after using the product for 31 days, simply return the item clean. We will replace the item, refund or credit your account the full purchase price of the product (minus Shipping & Handling charges).

Shipment Policy

Most in stock orders are shipped within 48 hours of placement. Shipping methods will vary depending on customer location and specification. Credit card orders will be billed when order is processed. Partial orders will be billed upon shipment.

Payment Acceptance

We accept Visa, Mastercard, American Express and Discover for phone and mail-in orders. We will also accept certified and personal checks and money orders. All personal checks must include current preprinted name, address, and phone number. All forms of payment must include the full price of the order including shipping and handling charges before any shipment will be made. Sorry, no C.O.D.'s accepted.

Product Backorders

At times of manufacturers unavailability or high demand for certain products, your order, or portion of, may be backordered. In the event of a backorder you will be notified of any delay beyond 30 days. Partial shipments may be made and you will not be charged for additional shipments.

Shipping and Handling Charges*

Order Subtotal	Regular	FedEx Two-Day	FedEx Next-Day
$24.99 or Less	$3.95	$8.50	$14.50
$25.00-$49.99	$4.95	$9.50	$15.95
$50.00-$74.99	$5.95	$11.00	$16.95
$75.00-$99.99	$7.95	$12.50	$18.50
$100.00 or More*	$9.95	$14.00	$19.95

* **Special Shipping Information**
Note: Canada orders add $ 7.00.
FedEx next-day and two-day delivery on in-stock items only. International shipping costs will vary.

Keep This Portion With Your Catalog

Once decisions are made on the size and number of pages, paper stock, layout, and illustrations, the copywriter's real job begins. Some catalogs use only a few lines of copy per item; others like L.L. Bean and J. Peterman use longer, narrative copy. A beginning catalog copywriter would do well to study the wealth of catalogs available, comparing size of copy blocks, treatment of headlines and subheads, placement of "the ask," and use of sentence fragments and abbreviations.

Your copy should definitely "put your prospect in the picture." Consider persuasive lines like these:

"Your bare feet are best qualified to judge this extra-soft, long wearing bath rug."

"This ribbed, merino-wool cape answers all your between-the-seasons dilemmas."

"You'll love the simplicity of our solid-oak rack."

The catalog copywriter may have to work "to spec"—fitting a certain number of characters (not words) into a space. Or, you may have to write a certain number of lines per inch. You should request whatever information the merchandiser can give you (e.g., product description sheets, product photos, billing/shipping options, terms of guarantee, opportunities for gift wrap or personalization, color, size variations), then convey this information as simply as possible to the reader (see Exhibit 8-3).

THE IMPORTANCE OF WORDS IN A VISUAL MEDIUM

Pat Friesen started her career—which now spans more than two decades as a direct response copywriter—as a catalog writer for Current Stationary and Fingerhut Corporation. When asked about the importance of copy in what many consider to be the primarily visual medium of catalogs, Pat says:

Pick up a catalog...your favorite catalog. Now block out, cross out, get rid of every word on the page so that you're left with only the photos. Then ask yourself this question, "Is catalog copy really so important?"

The unequivocal answer, "You're darn right it is!"

Go ahead and try to place an order quickly and easily without the copy. Look at the catalog spread in front of you and try to decide whether or not any given product is what you need and want. Is the photo, alone, enough to help you make your final buying decision? Whether the catalog is from the famous jewelry store Tiffany's, Reliable Office Supply, or any cataloger selling to consumers or busi-

Exhibit 8-3 A Page from the *Feelgood Catalog*

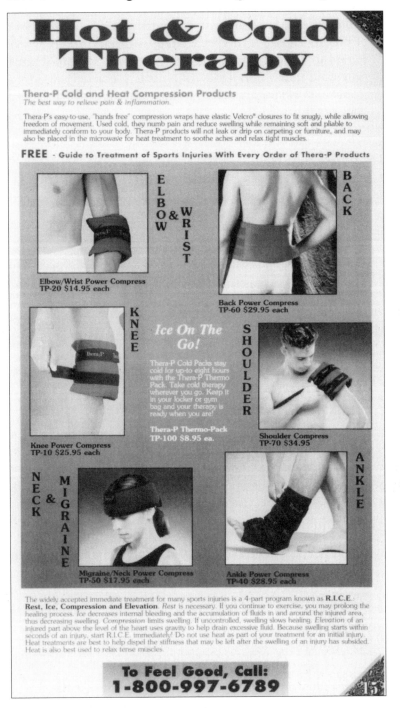

Source: Reprinted with permission of the *Feelgood Catalog*.

ness people, it's the copy that closes the sale. The product copy takes the customer through the buying process to the final buying decision based on size, color, quantity, price, and dozens of other important details that aren't obvious from a photo. Words are required to complete the picture. That's why it's important to invest time (and money) in good, solid catalog copy written by a professional experienced in selling using only a few short lines of power-packed copy.

What should you look for when writing and evaluating catalog copy? Use Pat Friesen's simple checklist as your starting point (see Exhibit 8-4).

Exhibit 8-4   A Catalog Copywriter's Checklist by Pat Friesen

1. **Catalog copy "voice."** What is your catalog copy's "point of view"? You'll find copy easier to write and more persuasive when it's consistently written using the same voice and from the same point of view. Study catalogs selling similar products (i.e. Lands' End and L.L. Bean) and compare the copy "voices." The easiest to read are conversational in tone without being annoyingly chatty.

2. **Product headlines/"identifiers."** Make it easy for your customer; use the headline to link the reader to the copy from the photograph. Types of product headlines include:

Label headlines—Women's 100% Cotton Turtlenecks

Value headlines—SAVE 25%! Spray Starch by the Case.

Benefit headlines—The World's Strongest Fiberboard Box

Plus, there are dozens of variations. No matter what type of product headline you use, remember that the purpose of the headline is to keep the momentum going by leading an interested customer from an enticing photograph into the sales copy.

3. **Product copy blocks**. A classic formula for writing successful catalog copy is called the Inverted Pyramid. It starts with the broad appeal of a major benefit. Next, it narrows the focus to secondary benefits that enhance product appeal. Then it supports these benefits with selling points and features. Finally, it closes with the all-important information necessary for ordering.

The catalog writer's challenge is to pay close attention to everything presented to him or her about the targeted audience as well as the product. From this, he or she must glean the one, two, or three shining benefits that appeal most to the customer, set the product apart from the competition, and accurately represent how the product answers the customer's question, "Why should I buy this product?"

4. **Headlines for spreads**. Headlines are used on page spreads to position the products featured on the spread (i.e., Software for Kids). They also can attract your reader's attention as he or she flips through your catalog (i.e., Gifts for Under $10). Every spread does not have to have a headline. Instead, use headlines to pace products, layout, and your reader's attention.

5. **The president's letter**. Traditionally featured on page 2 of a catalog, this one-sided dialogue establishes your catalog's niche, introduces new and valued customers to new products, and involves your reader in the catalog using specific page references. It's also an opportunity to talk about special offers. Frequently, but not always, the "voice" of the catalog product copy is first established in the president's letter. Don't use this very valuable space to ramble…use it to sell.

6. **Your guarantee**. While the guarantee doesn't get rewritten with each new catalog published, it is an important copy element that deserves to be highlighted on its own, as well as referred to in features such as the president's letter. Your guarantee should be as brief and to the point as possible. Excellent copy "hot spots" for your guarantee include the back cover, page 2, and the order form. If your catalog has more than 32 pages, you will want to include the guarantee in several places throughout the book.

7. **Page violators**. Copy for page violators (i.e. corner slashes, bursts, footers, headers, etc.) needs to be short, sweet, and to the point (i.e. 50% OFF, Exclusive, Prices Rolled Back!). It's always good to tie a benefit to a "housekeeping" detail such as a phone number (i.e., For overnight delivery, CALL 222-222-2222). Put key numbers and words either first or last in the violator copy so they're easily seen and quickly read.

8. **Photo captions and call-outs**. While product photos normally include an identifier (i.e., Two-Line Phone with Intercom), they can't all feature a full-blown benefit caption. Do include

photo captions with in-use and special feature shots. Your reader is drawn to these photos and wants to know more about them. Make sure to include benefit copy in all captions and call-outs (i.e., information connected to a visual by a line, designed to highlight a feature of the product).

Other important elements of the catalog copywriting process include:

- **Know your audience(s)**. Who are your primary and secondary buyers? Does your catalog have pass-along value? Always ask the question, "Who is the individual reading this copy?"

- **Know your products**. Each one has a different story. You need to know that product story in order to position a product within your catalog...and against the competition. Do your homework. Talk to your merchandise buyers. Read manufacturer information. Use the product yourself, when it makes sense. Check out what your competitors are saying about similar products.

- **Standardize your use** of punctuation, spelling, abbreviations, typefaces, etc. Make sure you have a style sheet or style book that documents how and when to use copy-related elements. This will make it easier for future and free-lance writers to write copy that presents your products in a consistent manner.

- **Vocabulary**. Every catalog has a copy style, which includes the copy tone and "voice." This is reflected by the choice of words. Short words charged with meaning work best because they're easily read by customers skimming copy for details. "Scarlet" may be right for a romance novel...but "red" tells the color story quickly, accurately and in less space.

There's a lot to writing successful catalog sales copy. The next time someone says to you, "I never read catalog copy," ask how he or she places an order without knowing if the product is really what it appears to be (Is that a miniature 6" hatbox or one large enough for a Stetson?). Ultimately, it's the copy that closes the sale.

9

DIRECT RESPONSE PRINT ADS

Words increase in value in direct response space advertising. Here, more than ever, every word counts. While there's still a lot of print advertising being done that isn't direct response (i.e., doesn't include a mail-back or fax-back order form or 800-number), for a direct marketer a sale, not an award for creativity, is the main objective. It's important to understand the similarities between direct response print ads and mailed packages. The goal of both types of promotions is to generate either orders (in a one-step campaign) or leads (for a two-step effort). It is **essential** for them both to do a sufficient selling job to obtain the desired response. In terms of our operatic acronym, A-I-D-A, a direct response print ad, like a direct mail package, seeks to take prospects through the entire sequence of Attention, Interest, Desire, and Action. Anything less than an order or, for two-step campaigns, a request for information, is considered a loss.

This similarity leads directly to another: the success of a direct response print ad can be tested and measured precisely. As a result, a considerable body of knowledge has been accumulated about what works and what doesn't. And you never want to underestimate that gap. The difference between a well-written ad and a mediocre one could increase sales nearly 20 times, according to Bruce Mattare, Marketing Manager of Louis Rukeyser's Mutual Funds. Mattare also notes in the February 1996 issue of *Marketing Advents* that the difference in pulling power between using the same headline and testing body copy can be 50% in an ad…while the difference in pulling power between different headlines using the same body copy can be as much as 400%!

A third similarity between direct response print ads and direct mail is the personal style—addressing the reader as "you" in a conversational manner and highlighting benefits of ordering, joining, subscribing.

The primary difference in the two types of promotion is simply the media involved. Magazine and newspaper advertisements allow much less space to get one's point across than direct mail. So the writing of a direct response ad must be a model of economy.

And it must clearly address its target audience right from the start. Mattare's favorite change to a space ad headline was the addition of two words, neither of which was "FREE." The original headline read "Save One Gallon Of Gas In Every Ten;" and the two words added were "Car Owners!"—a change that increased the ad's pulling power by 20%!

WRITING HEADLINES

Given this dual aim of economy of words and market specificity, how do you begin? Any promotional campaign must begin with a careful analysis of your objective, your prospects, and the key features and benefits of your product or service. Then, and only then, should you proceed to formulate what is far and away the most important component of your ad: the headline.

In *Tested Advertising Methods*, John Caples, author of some of the most successful direct response print ads of all time, presents five rules for writing headlines:

1. First and foremost, try to get self-interest into every headline you write. Make your headline suggest to the reader that here is something he wants. This rule is so fundamental that it would seem obvious. Yet the rule is violated every day by scores of writers.

2. If you have news, such as a new product, or a new use for an old product, be sure to get that news into your headline in a big way.

3. Avoid headlines that merely provoke curiosity. Curiosity combined with news or self-interest is an excellent aid to the pulling power of the headline, but curiosity by itself is seldom enough. This fundamental rule is violated more often than any other. Every issue of every magazine and newspaper contains headlines that attempt to sell the reader through curiosity alone.

4. Avoid, when possible, headlines that paint the gloomy or negative side of the picture. Take the cheerful, positive angle.

5. Try to suggest in your headline that here is a quick and easy way for the reader to get something he wants.

Caples adds a caution for writers who go for the "quick and easy" type of appeal. You must also, he says, strive for *believability*. If readers get a "too-good-to-be-true" feeling from your headline, you have not done your job properly, and your ad will yield disappointing results.

Let's look at the headline of one of the most famous direct response ads of all time—an ad Caples himself penned many years ago to promote a correspondence course in piano playing (Exhibit 9-1). The headline read, "They Laughed When I Sat Down at the Piano...But When I Started to Play!".

Why were people so drawn to this headline? There's certainly an element of curiosity, the desire to know what happened next and why. And there's self-interest; the headline implies that by reading further, the reader may be able to learn how to play the piano.

How powerful, then, is the scenario Caples created with just those few words in his headline—a story of triumph and vindication. This ad was so successful that it spawned a whole series of ads (from Caples and others) that began with some variation of "They Laughed." Each, in its own way, touched a raw nerve in a select group of prospects who saw themselves as underdogs in some respect. Such people identify with stories about one of their own who comes out on top, and the ads pioneered by Caples filled the bill nicely. So, too, did an ad for a correspondence course in French that effectively targeted people who felt embarrassment at not knowing that language with the headline, "They Grinned When the Waiter Spoke to Me in French...but their laughter changed to amazement at my reply."

These ads illustrate another powerful technique mentioned in the earlier chapter on direct mail letters: using a story to generate interest and boost sales. As a direct response copywriter, therefore, it will pay you to be alert to situations where you might be able to use a story to good effect.

We've seen how both curiosity and self-interest played a role in the appeal of Caples's "They Laughed" headline. Many successful headlines follow this pattern of incorporating several appealing elements. For instance, any ad that begins, "Announcing a Revolutionary Breakthrough in..." or "Announcing a New..." most likely combines news with self-interest. An example might be, "Announcing a New Scientifically Proven

Exhibit 9-1   Caples's Classic "They Laughed" Ad

Way to Lose Weight—Quickly and Easily." The "quick and easy" element is also explicitly introduced, but believability is preserved by use of the words "scientifically proven." Of course, if you say that something is scientifically proven, you'd better have a way of proving that to the reader in the body copy.

Let's look at a different example. The words "how to" have always held a special place in American advertising, and, as you might expect, these words figure prominently in many successful print ads. In *Successful Direct Marketing Methods* (Lincolnwood, IL: NTC Publishing Group, 1994), Bob Stone cites the example, developed by his own agency, of a headline from an ad promoting a correspondence course in engineering: "How to Become a "Non-Degree" Engineer in the Booming World of Electronics." This headline (Exhibit 9-2) builds in both curiosity, because of the implied promise to provide information, and also self-interest for those who see this information as the key to making a better life for themselves. Notice how much less compelling this headline is if we remove the "How to" at the beginning and simply say, "Become a Non-Degree Engineer in the Booming World of Electronics." Without the "How to," the headline becomes a command for the reader to carry out, perhaps adding another burden to his already busy life. With those two words, there is much more of a sense that someone will provide help in achieving the goal stated in the headline. A seemingly small consideration, perhaps, until you realize that most readers of the ad will decide in a matter of one brief second whether the headline is interesting enough to justify dipping into the body copy.

Here's a final testament to the importance of getting the headline right. John Caples has written about two headlines that were both actually tested in ads that were otherwise almost identical.

1. Are you afraid of making mistakes in English?

2. Do you make these mistakes in English?

The second headline had significantly better pulling power than the first. Experts agree that the use of the word "these" in the second sentence is what made the difference. "These" tells the reader, in effect, "Now, if you'll kindly read further, you'll find out about some of the mistakes I have in mind." It's the curiosity factor at work again.

In addition, the first sentence introduces what for many people may be a negative consideration as far as their command of the English language is concerned: fear. That is, many people may desire to improve their speak-

Exhibit 9-2 "How-To" Ad

How to Become a "Non-Degree" Engineer in the Booming World of Electronics

Thousands of real engineering jobs are being filled by men without engineering degrees. The pay is good, the future bright. Here's how to qualify...

By G. O. ALLEN
President, Cleveland Institute of Electronics

THE BIG BOOM IN ELECTRONICS—and the resulting shortage of graduate engineers—has created a new breed of professional man: the "non-degree" engineer. He has an income and prestige few men achieve without going to college. Depending on the branch of electronics he's in, he may "ride herd" over a flock of computers, run a powerful TV transmitter, supervise a service department, or work side by side with distinguished scientists designing and testing new electronic miracles.

According to one recent survey, in military-connected work alone 80% of the civilian field engineers are not college graduates. Yet they enjoy officer status and get generous *per diem* allowances in addition to their excellent salaries.

In TV and radio, you qualify for the key job of Broadcast Engineer if you have an FCC License, whether you've gone to college or not.

Now You Can Learn at Home

To qualify, however, you do need to know more than soldering, testing circuits, and replacing components. You need to really know your electronics theory—and to prove it by getting an FCC Commercial License.

Now you can master electronics theory at home, in your spare time. Over the last 30 years, here at Cleveland Institute of Electronics, we've perfected AUTO-PROGRAMMED™ lessons that make learning at home easy, even if you once had trouble studying. To help you even more, your instructor gives the homework you send in his undivided personal attention—it's like being the only student in his "class." He even mails back his corrections and comments the same day he gets your work, so you hear from him while everything is still fresh in your mind.

Does it work? I'll say! Better than 9 out of 10 CIE men who take the U.S. Government's tough FCC licensing exam *pass it on their very first try.* (Among non-CIE men, 2 out of 3 who take the exam *fail.*) That's why we can promise in writing to refund your tuition in full if you complete one of our FCC courses and fail to pass the licensing exam.

Students who have taken other courses often comment on how much more they learn from us. Says Mark E. Newland of Santa Maria, Calif.:

"Of 11 different correspondence courses I've taken, CIE's was the best prepared, most interesting, and easiest to understand. I passed my 1st Class FCC exam after completing my course, and have increased my earnings by $120 a month."

Mail Coupon for 2 Free Books

Thousands of today's "non-degree" engineers started by reading our 2 free books: (1) Our school catalog "How to Succeed in Electronics," describing opportunities in electronics, our teaching methods, and our courses, and (2) our special booklet, "How to Get a Commercial FCC License." To receive both without cost or obligation, mail coupon below.

CiE **Cleveland Institute of Electronics**
1776 E. 17th St. Dept. PS-6, Cleveland, Ohio 44114

Cleveland Institute of Electronics
1776 East 17th Street, Dept. PS-6, Cleveland, Ohio 44114

Please send me without cost or obligation:

1. Your 40-page booklet describing the job opportunities in Electronics today, how your courses can prepare me for them, your methods of instruction, and your special student services.
2. Your booklet on "How to Get a Commercial FCC License."

I am especially interested in:

☐ Electronics Technology   ☐ Electronic Communications
☐ First Class FCC License   ☐ Industrial Electronics
☐ Broadcast Engineering   ☐ Advanced Engineering

Name .... Age ......
　　　(Please print)

Address ....

City .... State .... Zip ....

Present Job Title ....

Accredited Member National Home Study Council
A Leader in Electronics Training...Since 1934

ing and writing skills, but they may be reluctant to admit, even to themselves, that they're afraid of making mistakes in English. The second headline solves this problem by avoiding the fear issue entirely.

It's important that you make it easy for your reader to picture himself or herself using your product, reading your magazine, joining your club. Like the teaser on the carrier envelope, your headline is your first, best chance to establish that one-to-one connection. And remember to tout whatever's new—a new product, a new price, a new ingredient.

Writing effective headlines is challenging work! Strive to make every word count, and don't settle for less than your best. If possible, create a number of versions and test them all. Remember: If your headline is weak, prospects won't take the time to read your body copy, and your goods won't sell.

WRITING THE RESPONSE FORM

Your response device should be easy to read and easy to complete. This isn't the place for colored backdrops or odd-shaped coupons like diamonds and circles. Position your order form nearest the outside edge of the page so it's easy for your reader to cut or tear out. Re-state your offer in succinct, benefit-oriented language. Use a check-off box to promote involvement just like you do on the response form of a mailed package. Make sure your entire sales message is repeated, in a short version. Include instructions for completing and returning the form to a stated address. Use positive, active words like "Yes, sign me up!" or "Yes, send my free book!"

WRITING BODY COPY

In a previous chapter, we saw how a direct mail letter can be developed in a variety of ways: with a story, by stressing the offer, etc. Likewise, the body copy of a direct response print ad can be developed in different ways. In *Profitable Direct Marketing*, Jim Kobs describes a general structure for writing body copy that can be adapted to almost any particular method:

1. The opening paragraph or two should enlarge on the headline. That's what attracted the reader.

2. Stack up the benefits and reasons to respond. The more the merrier, but cover the strongest ones first.

3. Include testimonials or use some other means to build credibility for your claims. This is a step that's often overlooked.

4. Explain the details of the offer and make a call to action. Try to include a believable reason to act now. "Orders are filled on a first-come basis" has a much more truthful ring than "Supplies are limited."

This structure is a lot like the one used for direct mail letters. That's not surprising because a lot of what works in direct mail also works with direct response print ads.

Regarding Kobs's second point, about stacking up the reasons to respond, here's a metaphor you may find useful: In developing your body copy, try to apply ever-increasing pressure, as though you were tightening a vise around your prospect. Keep piling on benefits, testimonials, a solid guarantee—whatever it takes until the prospect is "squeezed" to the point of throwing in the towel and placing an order.

Exhibit 9-3 is a good example of an ad targeted to a specific market.

The headline for this ad for *Parenting* magazine trumpets its desired audience right from the start: "Special Offer for New Mothers." The premium that is offered and also highlighted—a FREE Baby's Dish Set—has been selected for its certain appeal to this market. The body copy continues its direct appeal by answering the needs and concerns of new mothers—assuring them that in the pages of *Parenting* magazine they will find "tips on choosing the best-designed car seats, infant carriers, and high chairs. Everything that has anything to do with being a smart and loving parent today." This long-running ad was written by San Francisco-based copywriter Andrea Weingart and designed by graphic designer Karen Mandell.

Weingart and Mandell also teamed up to create an ad for *OS/2* magazine in Exhibit 9-4, one directed at a very different audience. Actually, the audience may overlap (a new mother may also be a potential subscriber to *OS/2*), but the ads address special promises that will resonate with the wants of particular prospects at a particular time.

This ad promises a free issue of the magazine. Weingart's copy literally "screams" the magic word "free" three times and also presents active-verb, benefit-oriented subheads like "Crank up your PC with power! Shift your hard-drive into over-drive! Make your software rumble and roar! Push your peripherals through the roof!" This copy does a good job of turning fairly dry technical material into an engaging, reader-involved scenario.

Exhibit 9-3   Print Ad from *Parenting* Magazine

Source: Reprinted with permission of *Parenting* Magazine, copywriter Andrea Weingart and Karen Mandell Graphic Design.

Exhibit 9-4   Print Ad from *OS/2* Magazine

Source: Reprinted with permission of *OS/2* Magazine, copywriter Andrea Weingart and Karen Mandell Graphic Design.

Another ad that does a good job of putting the target reader in the picture is one for *Portable 100* magazine. The ad, created by Marilyn Ewer of MKE Enterprises and Doug Hamer of D.S. Hamer Design Company, is shown in Exhibit 9-5.

Exhibit 9-5   Print Ad from *Portable 100* Magazine

The sky's the limit...
...with Portable 100 magazine.

On the road...at home ...in the office...in the air...the variety of tasks you can perform with your Tandy portable is expanding constantly.

To keep fully informed and up-to-date about current trends, new products, and new uses for your laptop, you need **Portable 100** magazine.

From sophisticated input/ output (I/O) calls and their applications, to simple disk drives, **Portable 100** magazine covers it all.

Portable 100 gives you features, news, columns, and reviews that are thorough and timely. And they are written in a fast-paced, easy-to-read style, by leading experts in the computer field.

In upcoming issues you will discover...

* how new peripherals can make you more productive.
* more efficient ways to communicate with your desktop.
* where to buy low-cost public-domain software.
* how your business can be more profitable with your portable at your fingertips.
* where to find the best bulletin boards and information services.
* and much more!

Don't miss even a single valuable monthly issue. Fill out the coupon below, or to charge it to your credit card, call

1-603-924-7949

Send no money now! We will gladly bill you.

SAVE **47%** OFF THE COVER PRICE!

☐ **YES!** I want to explore ways to be more productive with my Tandy portable...and save 47% off the newsstand price. Send me a year's subscription (12 issues) of **Portable 100** for $24.97.

☐ Payment enclosed   ☐ Bill me
Make checks payable to **Portable 100**

Name _____

Address _____

City _____ State ____ Zip ____

Canada $45.97 (Canadian funds), Mexico, $29.97. Foreign Surface $44.97. One year only. U.S. Funds drawn on U.S. banks. Foreign Airmail, please inquire. Please allow 6-8 weeks for delivery.   37DB4

MONEY BACK GUARANTEE:
If you are not completely satisfied with **Portable 100**, you may cancel your subscription and receive a full refund. Please allow 6-8 weeks for delivery of your first issue.

Mail to: Portable 100, Portable Computing International Corp., PO Box 428, Peterborough, NH 03458-0428

Source: Reprinted with permission of MKE Enterprises and D.S. Hamer Design.

They've literally hung the reader from a parachute and promised that "The sky's the limit…with *Portable 100* magazine." Body copy goes on to elaborate on the benefits of using a Tandy portable and subscribing. There's a lot of information imparted in a relatively small amount of copy, and the layout reinforces ease of reading.

A double-page spread also created by MKE Enterprises and D.S. Hamer Design again targets a different audience and uses both copy and visuals to help that audience select themselves (Exhibit 9-6).

Note how the order form is easy to cut out in its position at the far right of the spread. There's plenty of space left between the lines for the reader to complete the form. And selectivity is reinforced in the corner head, "Exclusive CD Offer! Not Available in Stores!"

One final ad illustrates how numbers can be put to good use in headlines and body copy (Exhibit 9-7). It was written by Jeff Laurie and designed by Karen Mandell.

The headline announces "9 reasons to send for *Baby On The Way*" and the body copy is effectively broken up into 9 benefits like "You'll trust it

Exhibit 9-6   Print Ad for Club CD

Source: Reprinted with permission of *CD Review* and MKE Enterprises.

because it comes from your obstetrician." And "It's totally free to expecting mothers like you!"

Exhibit 9-7   Print Ad for *Baby on the Way* Magazine

Source: Reprinted with permission of *Baby on the Way* Magazine, copywriter Jeff Laurie, and Karen Mandell Graphic Design.

WRAPPING IT UP

As it is with direct mail, so, too, with print ads. As much as you might like to reduce the process of writing a successful direct response print ad to a precise formula, it simply can't be done. But testing can help. The writer of direct response print advertising has one valuable tool the general advertising copywriter doesn't: a measurable, accountable medium that determines what works and what doesn't in the words you use. Analyze previous ads. Separate out the winners, the break-evens, the poor performers. Conduct postmortems on the bombs; try to determine what went wrong. Consider what elements the winning ads have in common— a particular premium, offer, benefit, headline—and repeat those elements in your next ad.

10

Copy That's Said, Not Read

TV, Radio, and Telephone Marketing

TV and Radio

Ever watch a TV commercial, get swept away by the visuals, but have no idea seconds later what product it was promoting? Or hear a funny commercial that got you laughing out loud but not reaching for your telephone?

Direct response TV and radio have the same goal as a direct mail effort: a buying decision or active expression of interest. But with TV and radio, you don't just paint word pictures, you let the reader see or hear them.

As a writer, the preparation you do will be the same as that for any direct mail package: know your product and know your prospects and customers. Translate product features into benefits. And remember how little time you have to "hook" your customer.

Your initial "hook" could include:

1. A promise: "You could look like this in 10 days."

2. An arresting fact or statistic: "Half of all American homes will suffer break-ins this year."

3. Or a personal question: "Tired of being hounded by bill collectors?"

When writing a commercial script for TV, you'll use two columns: video on the left and audio on the right, like this:

Video	Audio
1. *Close-up of puppy in kennel*	**Voice-over.** Sometimes, it's a long, cold wait to find a home.
2. *Hands pick up puppy*	**VO.** But it doesn't have to be. Share your life with a homeless animal.

Number the scenes and use storyboards with drawings to show the action taking place during the commercial.

How much can you write? In a live-action commercial, you can use approximately 135 words a minute. Delivery rate is hard to define, but the most effective commercials range in word count from 101 to 140 words per minute.

Pace your TV visuals. Try to allow a minimum of 3 seconds for viewers to orient themselves to a scene before moving on. In his book, *Or Your Money Back*, TV advertising expert Alvin Eicoff states, "To determine the length of your commercial, an advertiser must determine how long it takes to sell his product. Generally between one and two minutes is necessary to do an effective selling job. To dominate a 120-second break, you must create a commercial of at least 90 seconds in length; to own that break, your commercial must be the entire two minutes. If you don't do either of these two things, you run the risk of irritating viewers by being within a cluster of four 30-second spots."

In both radio and TV, your 800-number should be a constant presence. Web sites and e-mail addresses will gain increasing importance, too. Mention them in narration and display them on the screen.

The biggest challenge in writing radio copy is selling a product or service using the spoken word. Here are some practical hints:

• Read what you write out loud—not just once but several times.

• Use short words and short sentences.

- Use connectors like "and" or "but" to preserve the flow of the writing and give it a conversational tone.

- Sentence fragments sometimes work better than complete sentences.

- Contradictions (won't, can't) are fine to use.

- Punctuation is important—the announcer uses it as a road map as he or she reads. A double dash can give a dramatic pause. A hyphen can join two words to modify a third one (like baby-soft or squeaky-clean).

- Use words that are easy to pronounce. The letters "s," "z" and the soft "c" are often tongue twisters.

A guide to all the nuances of writing direct response radio and TV could be a book in itself. Clio Award winner Jean B. Hall has written TV and radio spots for the American Association of Retired Persons, National Public Radio, Bali Bras, and the American Florists Marketing Council. The following are a few tips from Hall on how to make your commercials more memorable and effective—and your experiences in the world of broadcasting more rewarding:

1. Take advantage of the medium. There are things you can do on radio that you can't do—or can't afford to do—anywhere else. Awhile back, comedy genius Stan Freberg created a spot promoting radio use that demonstrated this point to a tee. Right before your very ears, he drained a lake and conjured up an army of earthmovers to fill it with ice cream, hot fudge, and whipped cream. Then, helicopters flew in a giant maraschino cherry to top off the world's largest sundae! Creating this illusion on TV or in print would have taken a George-Lucas–sized budget or the Leonardo of airbrushing. But on radio, all it took was a few well-chosen sound effects.

In radio, you have two "dimensions" to work with: sound and time. Remember that sound includes not just words, but sound effects and music. Most recording studios have an extensive library of both music and effects from which to choose. And if you can't find what you need, specialists will search it out or even create it for you.

Take advantage of what radio does best, and use a variety of sounds to put together a clutter-cutting spot listeners will really remember.

2. Don't waste precious TV dollars on a "talking head." The same principle holds true for TV where, besides sound and time, you have the added dimension of visuals.

It's boring to watch an announcer—no matter how attractive—drone on for 30 or 60 seconds. Almost as boring as watching a "crawl" of words roll endlessly across the screen. If you're investing the big bucks it takes to produce and air a TV commercial, don't try to jury-rig a print ad or radio spot to do double duty. Start from scratch. Think about something you can *show* that will grab and hold the viewer's attention. Take maximum advantage of visuals to give the viewer a real eyeful.

3. Start with a "big idea." We've all been to movies that were lavishly produced, lavishly shot—and a complete waste of time! The same thing can happen to a TV or radio spot.

It's tempting to fall into the "production values" trap and convince yourself that a professional announcer's mellifluous baritone or the right props and lighting will rescue a second-rate idea and transform it into a thing of beauty. It won't.

If the script or storyboard seems dull when you read it, it will be dull on the air. The latest technology, the best cinematography, the most gifted director, and on-air talent still can't make a silk purse out of a sow's ear. You must have an exciting concept to hang your message on if you want results.

4. Keep your budget in mind as you write. A cast of thousands might make for an interesting commercial. Unfortunately, it would be a financial disaster for most advertisers. All those smiling faces—or happy voices—have to be paid. And at union rates, they don't come cheap. You can't get around it by calling them "extras" instead of "principals" either. The rule is, if their mothers can recognize them, they get scale…even if they don't speak a line!

Fortunately, you can create lots of terrific spots with one or two talents. For TV, you might even consider a visual that doesn't involve people at all—or shows them from the neck down—and relies on a voice-over or prerecorded character voices to carry the story. (The long-running 4-C Bread Crumbs campaign springs to mind as an example of how this device can be used effectively, although if you want elegantly manicured fingers picking up your product, you'll have to pay scale for a hand model.)

Whatever solution you come up with, just remember that every time you add a person to your commercial, every time you use a sound effect or "needle drop" of music, every time you switch scenes, you're adding extra dollars to your production budget.

5. But don't be penny-wise and pound foolish. The cheapest way to do a radio commercial is to use what's called "live-read" copy. You prepare a script (making sure it comes in within specified time limits), and give it to good old WXYZ. Then one of its station announcers reads it on air or prepares a cassette to play in your time slots.

If you're on a shoestring budget, live-read may be all you can afford. And because there's no studio time or union talent to pay, cost certainly is an advantage. But all too often, you get what you pay for—and less.

DJs are not commercial announcers. So you may find your exciting sales pitch lacks punch when read by an easy-listening host. Or that the person reading your copy has no feel for it and emphasizes all the wrong words.

A better—though admittedly more expensive—way to make sure you like what you hear on air is to do a studio session with a professional announcer who'll do the job right.

6. Use union talent. You may loathe unions. You may detest dealing with agents. You may think the current rates for an hour or so of an announcer's time are outrageous.

Use union talent anyway.

The fact is, all the best radio announcers are members of the American Federation of TV and Radio Artists (AFTRA). All the best television actors belong to the Screen Actors Guild (SAG). And if you want your product or service to be presented professionally, you need their services.

Maybe you think Joe in accounting would make a fine spokesperson. After all he's an attractive guy with a great voice. But can he squeeze an extra phrase or two of copy into a 60-second spot without making it sound rushed? Can he put a smile in his voice to end your commercial on an upbeat note? Or would he freeze up when confronted by an unfamiliar studio environment…or pop his p's by standing too close to the microphone? Resist the urge to use your staff in commercials. And resist the urge to be your own talent twice as hard. Unless you're *sure* you're the next Frank Perdue or Dave Thomas, writing a script that puts you in a starring role is a big mistake. One that can detract from your image, waste expensive studio time by necessitating costly retakes, and even land you on a union blacklist—so you can't get a decent announcer later when you discover your do-it-yourself effort isn't working.

7. Don't overwrite your commercial. You've got a dynamite concept and a general idea of the type of announcer and characters you want to use. Now it's time to get it down in black and white. (Double-spaced so it will be easy for your talent to read and you to edit.)

One of the biggest mistakes first-time scriptwriters make is packing their spots with wall-to-wall copy, so there's no time for the announcer to catch his breath or put a second's worth of extra emphasis on a key word or phrase.

How do you keep this from happening to you? Is there a magic formula for how many words to use?

The answer is no. Although some books give you general rules of thumb, the best way to figure out whether or not your copy will "fit" is to invest in a stopwatch and run through it yourself. Closet yourself in a quiet room, and read your script the way you want it to be read on air—slowly and with expression. Pause where you want the announcer to pause. Then go back, time each character's lines, and estimate how much time you'll need to fade up music and establish sound effects so they're recognizable. (Is 1 second enough for people to realize that they're hearing a vacuum cleaner instead of a car engine, or will you need 3?) If you're doing TV, make sure there's plenty of time for the action to take place. And make sure to leave at least 5 seconds for any product shots—or supers—you want your audience to actually read.

8. Give yourself some extra breathing room. Now add up the figures. Are you under your time limit?

Probably not. Even experienced writers usually produce a first draft that's 5, 10, or even 15 seconds too long.

The trick is to go back and cut the fat without cutting the essentials. Take out a word or two here and there—maybe an entire phrase or sound effect. You may have to reword a few sentences to make the copy shorter—or even sacrifice one of those golden expressions you congratulated yourself on earlier.

Do it. You'll wind up with a crisper, tighter commercial you'll like better in the long run. And one that won't have to be re-edited in the studio with the meter running.

It's a good idea to write 60-second radio spots that actually time out to 58 or 59 seconds—even shorter if you're using lots of sound effects. (You can always plug in an extra second of bells and whistles if you find yourself running short.) Keep 30-second TV commercials to 25 seconds or so. And plan a few extra "emergency cuts" in advance. (Pencil them in lightly on your copy of the script only.) That way, you won't have to go back to the drawing board in session while engineer and talent costs are mounting.

9. Make your product the star. People want to see your product. They want to know how it works. They want to hear what makes it speccial. And it's in your interest to accommodate them.

A clever, entertaining spot can be a real attention-getter. But you can get so clever and so entertaining that people remember the spot...and forget the product. Have fun with your commercial, and your audience will enjoy it. But don't let the fun get in the way of the message.

Avoid "borrowed-interest" spots, where the attention-getting device really has nothing to do with what you're selling. (A bathing beauty may get male viewers to sit up and take notice, but what they'll be noticing won't be the deluxe widget she's peddling.)

And avoid vague generalities. Words like "quality," "value," and "service" are millstones that weigh your copy down, and savvy consumers tune them out immediately. Instead, prove your claims with facts, delivered in punchy phrasing that's heavy on verbs and light on adjectives. Sell the sizzle, as well as the steak, by showing how what you're offering benefits buyers. And in TV, leave plenty of time to romance your product with "beauty shots" and demonstrate its unique features.

10. Tell them your name. Then tell them again. As mentioned earlier, one of the dimensions of both radio and TV is time. Unlike print, you can't reread a commercial or rip it out of a magazine to save the phone number. After it's gone, it's gone.

For this reason, it's wise to repeat your name and phone number often. Introduce your name early if you can. Then use it as an adjective to describe your product. It's not just a low price, it's "available at the low Time-Life price of just $14.95."

This repetition may sound a bit awkward at first, but consumers are used to it. And with all the competition on the airwaves, you really need this added emphasis to get your name to register.

11. What was that number again? Make sure you also repeat your phone number s-l-o-w-l-y at least twice—preferably toward the end of the commercial, so the brilliant phrasing that follows it won't eclipse this important information. And consider getting a number that spells out your name or a related phrase (like MCI's brainstorm 1-800-COLLECT) so harried commuters won't forget it by the next stoplight.

For TV, you'll want to allow plenty of time for supers. (Some telethons now run their number at the bottom of the screen throughout the entire program.) Make sure they're big enough to be read across the room by somebody who needs a new eyeglass prescription, in a color that contrasts sharply with the background, and in an easily discernible typeface (no Old English or other frilly typefaces).

Don't expect your audience to be speed-writers, either. If you're running an address, do your viewers and your response rate a favor by leaving plenty of time to copy it down. Better yet, read it aloud. After all, not everybody's sitting there glued to the screen. And you can't "act now" if you didn't quite catch where to send your money.

12. Make "real-life" spots sound real. There are several kinds of commercials that can be tricky to produce. One is the conversation spot.

You know—where Jane and Jill bump into each other in the washroom and start hashing out whose wash is whiter than white or why they use Band-Aid brand strips. Another is the testimonial given by actors playing "just plain folks."

Unless you have a playwright's ear, these spots can wind up sounding silly, stilted, and phony; and it's difficult to throw in the product name as often as you'd like.

Can you use this kind of spot effectively in direct response? Sure. Just realize from the start that it takes a special kind of talent and a bit of extra effort to pull it off.

13. Be wary of comedy, cabbies, kids, and dogs. Making a comedy spot work can also be a tough proposition.

If the jokes aren't genuinely funny—and delivered just right—the commercial can fall flat.

The same holds true for spots that depend on a special accent. You have to find an announcer whose reading is really convincing. And you can't just tell him or her to read your copy "with an Irish brogue" or "like a New York cabbie." You have to write with the effect you want in mind—and throw in phrases like "sure as the shamrocks come up in the spring," or "Where to, Mac?"

Kids and animals are easier to write for—but harder to direct. It's next to impossible to get a good performance from a 4-year-old when it's past nap time. Even with a professional trainer, it may take 20 takes before Fido's "woof" comes in on cue. And for some inexplicable reason, casting senior-citizen types can be a real bear. The good ones don't sound old, and the ones that sound old don't necessarily have the talent you're after. Don't chuck a good spot that relies on one of these elements. But be prepared to encounter a few difficulties. Build a little extra time into your schedule.

14. Make one spot do double duty. Maybe you'd like to save money by making a single commercial you can adapt for different cities or use with different deadlines or holiday offers.

You can do that by leaving room for the station announcer to read a live tag at the end of your commercial. Or you can prerecord different tags yourself so they'll have a more professional sound.

You also can leave a hole in the middle of your jingle or spoken radio commercial (called a "donut") for changing messages. And you can construct your TV commercials so you film a standard opening and closing and just change product shots and voice-overs in between.

Watching your language can result in substantial savings too. If you say "Call this number" instead of "Call 1-800-555-5555," you can simply change the super instead of re-recording the announcer a dozen times for each target market.

One word of caution, however: consult a talent payment expert about union rules for tags and donuts. What you consider a minor variation may be a separate spot in their book. And you could wind up owing more in penalties than you'll save in production costs.

15. Find the right radio announcer. Now that the spot's finally nailed down, who are you going to cast?

You've already ruled yourself, your kids, your Uncle Ned, and your star salesman out. So where do you find the caliber of professional talent you're after?

For radio spots and TV voice-overs, start by calling your local AFTRA office. (With luck, the number will be in the Yellow Pages. If not, check information in the nearest large city.) They'll send you a free directory with phone numbers of area talent or their agents.

Narrow the field by asking someone who's done commercials before to suggest who's a good bet. Or start calling at random; request tapes with samples of the announcer's previous spots, and settle in for a few hours of intensive listening—with a big legal pad beside you to jot down pertinent information. (If your tape recorder or cassette player has a counter, be sure to set it on zero at the beginning of each tape, so you can make a note of where to find the commercial that impressed you.)

Don't worry if all the voices sound the same initially. You'll soon pick up subtle differences and zero in on the qualities you want.

16. Think about going out of town. Even if you're not in a major market like New York, Chicago, or Los Angeles, you can call one or more of the big agents in those advertising meccas, describe your spot or fax a script, and tell them the tone you want (perky, authoritative, laid-back, yuppie, senior citizen, Generation X-er, etc.).

If they feel you're serious, they'll often arrange a free casting session and send you a tape of talent they think would be a good choice—reading your very own script in a variety of interpretations. At the very least, they'll send you a free master tape with samples of their leading male and female announcers' work.

Don't fret if the voice of your dreams is hundreds—or even thousands—of miles away. If you can't fly in for the session, you can arrange a "phone patch" with most major studios. Though it's not quite as good as being there in person, it lets you hear everything that's going on, request playbacks, make suggestions to the engineer and talent, and come away with a spot that's everything you hoped for—featuring a first-rate voice that's new to your market.

17. Find the right TV talent. When you're casting for TV, you want to see every gesture, every look, every wart the camera might pick up. The best way to do that is to arrange a session with a casting firm—either locally or in a major metropolitan area. The firm will need a script and detailed input on what you're looking for. (Is a pale complexion or curly hair unacceptable? Do you want a specific age range or ethnic mix? Actors who are attractive, but could stand to lose a few pounds? Freckle-faced kids 4 to 6 who can deliver a line with pizzazz?) Let your casting firm know—and let them beat the bushes for the talent you're after.

Be at the casting session in person if you can. But you can save time—or, if you're confident of your long-distance judgment, even do the whole job—by requesting a taped session. And you can play it back over and over until you're sure of your decision.

The decision may be clear-cut or a tough call. But if there's a choice between someone with the right look and someone who can act, don't hesitate. Choose the actor! And choose the actor with the intelligence to see what you're aiming for—and tailor his or her delivery to your goals.

18. Negotiate a better deal. You've bitten the bullet and are prepared to pay union scale. Now the agent wants…scale-and-a-half? Double scale? Triple scale?

Agents' demands can be staggering. They're in the business of earning their clients top dollar—and collecting a 10% commission on whatever they can convince you to pay—and they take that business very seriously.

Relax. You don't have to pay what they're asking. Even if you've written a spot with a specific celebrity in mind, you can probably make a few minor alterations and adapt it to another big name.

Don't take the negotiating process personally. And remember: You're paying; you're in the driver's seat.

19. Explain your situation, and negotiate some more. If you can possibly talk to the talent directly, call that number first. They often have a more modest idea of what their time is worth. They may have bills coming due that the agent doesn't know or care about. And chances are, they'll feel a scale spot is better than no spot at all.

If you must talk to an agent (and that probably will be the case, at least in a large market), explain your situation. If you're a small organization, plead poverty. "I'm sorry, but this is our first spot, and we really can't afford that much. Can you do a little better?"

If you're larger, plead reality. "I'm sorry, but we haven't got that much in our budget. Can you do a little better?"

If you've got multiple spots, explain that this could be a really lucrative deal—or hold out the carrot of future work. "If we get good results, we're planning to roll out a big campaign, and we want to use the same announcer on all six spots." But don't make promises you can't keep.

Be polite but firm. Bend a little if you can. Make a counteroffer and see what happens. (Inch up a little; let the agent inch down, and meet at the low end of middle.) You may be pleasantly surprised and get a top national talent for the same price you'd pay a local announcer.

20. Consider hiring a producer. You've never been in a studio? You're not really comfortable negotiating with high-powered agents or making decisions on sound effects and wardrobe? You're afraid the talent who reminded you so much of Orson Welles at the audition will turn up at the session sounding more like Mr. Ed?

A few "opening night" jitters on your first spot are natural. But if you're really nervous, pick up the phone. Hire a free-lance producer to do the worrying for you. Good producers know how to solve just about any problem you might encounter and seem to thrive on stress.

If a piece of stock music isn't right, they know where to get one that is. If the actors' plane is diverted to another airport, they'll get a driver to pick them up. If the director has made a decision you don't like, a word in the producer's ear can set things right without a major confrontation.

A producer can take the terror out of everything from budgeting to postproduction edits (of course, you'll still want to be there yourself to see that it all goes smoothly), and save you not only a succession of sleepless nights, but often, many times the fee you're paying for this help.

Your producer will probably be a union signatory. (Check to make sure.) Somebody's got to be before union talent will commit to doing your spot.

21. Don't try to do without a talent payment agency. You don't want union problems. If you take only one of the suggestions in this chapter, take this one: Get a reliable agency to handle your talent payment.

Over the years, AFTRA and SAG have evolved a set of rules that can only be described as Byzantine…complex requirements for session fees, demo rates, pension-and-welfare add-ons, and more. Plus a weighted point system where the amount you pay depends on how many markets you're in and how large they are.

You don't just deal with the union once and forget about it either. If your spot will be running for awhile, a new payment is due every 13 weeks. And if you stop running your commercial and then start again, you'll owe something for the period in between.

Missing a payment or paying the wrong amount (in fact, even rescheduling a session or serving lunch late at a TV shoot!) can mean hefty penalties. Or get you blacklisted if you can't straighten the problem out. So don't do it yourself. Call in an expert. If you can't figure out who to contact, ask your producer, TV director, or recording studio. Many studios offer this service as a sideline, and it's well worth the money!

22. Put in your two cents' worth. You are in the recording studio with a famous personality or an announcer with decades of experience. But his delivery isn't quite what you envisioned.

You are at a TV shoot, and the director says, "That's a wrap!" But you'd like one more take with a few minor changes.

You are at a jingle or casting session or postproduction edit. You see or hear something you think is a mistake.

Should you say something? (This is your first spot, and everyone else is presumably an expert.)

Absolutely! You owe it to yourself and your company—and to your client if you're doing the spot for someone else—to do everything in your power to make this commercial the best it can be. It's your duty to speak up. If you don't, you'll regret it every time the spot airs.

Do it politely. But don't settle for "almost there" when a few more minutes could make it perfect.

And one more thing about when you do get it perfect…don't get carried away by the excitement. Don't press the talk-back button or break silence on the set and yell, "That's it!" Force yourself to wait a few seconds. Count to ten in your head before you say anything. Because *your* words are being recorded, too. And if you're not careful, you could ruin that perfect take by "stepping on" the announcer before the last echoes of his or her voice have died away.

23. Make campaigns hang together. The people who called in response to your last spot are probably hot prospects for your new product, too. But will they recognize that it's the same dependable, responsive company making the offer?

The chances are a lot better if all your commercials use similar formats, similar music, similar typefaces on the supers, and maybe the same spokesperson or actors. Think a few spots ahead, and you won't have to start from scratch every time there's a new commercial to produce. But don't let this advice stop you from fixing a problem, introducing new elements, or updating a format that's starting to look tired.

24. Don't be afraid to break the rules. Finally, let your intelligence and your instincts guide you. With the exception of using union talent and a talent payment agency, feel free to break any of the rules above if you've got good reason.

Breakthrough spots *are* breakthroughs because they don't follow the conventional wisdom. Because they do something different—something that's never been tried before. And because that something different works like gangbusters!

TELEMARKETING

Benefits—answering the "What's in it for me?" question—are still of prime importance in writing for media other than mail. We will examine how one writer initially approached a telemarketing assignment for a midsize financial service organization that specializes in the buying and trading of common stocks.

The writer, Diane Bonavist, was told that the company would be offering a plan for reinvestment of dividends (called ROD) next quarter. This would allow customers to use dividends paid on stocks to automatically purchase new shares. The company wanted their telemarketing representatives to articulate the many ways customers could benefit from this new plan.

Bonavist was given system specifications written by computer programmers, and a customer agreement. The client was receptive to the writer's request to spend time on-site. She sat through two 4-hour shifts with the telemarketers after which she composed a list of ROD's key characteristics:

- Changes to reinvestment registration can be done by phone.

- Fractional as well as whole shares are reinvested.

- There is a 24-hour touch-tone inquiry system.

- All securities or some securities can be tagged for reinvestment.

- There are more than 4,000 securities eligible for ROD management.

- There are no fees charged for ROD transactions.

- Customers can receive discounts on the purchase price of certain ROD-managed securities.

Then she translated and expanded those features into customer benefits (Exhibit 10-1). This is where the reference materials and the information she gathered on-site proved essential.

Whether you're using the telephone to sell investment plans or raise funds for a charity, finding the right voice to appeal to each market segment can dramatically increase the effectiveness of your campaign. In the August 1990 issue of *The Donor Developer*, Michael J. Rosen cited a capital campaign for St. Joseph's University that brought a 62% increase in the pledge rate simply by changing the wording of the telephone solicitation.

Exhibit 10-1   Translating Features into Benefits

Feature:

1. Changes to reinvestment registration can be done by phone.

Benefit:

Expedience—Because written instructions aren't required, customers can easily change reinvestment strategy and take advantage of market fluctuations.

Feature:

2. Fractional shares are reinvested.

Benefit:

Customers don't have to have a dividend large enough to purchase a full share. It gives them access to buys they couldn't normally make in the marketplace.

Feature:

3. There is a 24-hour touch-tone inquiry system available.

Benefits:

Timely access to ROD information
Convenience

Feature:

4. All securities or some securities can be tagged for reinvestment.

Benefit:

Customers may register their entire account for reinvestment.
  –All current securities and all future purchases of new securities are automatically tagged by the ROD system for dividend reinvestment.
  –They are relieved of making ongoing investment decisions, yet they are secure in knowing they are fully invested.
Customers can pursue long-range investment goals.
Customers may register only select securities for reinvestment.
  –They can follow a carefully designed investment strategy.
  –They have flexibility in managing their investments.
  –They can take advantage of an individual approach.

Feature:

5. There are more than 4,000 securities eligible for ROD management.

Benefits:

This means an extensive range for potential reinvestments.

Customers don't have to reinvest through plans offered by individual stock companies.

Customers can consolidate their assets.

Feature:

6. There are no fees charged for ROD transactions.

Benefits:

This helps build equity faster.

All customers' capital goes to work for them.

This lowers the average cost per share.

Feature:

7. Customers can receive discounts on the purchase price of certain ROD-managed securities.

Benefits:

They can purchase more shares for their money.

Customers with large holdings will see a significant increase in shares purchased for reinvestment.

By listening to the alumni who were not responding to the appeal, the school was able to evaluate how people were receiving its message and respond with a new message that specifically targeted alumni by using an initial opening line of "When was the last time you stopped by Cavanaugh's (a local bar popular with university students)?" The alumni felt grateful to be recognized for who they were.

Targeted Scripts

TransAmerica Marketing Services, Inc., is a full-service agency based in Vienna, Virginia, that handles telephone marketing campaigns for fundraising, upgrading, prospecting, and more. In an article written for TransAmerica's newsletter, editor Marcia Calhoun asks:

> Where would telemarketing agencies be without phone scripts? Telephone marketing scripts give communicators vital information, useful terminology, and appropriate delivery techniques. And I think it's safe to say, in most cases, it's very difficult to give an effective presentation without a script.
>
> But how can one script appeal to every person we encounter on the phone? How can one approach be equally effective for "Mr. Aggressive," "Mrs. Easily Intimidated," and "Miss Say Nothing"?
>
> The truth is, one script can't do the job. An effective telephone marketing presentation must be geared toward the listener's personality type.
>
> Over the years we've spoken with millions of people on the phone. And, based on our experience, we conclude most individuals fall into just three personality types: Direct, Indirect, and Passive.
>
> Let me tell you a little about these three types of folks.
>
> Direct: These individuals respond with a lot of detail and questions. They appear to be "know-it-alls" and sometimes "complainers." They're aggressive and need to be in control of the situation.
>
> Indirect: Indirect individuals are unresponsive to your request. They need someone to take control of the situation and guide them into a decision.
>
> Passive: Many elderly people fall into this category. They're friendly, attentive, easy to talk to—but the bottom line is they won't commit.
>
> Our challenge as marketers is to determine the characteristics of the person we're encountering on the phone—and then deliver a presentation that will motivate him or her to take action.
>
> Our communicators are specially trained to listen, determine the personality type, and then choose the appropriate donor profile.

For example, a direct person requires a presentation that contains a lot of facts and details. An indirect person needs guidance and direction. And, the passive individual needs to be flattered and convinced they make a difference.

And, this donor profile approach works! We've increased our results by 65%.

It's crucial we realize telephone marketers aren't the only people who work from scripts. The person answering the phone has "a script" he or she uses, as well. And, to win them over, we must know how to effectively respond to their presentation.

Sample Scripts

Exhibits 10-2 to 10-4 provide examples of scripts with the "vital information, useful terminology, and appropriate delivery techniques" necessary for effective telemarketing. Exhibit 10-2 presents a closing method used by telemarketers for dealing with the indirect personality type. Exhibit 10-3 shows ten tailored telemarketing scripts created by Trans-America Marketing Services for its client, Trans World Radio. And, finally, Exhibit 10-4 contains samples of five letters used to follow up telemarketing calls. The letters were created for Trans World Radio by Trans-America Marketing Services.

Exhibit 10-2   Closing Method

Don't get me wrong, a "strong, silent type" can be desirable in the right situation. But, the recipient of a telemarketing call certainly isn't one of them.

Picture this…You've made the perfect presentation, and now all you have to do is wrap up the call and get the person to commit. He hasn't posed an objection throughout your entire presentation, so you feel pretty confident you both agree on the next step.

But when you pop the question, he says "no." Just "no." He doesn't pose a real objection and you're left guessing what's going on in his mind. It happens to the best of us.

I call these people "Indirect Personality Types." They respond negatively, but don't give you a reason why they're refusing your offer. You can handle these types of people in two ways.

First, you can ask them open-ended questions to discover the underlying reason to their objections. For example:

"Sir/Ma'am, I'm sorry to hear you're not interested right now. Is there some reason why you've chosen not to renew with us again this year?"

Once the person responds with a reason, you now have specific information—not simply a "no" to work with.

Or, you can use the Three-Question Close. This approach puts the person into a positive frame of mind by asking three, short, rapid-fire questions that you know will elicit agreement. Then, you follow with a simple close. For example:

"Faster monthly turnover is an important objective, right?"

"Yes"

"You do want a short payback period, don't you?"

"Yes."

"And, you want to maximize your parts department's productivity, correct?"

"Yes, that's correct."

"Well, this new inventory control system will do all three of these things. Can I go ahead and sign you up, so you can start achieving all these crucial goals?"

Keep in mind the questions should be benefit related and cover points already discussed in the presentation.

Source: From *Telephone Selling Report*'s "13 Proven Closing Ideas for Telephone Salespeople," Copyright 1988. Reprinted with permission of TransAmerica Marketing Services, Inc.

Exhibit 10-3   Targeted Telemarketing Scripts

1. Introduction to person answering phone

Hello, may I please speak with Mr.(s)_____?

    IF YES: Thank you. **(PROCEED TO APPROPRIATE INTRODUCTION)**

    IF WHO IS THIS/WHAT IS THIS REGARDING?: This is _____, and I'm calling on behalf of Trans World Radio. Should I speak directly with **(him/her)**, or can you help me?

        IF YES: PROCEED TO APPROPRIATE INTRODUCTION

        IF NO: GO TO NOT AVAILABLE

    IF NOT AVAILABLE: When would be the best time for me to reach Mr.(s)_____? **(RECORD TIME)** Thank you very much. I'll try back then. Goodbye.

Exhibit 10-3 **Targeted Telemarketing Scripts** *(continued)*

2. Introduction to telemarketing responders and lapsed donors

Hello, Mr.(s)_____, this is_____, and I'm calling on behalf of Trans World Radio to thank you so much for helping bring thousands to the Lord through Gospel radio.

You've been such a dedicated supporter of the ministry in the past, and our situation is so urgent right now that there wasn't time to write to you, so we wanted to call you personally.

Some months ago, we had to replace a failed transmitter tube on Bonaire, which as you may know allows us to broadcast into most of Latin America. Since then, we've been operating without a spare tube, which means if the one we have installed goes out, we'll lose all our broadcasts into Latin America, and we can reach nearly 250 million people there! We couldn't take our chances any longer, so we've gone ahead and ordered the replacement tube. But we still need to raise the $116,000 needed to pay for it, and we're hoping you can help us during this critical time.

Mr.(s)_____ can we count on your help with a gift of $MRC+$10 or even $MRC+$20?

NOTE: IF ASKED WHEN TUBE WENT OUT, IT WAS LAST DECEMBER (1994)

IF DONOR HAS FINANCIAL OBJECTION, BUT IS INTERESTED IN TWR

AND ISSUE: GO TO EFT OPTION

Exhibit 10-3 Targeted Telemarketing Scripts *(continued)*

3. Introduction to missionary/nondonors

Hello, Mr.(s)_____, this is _____, and I'm calling on behalf of Trans World Radio to thank you so much for your interest in one of our missionaries. Are you familiar with our international Gospel radio programs, as well?

IF YES: That's wonderful. **(CONTINUE)**

IF NO: Well, we are currently broadcasting Gospel radio programs in over 100 languages and reaching potentially 80% of the world's population. We're bringing Christ's message to the furthest corners of the world <u>where not even missionaries can go.</u> **(CONTINUE)**

CONTINUATION

The reason I'm calling is because some months ago, we had to replace a failed transmitter tube on Bonaire, which as you may know allows us to broadcast into most of Latin America. Since then, we've been operating <u>without</u> a spare tube, which means if the one we have installed goes out, we'll lose <u>all our broadcasts</u> into Latin America, and we can reach nearly <u>250 million people</u> there! We couldn't take our changes any longer, so we've gone ahead and ordered the replacement tube. But we still need to raise the $116,000 needed to pay for it, and we're hoping you can help us during this critical time.

Mr.(s)_____ can we count on your help with a gift of $MRC+$10 or even $MRC+$20?

*NOTE: IF ASKED WHEN TUBE WENT OUT, IT WAS LAST DECEMBER (1994)

IF DONOR HAS FINANCIAL OBJECTION, BUT IS INTERESTED IN TWR AND ISSUE: GO TO EFT OPTION

Exhibit 10-3   Targeted Telemarketing Scripts *(continued)*

4. EFT Option

I can appreciate if that's too much for you to help with all at once. If it's more convenient for you, you can fulfill your pledge through monthly installments through electronic funds transfer. Are you familiar with EFT, Mr.(s)____?

IF YES: Would it be easier for you to fulfill your $XX gift through automatic monthly deductions?

IF NO: Well, we would send you a very brief form to fill out which includes you checking account number. Then, the amount you indicate would automatically be deducted from your checking account for each month you request. The great thing about EFT is there's nothing for you to do once you send us your form — the bank does everything for you, and your transactions appear on your monthly statement. Are you interested in taking advantage of EFT?

Exhibit 10-3　Targeted Telemarketing Scripts *(continued)*

5. Close for will pledge/specific amount

That's wonderful, Mr.(s)_____. We'll be writing you a letter to thank you for your $XX contribution, so let me just verify your address.   **(VERIFY FULL ADDRESS INCLUDING APARTMENT # AND ZIP CODE)**

In with our letter will be a special envelope to mail back your $XX gift. We would greatly appreciate it if you could return your contribution within 10 days of receiving our letter. Are you able to do that, (NAME)?

IF DONOR IS HESITANT ABOUT TIME-FRAME, REMIND THEM THAT WITH MAIL TIME, IT SHOULD BE ABOUT TWO WEEKS FROM NOW.

(RESPOND) Thank you again. Your support will really make a tremendous difference. Goodbye.

Exhibit 10-3   Targeted Telemarketing Scripts *(continued)*

6. Close for will pledge/no specific amount

That's terrific, Mr.(s)_____. We'll be sending you a letter to thank you for your contribution, so let me just verify your address. **(VERIFY FULL ADDRESS INCLUDING APARTMENT # AND ZIP CODE)**

Mr.(s)_____, so we have an idea of how close we're getting to raising the money needed to purchase the tube, is there a minimum amount you feel comfortable with?

(IF PERSON IS LAPSED DONOR AND YOU HAVEN'T SUGGESTED $MRC, SUGGEST THAT. IF NONDONOR, SUGGEST LOWER GIFT AMOUNT)

IF YES/VOLUNTEERS AMOUNT: Great! That will help so much! In with our letter, there will be an envelope to return your $XX gift. We would greatly appreciate it if you could return your contribution within 10 days of receiving our letter. Are you able to do that, **(NAME)**?

IF DONOR IS HESITANT ABOUT TIME-FRAME, REMIND THEM THAT WITH MAIL TIME, IT SHOULD BE ABOUT TWO WEEKS FROM NOW.

(RESPOND) Thank you again. Your support will really make a tremendous difference. Goodbye.

IF STILL WON'T COMMIT TO AN AMOUNT: That's fine. We'll just go ahead and send you our letter. Thank you again. Your support will really make a tremendous difference. Goodbye.

Exhibit 10-3   Targeted Telemarketing Scripts *(continued)*

7. Close for may pledge

Thank you for your consideration, Mr.(s)_____. Let me just verify your address, and we'll get a letter off to you right away, along with a return envelope. (VERIFY ADDRESS IN FULL, INCLUDING APARTMENT # AND ZIP CODE.)

Please watch for our letter in the mail. Thank you for taking the time to speak with me today, and we hope to hear from you soon. Goodbye.

Exhibit 10-3   Targeted Telemarketing Scripts *(continued)*

8. Close for will pledge/specific amount EFT (installments)

That's wonderful, Mr.(s)_____. We'll be writing you a letter to thank you for your $XX contribution, and enclosed will be that brief form we talked about for you to fill out and return, indicating the amount you would like deducted from your account monthly. Please be sure to fill out the entire form and return it to us in the envelope we'll provide.

Let me just verify your address.   **(VERIFY FULL ADDRESS INCLUDING APARTMENT # AND ZIP CODE)**

Do you have any questions about EFT that I can try to answer for you?

    IF YES: TRY TO ANSWER QUESTION. IF YOU CAN'T ANSWER,

    RECORD AS SPECIAL COMMENT TO BE PASSED ALONG TO

    TWR.

Thank you again for your generous $XX gift, Mr.(s)_____. It will make a tremendous difference. Goodbye.

Exhibit 10-3   Targeted Telemarketing Scripts *(continued)*

9. Close for not interested

I can appreciate if this isn't a good time. Even if you waited 30 days to return your contribution, it would still make a tremendous difference. Do you feel you could help with $XX in the next 30 days?

IF YES: GO TO CLOSE FOR WILL PLEDGE IN 30 DAYS

IF NO: I'm sorry to hear you won't be able to help us right now, **(if appropriate: but we thank you so much for the support you've given us in the past.)** We hope you will pray for our work. Thank you for taking the time to speak with me (today/tonight.) Goodbye.

Exhibit 10-3   Targeted Telemarketing Scripts *(continued)*

10. Close for will pledge in 30 days

That's wonderful, Mr.(s)_____. We'll be writing you a letter to thank you for your $XX contribution. Let me just verify your address.   (VERIFY FULL ADDRESS INCLUDING APARTMENT # AND ZIP CODE)

In with our letter will be a special envelope to mail back your gift in 30 days. Or, if your situation changes and you can return it sooner, that would be even a greater help to us. Thank you again. Your support will really make a tremendous difference. Goodbye.

Exhibit 10-4   Telemarketing Follow-Up Letters

FOLLOW UP TO THOSE WHO WILL PLEDGE/SPECIFIC AMOUNT
TRANS WORLD RADIO

TOM LOWELL, PRESIDENT
TRANS WORLD RADIO
P.O. BOX 8700
CARY, NORTH CAROLINA 27512

XXDATEFILLXX

XXNAMEFILLXX
XXADDRESSFILLXX
XXCITYXXSTATEXXZIPXX

THANK YOU FOR SPEAKING WITH **XXNAMEFILLXX** ON THE TELEPHONE AND FOR AGREEING TO SEND A **$XX** GIFT TO HELP TRANS WORLD RADIO RAISE THE $116,000 NEEDED TO PAY FOR A NEW TRANSMITTER TUBE FOR OUR BROADCAST SITE ON BONAIRE.

AS **XXFIRSTNAMEXX** EXPLAINED WHEN **XXHE/SHEXX** RECENTLY SPOKE WITH YOU, OUR TRANSMITTER TUBE ON BONAIRE FAILED BACK IN DECEMBER, FORCING US TO REPLACE IT WITH THE ONLY SPARE WE HAVE.

RIGHT NOW, WE ARE OPERATING WITHOUT ANY BACKUP -- WHICH MEANS THAT <u>IF THE TUBE WE HAVE INSTALLED FAILS, WE WILL BE COMPLETELY OFF THE AIR, WITH NO HOPE OF RESUMING BROADCASTS UNTIL WE CAN INSTALL A NEW TUBE!</u>

IF WE GO OFF THE AIR IN BONAIRE, <u>OUR MINISTRY TO POTENTIALLY 250 MILLION PEOPLE IN SOUTH AMERICA, THE CARIBBEAN AND MEXICO WILL BE SILENCED!</u>

FOR COUNTLESS BELIEVERS, TWR PROGRAMS ARE THEIR ONLY SOURCE OF SPIRITUAL STRENGTH. THAT IS WHY I FELT IT WAS ABSOLUTELY URGENT THAT WE GO AHEAD AND ORDER THE NEW TUBE BEFORE WE FACE A CRISIS SITUATION.

GOD BLESS YOU FOR STEPPING FORWARD AT THIS VERY IMPORTANT TIME. YOUR **$XX** GIFT WILL GO A LONG WAY, AND I'M CONFIDENT THAT WITH THE PRAYERS OF DEDICATED FRIENDS LIKE YOU, WE'LL MAKE SURE THE GOOD NEWS CONTINUES TO BE SHARED IN LATIN AMERICA AND ACROSS THE WORLD.

YOURS IN CHRIST,
TOM LOWELL, PRESIDENT

P.S.   IF YOU WOULD POSSIBLY CONSIDER MAKING A MONTHLY CONTRIBUTION TO TWR, IT WOULD BE A GODSEND IN OUR EFFORTS TO KEEP OUR PROGRAMS ON THE AIR AROUND THE WORLD. I'VE ENCLOSED A VERY BRIEF FORM WHICH EXPLAINS MONTHLY GIVING. I'D APPRECIATE YOUR TAKING A MOMENT TO READ IT OVER AND PRAYFULLY CONSIDER IF IT'S RIGHT FOR YOU. THANK YOU AGAIN.

(continued)

Exhibit 10-4   Telemarketing Follow-Up Letters *(continued)*

**FOLLOW UP TO THOSE WHO WILL PLEDGE IN 30 DAYS
TRANS WORLD RADIO**

TOM LOWELL, PRESIDENT
TRANS WORLD RADIO
P.O. BOX 8700
CARY, NORTH CAROLINA 27512

XXDATEFILLXX

XXNAMEFILLXX
XXADDRESSFILLXX
XXCITYXXSTATEXXZIPXX

THANK YOU FOR SPEAKING WITH **XXNAMEFILLXX** ON THE TELEPHONE AND FOR AGREEING TO SEND A **$XX** GIFT IN THE NEXT 30 DAYS TO HELP TRANS WORLD RADIO RAISE THE $116,000 NEEDED TO PAY FOR A NEW TRANSMITTER TUBE FOR OUR BROADCAST SITE ON BONAIRE.

AS **XXFIRSTNAMEXX** EXPLAINED WHEN **XXHE/SHEXX** RECENTLY SPOKE WITH YOU, OUR TRANSMITTER TUBE ON BONAIRE FAILED BACK IN DECEMBER, FORCING US TO REPLACE IT WITH THE ONLY SPARE WE HAVE.

RIGHT NOW, WE ARE OPERATING WITHOUT ANY BACKUP -- WHICH MEANS THAT <u>IF THE TUBE WE HAVE INSTALLED FAILS, WE WILL BE COMPLETELY OFF THE AIR, WITH NO HOPE OF RESUMING BROADCASTS UNTIL WE CAN INSTALL A NEW TUBE</u>!

IF WE GO OFF THE AIR IN BONAIRE, <u>OUR MINISTRY TO POTENTIALLY 250 MILLION PEOPLE IN SOUTH AMERICA, THE CARIBBEAN AND MEXICO WILL BE SILENCED</u>!

FOR COUNTLESS BELIEVERS, TWR PROGRAMS ARE THEIR ONLY SOURCE OF SPIRITUAL STRENGTH. THAT IS WHY I FELT IT WAS ABSOLUTELY URGENT THAT WE GO AHEAD AND ORDER THE NEW TUBE BEFORE WE FACE A CRISIS SITUATION.

GOD BLESS YOU FOR STEPPING FORWARD AT THIS VERY IMPORTANT TIME. YOUR **$XX** GIFT WILL GO A LONG WAY, AND I'M CONFIDENT THAT WITH THE PRAYERS OF DEDICATED FRIENDS LIKE YOU, WE'LL MAKE SURE THE GOOD NEWS CONTINUES TO BE SHARED IN LATIN AMERICA AND ACROSS THE WORLD.

YOURS IN CHRIST,
TOM LOWELL, PRESIDENT

P.S.   IF YOU WOULD POSSIBLY CONSIDER MAKING A MONTHLY CONTRIBUTION TO TWR, IT WOULD BE A GODSEND IN OUR EFFORTS TO KEEP OUR PROGRAMS ON THE AIR AROUND THE WORLD. I'VE ENCLOSED A VERY BRIEF FORM WHICH EXPLAINS MONTHLY GIVING. I'D APPRECIATE YOUR TAKING A MOMENT TO READ IT OVER AND PRAYFULLY CONSIDER IF IT'S RIGHT FOR YOU. THANK YOU AGAIN.

Exhibit 10-4   Telemarketing Follow-Up Letters (*continued*)

FOLLOW UP TO THOSE WHO WILL PLEDGE / EFT
TRANS WORLD RADIO

TOM LOWELL, PRESIDENT
TRANS WORLD RADIO
P.O. BOX 8700
CARY, NORTH CAROLINA 27512

XXDATEFILLXX

XXNAMEFILLXX
XXADDRESSFILLXX
XXCITYXXSTATEXXZIPXX

THANK YOU FOR SPEAKING WITH **XXNAMEFILLXX** ON THE TELEPHONE AND FOR AGREEING TO SUPPORT TRANSWORLD RADIO WITH A **$XX** GIFT THROUGH OUR CONVENIENT ELECTRONIC FUNDS TRANSFER PROGRAM. I HAVE ENCLOSED A BRIEF FORM FOR YOU TO FILL OUT AND RETURN IN THE ENCLOSED ENVELOPE.

AS **XXFIRSTNAMEXX** EXPLAINED WHEN **XXHE/SHEXX** RECENTLY SPOKE WITH YOU, OUR TRANSMITTER TUBE ON BONAIRE FAILED BACK IN DECEMBER, FORCING US TO REPLACE IT WITH THE ONLY SPARE WE HAVE.

RIGHT NOW, WE ARE OPERATING WITHOUT ANY BACKUP -- WHICH MEANS THAT <u>IF THE TUBE WE HAVE INSTALLED FAILS, WE WILL BE COMPLETELY OFF THE AIR, WITH NO HOPE OF RESUMING BROADCASTS UNTIL WE CAN INSTALL A NEW TUBE!</u>

IF WE GO OFF THE AIR IN BONAIRE, <u>OUR MINISTRY TO POTENTIALLY 250 MILLION PEOPLE IN SOUTH AMERICA, THE CARIBBEAN AND MEXICO WILL BE SILENCED</u>!

FOR COUNTLESS BELIEVERS, TWR PROGRAMS ARE THEIR ONLY SOURCE OF SPIRITUAL STRENGTH. THAT IS WHY I FELT IT WAS ABSOLUTELY URGENT THAT WE GO AHEAD AND ORDER THE NEW TUBE BEFORE WE FACE A CRISIS SITUATION.

GOD BLESS YOU FOR STEPPING FORWARD AT THIS VERY IMPORTANT TIME. YOUR **$XX** GIFT WILL GO A LONG WAY IN HELPING US RAISE THE $116,000 NEEDED TO PAY FOR THE NEW TRANSMITTER TUBE. I'M CONFIDENT THAT WITH THE PRAYERS OF DEDICATED FRIENDS LIKE YOU, WE'LL MAKE SURE THE GOOD NEWS CONTINUES TO BE SHARED IN LATIN AMERICA AND ACROSS THE WORLD.

YOURS IN CHRIST,
TOM LOWELL, PRESIDENT

P.S.   PLEASE BE SURE TO COMPLETELY FILL OUT THE EFT FORM AND SEND IT BACK TO US RIGHT AWAY IN THE ENVELOPE I'VE ENCLOSED FOR YOUR CONVENIENCE.   THANK YOU AGAIN FOR YOUR $XX CONTRIBUTION.

Exhibit 10-4 Telemarketing Follow-Up Letters *(continued)*

**FOLLOW UP TO THOSE WHO WILL PLEDGE/NO SPECIFIC AMOUNT
TRANS WORLD RADIO**

TOM LOWELL, PRESIDENT
TRANS WORLD RADIO
P.O. BOX 8700
CARY, NORTH CAROLINA 27512

XXDATEFILLXX

XXNAMEFILLXX
XXADDRESSFILLXX
XXCITYXXSTATEXXZIPXX

THANK YOU FOR SPEAKING WITH **XXNAMEFILLXX** ON THE TELEPHONE AND FOR
AGREEING TO HELP TRANS WORLD RADIO RAISE THE $116,000 NEEDED TO PAY FOR
THE NEW TRANSMITTER TUBE FOR OUR BROADCAST SITE ON BONAIRE.

AS **XXFIRSTNAMEXX** EXPLAINED WHEN **XXHE/SHEXX** RECENTLY SPOKE WITH
YOU, OUR TRANSMITTER TUBE ON BONAIRE FAILED BACK IN DECEMBER, FORCING
US TO REPLACE IT WITH THE ONLY SPARE WE HAVE.

RIGHT NOW, WE ARE OPERATING WITHOUT ANY BACKUP -- WHICH MEANS THAT <u>IF
THE TUBE WE HAVE INSTALLED FAILS, WE WILL BE COMPLETELY OFF THE AIR,
WITH NO HOPE OF RESUMING BROADCASTS UNTIL WE CAN INSTALL A NEW TUBE!</u>

IF WE GO OFF THE AIR IN BONAIRE, <u>OUR MINISTRY TO POTENTIALLY 250 MILLION
PEOPLE IN SOUTH AMERICA, THE CARIBBEAN AND MEXICO WILL BE SILENCED!</u>

FOR COUNTLESS BELIEVERS, TWR PROGRAMS ARE THEIR ONLY SOURCE OF
SPIRITUAL STRENGTH. THAT IS WHY I FELT IT WAS ABSOLUTELY URGENT THAT
WE GO AHEAD AND ORDER THE NEW TUBE BEFORE WE FACE A CRISIS SITUATION.

GOD BLESS YOU FOR STEPPING FORWARD AT THIS VERY IMPORTANT TIME. YOUR
GIFT WILL GO A LONG WAY, AND I'M CONFIDENT THAT WITH THE PRAYERS OF
DEDICATED FRIENDS LIKE YOU, WE'LL MAKE SURE THE GOOD NEWS CONTINUES
TO BE SHARED IN LATIN AMERICA AND ACROSS THE WORLD.

YOURS IN CHRIST,
TOM LOWELL, PRESIDENT

P.S. IF YOU WOULD POSSIBLY CONSIDER MAKING A MONTHLY
        CONTRIBUTION TO TWR, IT WOULD BE A GODSEND IN OUR EFFORTS
        TO KEEP OUR PROGRAMS ON THE AIR AROUND THE WORLD. I'VE
        ENCLOSED A VERY BRIEF FORM WHICH EXPLAINS MONTHLY GIVING.
        I'D APPRECIATE YOUR TAKING A MOMENT TO READ IT OVER AND
        PRAYFULLY CONSIDER IF IT'S RIGHT FOR YOU. THANK YOU AGAIN.

Exhibit 10-4   Telemarketing Follow-Up Letters *(continued)*

**FOLLOW UP TO THOSE WHO MAY PLEDGE
TRANS WORLD RADIO**

TOM LOWELL, PRESIDENT
TRANS WORLD RADIO
P.O. BOX 8700
CARY, NORTH CAROLINA 27512

XXDATEFILLXX

XXNAMEFILLXX
XXADDRESSFILLXX
XXCITYXXSTATEXXZIPXX

THANK YOU FOR SPEAKING WITH **XXNAMEFILLXX** ON THE TELEPHONE. I'M VERY GRATEFUL THAT YOU ARE CONSIDERING SENDING A GIFT TO HELP TRANS WORLD RADIO RAISE THE $116,000 NEEDED TO PAY FOR A NEW TRANSMITTER TUBE FOR OUR BROADCAST SITE ON BONAIRE.

AS **XXFIRSTNAMEXX** EXPLAINED WHEN **XXHE/SHEXX** RECENTLY SPOKE WITH YOU, OUR TRANSMITTER TUBE ON BONAIRE FAILED BACK IN DECEMBER, FORCING US TO REPLACE IT WITH THE ONLY SPARE WE HAVE.

RIGHT NOW, WE ARE OPERATING WITHOUT ANY BACKUP -- WHICH MEANS THAT <u>IF THE TUBE WE HAVE INSTALLED FAILS, WE WILL BE COMPLETELY OFF THE AIR, WITH NO HOPE OF RESUMING BROADCASTS UNTIL WE CAN INSTALL A NEW TUBE</u>!

IF WE GO OFF THE AIR IN BONAIRE, <u>OUR MINISTRY TO POTENTIALLY 250 MILLION PEOPLE IN SOUTH AMERICA, THE CARIBBEAN AND MEXICO WILL BE SILENCED</u>!

FOR COUNTLESS BELIEVERS, TWR PROGRAMS ARE THEIR ONLY SOURCE OF SPIRITUAL STRENGTH. THAT IS WHY I FELT IT WAS ABSOLUTELY URGENT THAT WE GO AHEAD AND ORDER THE NEW TUBE BEFORE WE FACE A CRISIS SITUATION.

YOUR GIFT WILL GO A LONG WAY, AND I'M CONFIDENT THAT WITH THE PRAYERS OF DEDICATED FRIENDS LIKE YOU, WE'LL MAKE SURE THE GOOD NEWS CONTINUES TO BE SHARED IN LATIN AMERICA AND ACROSS THE WORLD.

YOURS IN CHRIST,
TOM LOWELL, PRESIDENT

P.S.   IF YOU WOULD POSSIBLY CONSIDER MAKING A MONTHLY CONTRIBUTION TO TWR, IT WOULD BE A GODSEND IN OUR EFFORTS TO KEEP OUR PROGRAMS ON THE AIR AROUND THE WORLD. I'VE ENCLOSED A VERY BRIEF FORM WHICH EXPLAINS MONTHLY GIVING. I'D APPRECIATE YOUR TAKING A MOMENT TO READ IT OVER AND PRAYFULLY CONSIDER IF IT'S RIGHT FOR YOU. THANK YOU AGAIN.

Source: Reprinted with permission of Trans World Radio and TransAmerica Marketing Services, Inc.

11

COPYWRITING FOR ONLINE MEDIA

by Jeff Laurie

All the copy techniques you've learned in this book apply to online direct marketing as well. A Web site or online ad can be as persuasive as a direct mail package or space ad. But online media is also significantly different from traditional media, and many copywriting techniques must be recalibrated to fit. In this chapter, you'll learn how to transfer your copywriting skills to the new, user-controlled online media.

The Internet and the commercial online services are powerful communication tools, but they are not inherently *selling* venues. To make Web sites and online ads *sell* requires that your copy and design exploit the strengths and overcome the weaknesses of online media.

Three aspects of creating persuasive, response-oriented online sites are in your control: copy, screen design, and site design (architecture). Technology is too complex an area to be dealt with here. Just like you expect to work with a graphic artist in print media and with a director for direct response television, so too should you expect to work with an experienced developer when implementing a Web site or electronic ad. You should work with a graphic artist also. Creating Web sites or online ads requires that you think visually. A graphic artist can help with the many traditional visual considerations like typeface, color, and illustration selection that are involved.

We will be more focused on structuring an online site than you might expect from a copywriting text. This is because the unique, user-controlled attributes of online media force you to pay more attention to navigation (and hence, structure) than you must with other direct response media. We also will spend more time than you might expect talking about visual images. Because online media is inherently graphical, you have to think more visually at the concept level than you do for traditional forms of direct marketing (except television).

To many copywriters, narrative flow and eye movement aren't foreign concepts. The majority of writers conceptualize direct response projects with a mind to copy flow from package element to package element in the case of envelope packages, panel to panel for self-mailers or brochures, and sequence-to-sequence for television. And, if they aren't working closely with an art director in an agency setting, many writers include "copywriter's roughs"—thumbnail sketches—with their first drafts.

In traditional media, thinking visually helps you write copy that moves with compelling logic from envelope to letter, from letter to order form, and from panel to panel on a brochure. This builds the drama and promise of your package, as well as sets up an ideal slippery slope from outer envelope to reply form.

When you write for online media, this applies to an even greater degree.

Online, every screen is a bite-sized morsel of information and potential involvement. To move to the next screen the prospect must act by clicking the mouse. Every click is a promise with a payoff. So you have to be an information architect as well as a writer. You have to lay out your site as you would rooms in a shop through which you will accompany your prospect.

What follows is a road map for a single product or service site—not a multiple product or service site—much like that of a single direct mail package. If you are constructing a multiple product site, the suggestions can be applied to the tree for each separate product or product line.

There are as many variations on information design as there are products, online sites, and creative people writing and designing them. You can use the following as touchstones as you create the Web site or online ad that is appropriate to your company, your product or service, or your industry.

Basic Principles of Online Media for Copywriters

Some basic attributes of online media influence what you write and how you interact with the prospect. Cyberspace has several important things going for it—and some things going against it—which you must understand to succeed. Some of these overlap, but each highlights a particular aspect of the online experience that you must keep in mind when writing for online media.

Online Is Personal, Private, and Intimate.

Although it appears that your online prospect is merely looking at a computer screen, he or she is in fact enmeshed in a deep personal experience of inner space, with visual, verbal, and often auditory senses being stimulated. This opens the door for you to communicate with the privacy of the mailbox and the intimacy of a one-on-one conversation. Make the Web site or electronic ad about your prospect and his or her needs and wants, and the prospect will buy.

Cyberspace Is a Multimedia Environment.

The technical capabilities of online communications allow text, graphics, sound, and motion to be delivered to the desktop. You can harness this cornucopia of media to enhance your sales effectiveness.

Show your prospects something and they will see. Involve them with pictures, narrative, touch, sound, and video, and they will experience and participate. The more they experience and participate, the more involved prospects will be. The more involved, the more receptive to buy. As more users become comfortable with online technology and more of your competitors employ multimedia, the more your selling efforts will have to include multimedia.

Cyberspace Is Inherently Interactive.

An online site is not a brochure. Going online is something people *do*. It is an activity. Your visitors expect to act, to click. They expect to jump from screen to screen, to fly from site to site or subject to subject.

That's the good news. Interactivity produces involvement and promotes empowerment; empowerment increases engagement. Engaging the prospect is the first task no matter what the medium.

On the other hand, the bad news is that everything in cyberspace is interactive to some degree. So the threshold for involvement is rising. You will have to be increasingly savvy about new technologies like Sun Microsystem's Java and Macromedia's Shockwave in order to engage the user.

The User Is in Control.

Online, the user is the master of his or her universe. His or her visit to your site is self-selected. And changing channels is as easy as clicking a TV remote. In addition, the prospect has to do all the work to find you and order from you.

This means that while cyberspace is an active, vital, robust experience for the user, it's an essentially passive venture for the marketer (after the active period of writing and launching your online site is completed).

This makes cyberspace a relatively unfriendly direct response environment. As Denny Hatch wrote in *Target Marketing*, "Forcing the prospect to be pro-active and go hunting for your product in cyberspace is 180 degrees apart from thrusting your offer into the prospect's hands, mailbox, newspaper, magazine, telephone, or TV screen." On the other hand, because the user selects your site and decides how long to stay there, his or her length of engagement can be much longer than in other direct response media.

The User Is Conditioned to Look for Options.

The key here is action. Cyberspace users expect first and foremost to engage in action choices. They expect to deliberate and decide. They expect to click. This reduces attention span and increases expectations, putting more pressure on you to keep your visitor interested. You don't get a second chance to be dull. By the same token, the action culture works in your favor because it encourages response.

Hyperlinks Are Built-In Action Devices That Stand Out by Definition.

The act of clicking on a hyperlink initiates anticipation. Each new screen is a new experience, with a promise and a payoff. Hyperlinking is more powerful than scrolling. Clicking on hyperlinks is a more conscious decision than fingering through elements of a direct mail package. Hyperlinks are a built-in action resource that works in your favor as a direct marketer.

It Costs Money to Be Online.

Your target is *paying* to read your promotion. This is extremely important, and makes online media different from direct mail, space ads, and television. It's as easy to click to another cyberspace address as it is to toss an envelope in the round file. As a direct response copywriter, you're on highly leveraged time.

There Are No Built-In Affinity Groups.

In cyberspace, access is separate from content. You can't automatically hone-in on a market like you can with a well-targeted mailing list, by placing a space ad in a magazine that caters to your exact audience, or by running a commercial on a particular TV show. The channel that brings the user to you is the same channel that can take the user to thousands of other online locations.

Imagine that instead of many magazines published every month, only one magazine was published. Imagine that it was a 10,000-page behemoth that readers opened anywhere and just started reading. How could you be sure your ad reached the right people, no matter where it was placed? This is essentially the dilemma in cyberspace.

You Can't Do Unsolicited E-Mailings.

As of this writing, online culture is militantly resistant to unsolicited commercial e-mailings. Like junk fax and telephone calls at dinnertime, commercial e-mail is perceived as intrusive and obnoxious. Those who violate this principle risk engendering hostility and even retaliation. For example, because everyone in cyberspace is a publisher (everyone can initiate postings to e-mail lists and forums), and there are no gatekeepers on the Internet (and relatively few for the commercial online services), an angry recipient can cause you a public relations nightmare by damning your offense on forums and bulletin boards. This is a problem you don't have to worry about with traditional media.

Worse, an offended party can wreck havoc on your computer system. Imagine someone retaliating against you for the offense of unsolicited e-mail by sending you their operating system 500 times. It can be done fairly easily.

Revenge for them. A disaster for you.

The Space Metaphor Is Real.

The terms "cyberspace" and "marketspace," "chat rooms," and "online malls" are expressions of the "inner space" of the online experience. Users appear to be looking at computer screens, but they are actually in imaginary *places*, much as they are when watching a movie. The multimedia and interactivity of cyberspace allows the imagination to spatially "enter" the online experience. And it won't be long before virtual reality software enhances this perception.

The Internet and Online Services Are Nondiminishing Resources.

An unlimited number of bits are at your disposal. This means you can use as many bits as you need to tell your story and not use them up—provided that you can keep the prospect involved. As much time and space as you can win by your benefits and presentations can be yours.

Cyberspace Is International.

Information about your product or service is available anywhere in the world, 7 days a week, 24 hours a day. The upside is that English is the language of cyberspace, so if you don't invest in alternate language versions of your online site, you probably won't harm yourself. (Although some Internet sites offer options that allow the visitor to choose the language in which the site appears.) On the other hand, you should be prepared to deal with international postal issues and currency exchange issues if you plan to accept orders from other countries.

People Don't Go Online Just for Information.

The popular conception that cyberspace is a giant library where people go for information is wrong. For consumers, cyberspace is more like a pub. Most consumers are looking for communication and community first. And fun and adventure second. Sometimes consumers use cyberspace for information.

Business users are more often looking for information, but not necessarily hard business data. Often, business users are seeking solutions to problems, competitive intelligence, quick answers to customer service questions, or product specifications.

PREPARE TO WRITE

So, what do these inherent characteristics of cyberspace mean for your copy and the design of your persuasive Web site or online ad?

To begin we must ask two basic questions that you will recognize from your experience in traditional media. And then you make the first mental leap into cyberspace.

What Is the Mission of Your Site?

Your first step is to be clear about the goal of your site. Are you looking for new business? Lead generation? Follow-up business with continuing customers?

Are you selling a low-cost item that can be ordered online? Or an expensive product that requires a multiple-contact, consultative selling effort?

Your answers to these questions will determine what you write and how you structure your online presence.

Because our subject is direct response copywriting, we will focus only on goals that require persuasion. But make no mistake, you can use online media for many things—pre-sales information, product catalogs, manuals, directories, spec sheets, price schedules, service and support, media relations, investor relations, and employment information, to name a few.

Is Your Audience Corporate Users or Home Users?

Online users are intelligent, educated, upscale, and busy. But beyond that, what characteristics do they have that you can use when planning and writing your site?

First, you have to know your prospect's needs and interests to make your copy irresistible, just as you do for traditional direct response media.

Second, you must define the technical limits of your audience.

Are they corporate users (or a highly technical consumer niche) with access to fast data connections? If so, you can include large graphics and sound, video, and other interactive bells and whistles in your design.

Is your target consumers with standard (slow) modem connections? If so, you'll have to restrict the size and number of your graphics, and be aware of download times for every screen you put up.

Think of your site in terms of a traditional direct mail package or a direct response space ad.

The techniques of direct response copy have been developed by generations of marketers, who have conducted tens of thousands of tests. The rules for creating direct response vehicles have been finely honed to be as effective as possible, and presented in an order that is natural for human modes of perception.

This knowledge can be carried over to your online direct response copy and site design. Exhibit 11-1 has guidelines to help you think about the roles of the different elements of your online site.

FIVE CRUCIAL STEPS TO TARGET YOUR AUDIENCE

Because there is no built-in affinity group and you can't do unsolicited e-mailings online, you have to help your market find you. This makes cyberspace a "pull" medium rather than a "push" medium. High-tech marketing consultant Kristen Zhivago uses a water analogy to illustrate this:

- Broadcasting is like spraying a crowd with a hose.

- Narrowcasting [and direct marketing] is like aiming a small hose at people who have asked to get wet.

- Cybercasting is the act of creating a pond in cyberspace and inviting people to come in and swim.

Exhibit 11-1   Guidelines for Online Copy

- Outer envelope—"Home page" or "splash page."
- Letter—The first few pages of your site. Here's where you sell benefits and get the user involved.
- Offer—Should be at the top of the site, just as you would have it on your envelope or on the first page of your letter.
- Brochure—Screens that are deeper in your site, to provide information to back up your benefit claims.
- Reply Form/BRE—Make it reachable by hyperlink from all screens.
- Inserts and buck slips—Separate sections highlighting subjects of particular interest, reachable by hyperlink from selected screens.

To get people to come to your pond, you must take five crucial steps. (The following applies to Internet marketing. If you have an ad on a commercial online service, you'll have to concentrate on getting correctly indexed, well-placed, and possibly buying banners to attract attention.)

1. Choose an Intuitive Domain Name. Your domain name is a word. One of the most important words in your online direct marketing arsenal. It should express your product name or your lead benefit. Think of it as a billboard: short, simple, and easy to remember. Having an intuitive domain name makes it easier for people to return to your site and easier to pass along word of your site to others.

If your domain name isn't intuitive, register a new name. It's an inexpensive procedure. You'll have to clear this with your top marketing management, but there is no law that says your company can't register multiple domain names. If your site is dedicated to a single product, you should certainly try to register the product name as the domain name. If your site is a catalog of products, think about choosing multiple domain names, one for each major segment of your product line. Whatever you do, don't use the address of your host system if you are outsourcing your site. This creates a long, cumbersome address that is hard to remember and hard to type. And it implies that your company is not serious or substantial enough to have its own Web server. Most hosting services will allow you to create a virtual domain name.

2. Register with the Web Directories and Search Engines. On the Internet, searchability is everything. Because access is separate from content, you must put up as many pointing signs to your site as possible to flag down prospects as they speed by on the highway.

The best pointing signs are the Web directories and search engines like Yahoo, Lycos, OpenText, Alta Vista and WebCrawler, to name a few of the larger ones. Registering your site under the appropriate classifications is analogous to placing ads in highly targeted print media. When a prospect wants to know about something that you're selling, chances are they will start searching by keyword at a Web directory. You want to be one of the sites that come up on the search.

3. Carefully Choose Index Keywords to Help Your Market Find You. Some directories do their own indexing through robots (alternately called bots, worms, crawlers, or spiders), which are search engines that poke around the Web identifying and indexing sites. And all the major directories allow visitors to mount their own key word searches.

When a crawler trolls through your site, you want to make sure that it picks up and registers all the key words that express the appeal of your product or service. The way to do this is through the copy on your home page, and an Index Keyword file. A keyword file is a "commented out" section on your home page that is not visible on users' screens, but can be read by robots, crawlers, and spiders.

Think of this file as a thesaurus of the concepts about, and benefits of, your product or service. You must pick these words well. The more you dilute your concept with tangential words, the more tangential your visitors will be. Instead, key off benefits, features, and the category of product or service you are offering. Key off words that express your solution, your product name, and your company name.

For example, keywords for a free-lance copywriter who specializes in magazine circulation promotion might include these words:

Circulation

Copy

Copywriting

Creative

Direct mail

Direct marketing

Direct response

Free-lance

Magazine

Promotion

Response

Writer

4. Get the Word Out to Your "Virtual Community." Your virtual community is the affinity group you are seeking to locate. It is comprised of individuals spread all over cyberspace. Getting the word out means—

- Buying links or banner ads on related online locations, including the all-important directories. (I say buying and not "trading" because I don't recommend linking out of your site. More on that below.)

- Posting notices on the commercial services' discussion forums.

- Posting notices to Usenet's newsgroups.

- Contributing to electronic mailing lists in the subject interests of your audience and including your cyberspace address in your signature file.

- Sponsoring an electronic mailing list or discussion forum of your own.

- Consider locating in an online mall, if you find one that specializes in your product, service, or area of interest.

5. Publicize Your Online Address through Traditional Media. Include your cyberspace address in all your print advertising and marketing materials. Make sure it appears on your stationery and business cards. Send press releases announcing the launch of your site or changes to your existing site to newspapers, magazines, and newsletters, as well as online publications like electronic magazines.

NAVIGATION AND DESIGN ISSUES

Structure Your Site around the Offer—And Ask for a Response.

Just as in traditional direct marketing, you must make an offer. And to be most effective, your offer must be the centerpiece of your site. Why make an offer? For the same reasons you make one in traditional direct marketing: because the offer is the action lever that motivates the prospect to respond, to respond *now*. Your offer should appear on every screen, along with your call to action.

How Well You Structure Your Site Is as Important as How Well You Express Benefits.

Moving through cyberspace requires more conscious decision making than traditional media. Online navigation is analogous to movement from piece to piece in a traditional direct mail package or section to section in a space ad. Although you cannot control the order in which people read your print pieces, you try to coordinate headlines and subheads so every element combines to tell a compelling story that leads to the order form.

Online media gives you more control over the narrative flow, but you're in more danger of losing the prospect to an impulsive click out of your site. The visitor consciously chooses to make each move. The option to continue is more conscious because clicking the mouse is required anyway—it's either click to the next panel of your narrative, or click out of your site. So you're on a higher tightrope. That's why the design and architecture of the pathways through your online location are very important.

Control the Visitor's Experience.

The key to success is limiting the user's options from any given screen. Instead of creating paths that lead to confusion and exit, you must control your benefit story so the prospect learns about your product or service in the order you want him to.

Just as you order the progression of benefits on your envelope and letter (and columns on a space ad) to heap benefit upon benefit and make your product or service irresistible, so you must order the flow of screens.

A fundamental tension is at work here. People expect freedom in cyberspace. How to reconcile these divergent goals? The answer is to give navigation options, but only limited ones. This applies most at the top portion of your site, while you are telling your benefit story. After the user has experienced the benefits, you can open up the structure and allow more freedom of movement, allowing the prospect to revisit the benefits or leap forward to satisfy a curiosity.

When planning the architecture of your site, take these two initial steps:

1. Make a detailed list of what you want to cover.

   - Benefits
   - Features
   - Illustrations
   - Testimonials
   - Case studies
   - Success stories
   - News releases
   - Data sheets
   - Other information

2. Make a flowchart of how you want the prospect to move through these details. As you design each level or area of your site, you'll develop a logical plan to divide each section into screens.

Design in Tiers.

As a general approach, think of your online site as a building with the lobby on the top floor and the sales and demonstration suites—each with its own small lobby—on the lower floors.

Your home page is where your prospect gets off the elevator, having arrived from the busy highway below. From the lobby, the visitor travels down from level to level, entering sublobbies, which are jumping-off points to suites where you present your sales talk and displays. Each suite represents a group of screens on closely related topics.

The deeper the visitor explores your site, the more specific and feature oriented your screens should be. For example, you might think of a site as a five-story building (Exhibit 11-2).

Start with Benefits, Follow with Features.

Just as you lead with your strongest benefits when writing traditional direct response copy, so you should make sure that your most powerful benefits appear on the first few screens your visitor sees. What better way to keep someone interested and moving through your site than to engage him or her with all the great things that will come from buying your product?

Make Pages Short and Easy to Peruse.

Think in "sound bites." The shorter a screen is, the faster it comes up and the more quickly the user satisfies the drama of anticipation that begins with the click of an icon or hyperlink.

When the user is repeatedly satisfied in this way, he or she experiences a sense of emotional well-being, confident in the intelligence behind the site. And this translates into confidence in your product or service.

If you must have long pages, break them up with links that allow quick navigation to points farther down the long screen.

Restrict the Number of Icons or Links.

Just as you should be brief with your copy, you should restrict navigation options to four to six links or icons. Restricting options also guards

Exhibit 11-2   Architecture of a Direct Response Web Site

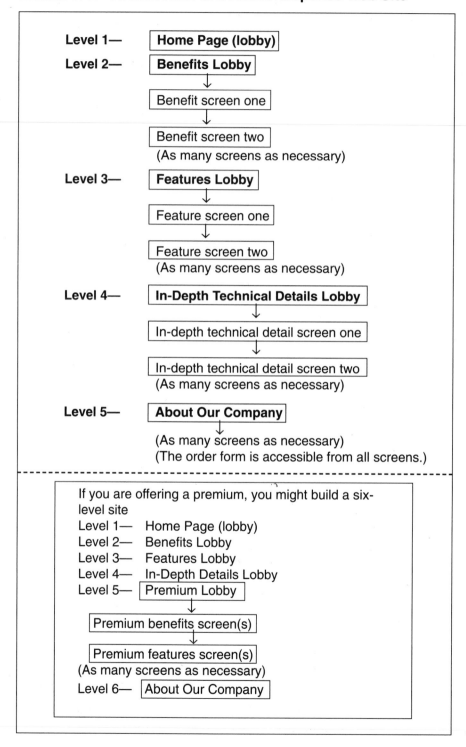

against information overload and confusion. Recent research indicates that people read computer screens 25 percent slower than they read paper-based documents. Also, people are conditioned to looking at TV monitors, where quick glances are necessary to scan information.

Put a Table of Contents or Site Map in the Bottom Half of Your Site.

After you have controlled the visitor's experience at the benefits section at the top of your site, you must recognize the user's inherent freedom by giving him or her the opportunity to navigate at will. So you can "open up" your site after the benefits section. This can be achieved with a wider range of navigation options, or a table of contents, or a map of the site (the ultimate in self-direction) with hot links to each subject entry.

Express Your Navigation Commands as Benefit Headlines.

If you can create a benefit chain that keeps the reader moving from screen to screen, you've got them on the "slippery slope" to a response. Don't force your visitor to go back to a lobby after clicking to a screen. Instead, sell the benefits of moving to the next screen at the same time you sell your product or service. For example, don't write "Next page, please"; write "Click here for fabulous profit opportunities."

Think Visually—Use Images like Words.

Cyberspace is a multimedia, not a text-based, environment. In cyberspace, icons, navigation bars, and other visual stimuli serve as directional and emotional signs. Call it the return of hieroglyphics—or is it the triumph of ideograms?

As a copywriter, you must identify physical world metaphors and invest them with emotional values that will make your visitor act—either to click to the next screen of your narrative, or to respond.

The more you can use the inherent graphical qualities of cyberspace, the better direct response writer you will be. Here's how you can enhance benefit statements by using images that suggest benefits:

Instead of writing "Click here for fabulous profit opportunities," you can shorten your message and quicken its impact with "Fabulous profit opportunities" beside an icon in the form of a dollar sign.

Instead of writing "Click here to save on tires," you can write "Save 25% on tires!" beside an icon in the form of a tire.

Use Visual Metaphors.

Because the experience of "space" is real when the user is online, and the user "enters" your site, visual metaphors are an excellent way to further involve your visitor. For example, you can present screens as offices, showrooms and retail spaces, or express links as items in a room or on a desktop. You can inspire navigation through travel metaphors like doors, archways, paths, and gates. Beware, however, of cliches or overused images.

Create Compelling Cul-de-Sacs.

Just as you include buck slips and lift letters to draw attention to elements you want to highlight in a direct mail package, so you can use "islands" or "cul-de-sacs" as compelling asides to reinforce your selling argument. A cul-de-sac is a screen that leads back to the screen immediately preceding it (and nowhere else). It's a one-stop train that, by virtue of being set aside from the narrative flow, interrupts the user's rhythm and stands apart. In doing so, it reinforces its point. For example:

 Don't Click Here

After visiting the screen, the reader must return to the previous screen to move along on the narrative, and the message in the cul-de-sac stands out.

Don't Link Out!

The technical ability to hyperlink, the cyberspace "gift culture" that values cooperation and giving free information, and efforts to financially support general interest online sites through selling icons and banners has led many people to pack their sites with signposts to other sites.

For someone with a product or service to sell, this is equivalent to greeting customers at your store with directions to your competitors' stores and other interesting places in town.

You want to keep your visitor in your control. Don't link out! Or, if you must include links to other sites, place the links in a special section deep in your site where they will not be discovered until late in the sales visit.

Some sites have an intervening page that stops the visitor when he or she clicks a hyperlink out of the site. It says something like, "You are about to leave our site. Are you sure you want to go? Bookmark us before you leave!"

Make Every Decision Reversible.

No matter how much you must control the user's experience, you also must acknowledge his inherent freedom in cyberspace. Therefore, you should make every decision reversible within an acceptable range of motion.

A general rule of thumb is that users should always be able to move to:

- Home page at the top of your site

- Back one screen

- Forward one screen

- If the reader is deep in a site with multiple tiers, he or she should be able to get back to the top of each tier.

16 Touchstones for Persuasive Online Copywriting

1. *Start strong: Your "Home Page" or "Splash Page" is your outer envelope and your headline.* As in all forms of direct response copywriting, you have 3 to 5 seconds to make an initial impression and hook the visitor's attention in cyberspace. This means that the first screen your prospect sees is the most important screen in your site. That's where you have to inspire your visitor to click into your selling narrative. You do this by leading with your strongest benefit, or the most provocative or informative thing you can say, as you do with teaser copy on your outer envelope or the headline on your space ad.

   All the rules of headline writing apply to your home page. A few additional rules are unique to cyberspace:

   - Don't burden your home page with a large, slow-loading graphic. When a user accesses your site, he or she wants a quick climax to the drama of anticipation.

- Don't try to be "cool." The price you'll pay in slow loading isn't worth the impression you'll make.
- Don't fill up your first screen with your logo. Your logo isn't as interesting as you think it is. It doesn't promise a benefit or impart useful information. Instead, favor a bold, attention-getting headline.
- Get the reader off the first screen as soon as possible and into the narrative flow of your benefit story.
- Make sure your navigation buttons or bar do not extend below the live portion of the screen. Don't start people off scrolling. Start them clicking.

2. *Include a letter!* Put a short introductory letter on your home page or second page! Don't be afraid of importing this technique from traditional mail. What's more personal than a letter? What adds intimacy and a human touch better than a me-to-you voice? The letter can be straight text, without embedded hyperlinks, followed by benefit-oriented icons or navigation buttons. Or it can be sprinkled with hyperlinked benefit statements. You can even include a photo of the signatory for a more emotional effect.

3. *Use a second letter—like a lift note or "publisher's letter."* A second letter, which operates like a cul-de-sac, gives the user a chance to interact with a second voice. This adds a further degree of humanness to the site and emphasizes the message being offered in the second letter.

4. *Clickable words, phrases, and sentences automatically stand out as action devices. Take advantage of them!* Clickable words function like subheads. By virtue of their blue color, the fact that they are underlined, and the drama of anticipation they raise in the user, they immediately draw the eye.

   They are participation devices. Involvement devices. To make them work for you, they should be phrased as benefit statements or headline-type statements. Here are hyperlinked benefit statements from the text of a letter: "You can launch with full editorial independence and complete freedom from technology concerns. For a low cost that will surprise you."

Underlined phrases work as independent benefit statements to the reader who is scanning. This copy accompanied icons at the bottom of a screen:

 "<u>Your investment can be as low as $zero</u>."

 And "<u>Earn income from four sources.</u>"

5. *Every screen should have a call to action or a hyperlink to a response mechanism.* You can't know on which screen your prospect will decide to respond, or when he or she will have a question you can answer. So every page must remind your visitor that help—or the satisfaction of ordering—is quickly at hand. A call to action on every screen (even if it's a helping statement and not a request for the order) also reinforces the idea that you want a response. The call to action can include buttons or live e-mail links.

"If you'd rather skip this and talk with a person, call Donna Baier Stein at…"
"Interested in finding out more? Print this page and call us at your earliest convenience."
"Have a question? <u>Click here</u> and we'll get right back to you."

6. *Put your online address and your phone number on every screen.* Often visitors will print your Web site or online ad and save it to read later. Because you can't control whether the user's browser will print your address, you should make sure that every page contains your online address to that users can find their way back to you. Also, include your phone number because some people will want to ask questions or place an order "in person."

7. *Create customer intimacy.* Users are in "inner space"; the online experience is inherently intimate. You can exploit this advantage to make your online presence as personal as possible. Some ideas:

- Write to the prospect—use the word "you."
- Establish affinity with the visitor by using the language of his or her profession or interest group.
- Keep the prospect involved.

You can also use personalization to further the sense of one-to-one marketing. With technologies that allow personalization on the fly, it's possible to personalize every panel of your Web site or online ad. This requires the user to sign in at top of the site. Many consumers are resistant to this, however, either for privacy's sake or due to inertia, so you'll have to make a great promise or offer a premium to get visitors to enter information about themselves at the top of your site.

8. *Keep the reader surprised and engaged.* What's deadly to all copywriting—for all media—is predictability. If the prospect can anticipate what's next, they're bored. If they're bored, they're emotionally disengaged. If they're disengaged, they're ready to exit.

Be bold and inventive with words and images. This will get attention and provoke action. Ask a provocative question. Give information. Promise a giant benefit. All the tricks to good copywriting apply. The important thing is that the payoff must be commensurate with the promise. Otherwise you risk alienating your prospect. And you can't be trivial. Being trivial destroys your credibility. These examples show inventive use of narrative directions:

  Secret #3

  Are you ready for the price?

Upon clicking the icons and arriving at these screens, your prospect must be satisfied with the payoff. Otherwise, you lose him or her.

9. *Write in commands—give instructions.* Begin action sentences with verbs. Cyberspace is more of an action medium than any other

direct response venue. Because the reader must propel himself or herself to the next screen or activity, you must be constantly but subtly directive, as you might be in an instructional manual:

Press here...

Enter here...

To keep the reader surprised and engaged, try giving operational commands gently and with a light touch (and whenever possible in the language of the product or service you are selling). Imagine these lines as hotlinks beside appropriate icons:

Experience the wonder of...

Take an amazing trip to...

Delight your imagination with...

Challenge the status quo at...

10. *Use visual images to break up copy.* Cyberspace is inherently visual, and reading text on a computer screen is harder than reading text on a piece of paper. Don't overwhelm visitors with a tidal wave of words. Use photos, drawings, cartoons, charts, and diagrams to open up your screens. Also, always include a caption with an image. The eye is first drawn to the image, then invariably to the caption. Captions are great places to state a benefit or tout an important feature.

11. *Use image maps to sell.* Image maps are graphic images like photographs or drawings that allow users to click on sections of them to link elsewhere. (See Exhibit 11-3). One image map can have many discrete clickable areas. Image maps are ideal for product shots. The user can click on a part of the product to receive more detailed information about the benefits and features of that part. You can link to video or audio clips to bring alive parts of an image. It is important that you make sure the clickable regions are obvious. And it is a good idea to include hotlinked call-outs for those with their graphics turned off.

12. *Make image choices based on download time.* You must always be aware of download time. The most important consideration is

Exhibit 11-3   Image Map

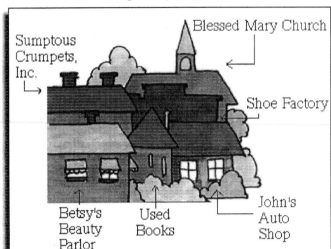

Source: Reprinted with permission of Holland Mark Martin.

whether your audience is comprised of corporate users with fast data access or consumers online with slow modems.

A good rule of thumb is: Don't make your visitor wait more than 15 to 20 seconds for a page. If you are appealing to consumers or small businesspeople, that means you'll have to restrict yourself to small images. Some hints:

- Don't use backgrounds unless your audience has fast data access.

- Use "thin graphics"—two-color images or minimized color palettes.

- Design horizontally oriented graphical elements where possible. The commonly used GIF format is oriented from the top-left across each line, down to the subsequent line until the bottom right point is reached. Vertical expanses of color do not see as much savings in graphic size.

13. *Make your site as long as it needs to be to tell your story.* Long copy or short copy? Deep site or shallow? The age-old debate continues into the new realm of online media. And the answer remains today what it has always been. People will read long copy—or stay at your online location for an extended period of

time—if you keep their attention riveted. So include as much content as necessary to tell your story.

14. *Include a total product summary screen that leads only to the response form.* At some point your visitor may tire of your screen-by-screen narrative and want the big picture fast. Try putting all the major features and price details on a single screen and locate the screen at the end of the benefits section, and at subsequent intervals. Allow only two links out: to the order form, or back to the previous screen.

15. *Forget about "cool," think "effective."* Although this book isn't about design, copy is so tightly related to traditional design considerations in online media that a few comments are in order:

    - First and foremost, cool (trendy) is not synonymous with good. Response-oriented simplicity and purposeful interactivity are more important than "Wow!"
    - There is an inherent tension between the desire to create a clean, organized, minimal visual presentation (to conserve bits and speed downloading time) and the need for visual variety. Don't be a slave to consistency! As direct response master Denny Hatch puts it, "Consistency rejects involvement." Keep the eye moving.
    - Consider how the graphics may appear on various browsers.
    - Make sure your menu bar or basic navigation area is simple, clear, and intuitive to use.
    - Don't use hot new technologies just because they're available. Your presence in cyberspace can include images, sound, and video. But do your visitors have the technology to use these applications? If they don't, their confusion and frustration will cost you sales.

16. *Show your face!* People respond emotionally to faces. By "showing your face" you will make an emotional connection to visitors. Demonstrate that there are living, breathing people on the other end of the wire to offer help and solutions.

    How to do this? Because you have an unlimited number of bits at your disposal, reserve a section near the bottom of your online presence where you—

    - Include photos and biographical profiles of employees who have contact with customers.

- List your company's officers, with their areas of responsibility, professional biographies, and e-mail addresses.
- Encourage prospects to contact your executives.
- Tell your corporate story. Show your offices.

THE REPLY FORM

Just as in print-based direct marketing, the reply form is the moment of truth. Whether your goal is to receive an order, get permission to send more information, collect answers to a survey (or anything else), all the tactics and techniques you learned in Chapter 5 apply. In addition, you can do several things to enhance the power of your electronic reply form.

Place a Hyperlink to the Reply Form on Every Screen.

The first rule of reply forms is to keep them in front of the prospect. In cyberspace, you do this by making your response form accessible from every screen. Not only does this allow your prospect to respond on impulse, but the reply form's presence is a constant reminder that you are requesting an action.

This is a distinct advantage over direct mail, where a reply form can get lost in the shuffle of paper. It's more like a space ad, where the coupon is always visible, or a TV commercial where the 800-number remains on the screen.

Make the Reply Form Look Like a Reply Form.

Some direct marketers restate savings and benefits on the reply. Others include a photograph of the product. Still others favor a clean, utilitarian form with no extraneous information. No matter which camp you are in, tip your hat to tradition and give your reply form a familiar look. For example:

- Place an offer-reinforcing headline and subhead at the top of the screen.

- Clearly state what you want the user to do.

- Use simple fields that are easy to understand and easy to complete.

- Make sure your contract language spells out your offer clearly.

- Don't ask for too much information from the respondent.

- Don't force the respondent to choose between too many product or offer options. Choices inhibit response.

- Use graphics such as postage stamp images or a "BRE look" (with appropriate postal markings) to reinforce the idea of response.

Give Alternatives for Placing the Order.

Because some people may be uncomfortable with online ordering, the order form should include all the options available for ordering. (This is not the same as offering too many product/offer choices.) Your online order form should include your:

- E-mail address

- Fax number

- Telephone number

- Postal mail address

Remember to tell the user they can respond in these ways.

Address Security and Satisfaction Fears—Offer a Guarantee.

Prominently place a guarantee on or adjacent to the ordering area. Encourage your customer to print out the guarantee and the order form. As you have already learned, the more generous the guarantee, the better. Your guarantee should include assurances about the security of credit card transactions at your online presence, if you are soliciting them. You might consider placing the guarantee in a cul-de-sac for emphasis.

Say "Thank You" to All Respondents—and Give Them a Receipt.

After the prospect places an order, program your server to produce a personalized thank-you note that appears as the order is received. In addition to thanking the user for the order, make the thank you a receipt: give customer service names and phone numbers, when to expect delivery, a confirmation number, a guarantee, and any other relevant information to make the prospect feel appreciated and well taken care of. And remind the respondent to print out the thank-you form.

A word about following up via e-mail: It is perfectly legitimate to try to capture e-mail and postal addresses and other customer contact information in cyberspace. However, you must take particular care if your plan includes following up via e-mail.

You might suspect that if a visitor has responded, you have the visitor's implicit permission to e-mail commercial solicitations in the future. Although logic suggests this, you would be wise to exercise caution. The respondent might not remember responding to you, and so whether you are "right" or not, you may be perceived as inappropriate and intrusive.

The best approach is to ask for permission to send follow-up materials by e-mail. For example, position your future e-mail as a service: "To receive continuing updates by e-mail, click here." Or, "May we contact you by e-mail with future details?"

CONCLUSION

Online direct marketing is still a developing art, and we have only touched the surface here. The more you study this book and develop your copywriting skills, the more effective you will be at persuading people to act using words. And the more you explore the multimedia possibilities of online marketing, the more you will be able to link words with images, sound, video, and narrative structure to inspire responses from your online visitors. Three checklists follow and provide a wrap-up of ways to find your prospects and leads in cyberspace, as well as suggestions for measuring traffic on your Web site.

CHECKLIST A: TEN WAYS TO FIND YOUR PROSPECTS IN THE DISAGGREGATED MASS OF THE INTERNET.

As you have learned, a postal mailing list is an affinity group. It is also a luxury you do not have in cyberspace. So your marketing efforts must include identifying and assembling your affinity group on your own. This is like flagging down prospects as they speed by on a highway. It's not easy, but here are some ways it can be done:

☑ House your online site or presence in an "Internet Mall" where your target audience is likely to congregate.

☑ Use Index Keywords words so robots and crawlers looking for specific products, services, or topics will find you.

☑ Buy banners (advertisements) in the right classifications on the Web directories or appropriate sections of the online services.

☑ Participate in relevant Usenet discussion groups and include your online address in your signature file.

☑ Participate in e-mail lists on your subject.

☑ Participate in forums on all the commercial online services and include your online address in your signature file.

☑ Put your online address on your print advertisements, stationery, business cards, bumper stickers, shop windows, and any other communications vehicles you maintain with customers.

☑ Send a postcard direct mailing to announce your online presence and invite prospects to visit.

☑ Distribute news releases to the media about your new site or changes to a current site.

☑ Send e-mail selectively to people notifying them of your site. (See Checklist B on e-mail etiquette.)

CHECKLIST B: TEN WAYS TO GET ONLINE LEADS

Here are some tactics for getting leads. You will recognize several of these as traditional direct response techniques, but others are unique to cyberspace.

☑ Offer a premium. Give away an online document, downloadable software, a disk, a T-shirt, a white paper, additional print information—anything that will appeal to your audience—in return for submitting name and address.

☑ Offer a free e-mail newsletter. Newsletters are much less expensive to distribute in cyberspace than via postal mail. Using relationship building as a guiding principle, consider an e-mail newsletter as a way to keep prospects informed about what you're doing, and keep your name in front of them. Position your e-mailing as a service. Say something like "Please register to receive ongoing news about our [product]." After you have them on your list, send short, informative newsletters on a regular basis.

☑ Require registration to enter a portion of the site. After whetting your visitor's appetite with benefits at the top of your Web site or online ad, follow with a gateway to the rest of the site (or a particular tree) that can only be entered by signing up.

☑ Require registration to get access to an online document. Instead of restricting a section of your site, require registration to see a particularly valuable document.

☑ Require registration to receive a demo of the product or download software. Try not restricting anything—but offer more to those who are willing to register. Downloadable software and video and audio clips are possibilities.

☑ Include a worksheet. A worksheet is a particularly valuable vehicle. It is interactive and therefore involving. The prospect's needs and interests are the centerpiece. It provides free information that the prospect can use (i.e., it is a service), and the prospect supplies his or her own data input.

☑ Offer a sign-in guestbook. Solicit comments about your Web site or online ad, your product, or any other relevant topic. If the comments can be read by others, like on an online forum, your guestbook can be a stopping point for visitors.

☑ Ask visitors to fill out a survey. You'll have to offer a significant incentive to make a survey work, because you're asking for the visitor's time and effort, and you're seeking information that may be perceived as private. Nevertheless, with the right incentive (an offer), a survey is worth a try.

☑ Encourage a dialog with prospects. Actively solicit questions by e-mail directed at your sales department or top executive.

CHECKLIST C: HOW TO CODE SPACE ADS OR OTHER MEDIA TO MEASURE THE AMOUNT OF TRAFFIC THEY GENERATE ON YOUR WEB SITE.

If you are running your online address in space ads or other media, you'll want to track which ads or media are most effective in attracting visitors to your site. You can achieve this by coding the Internet address you give. You have probably seen the familiar "Dept. xxx" on reply addresses, or "Ext. xxx" on 800-telephone numbers. These are response codes for situations where a precoded order form is not being returned.

☑ An analogous coding strategy for the Web is to assign a different online address (URL) for each space ad or media source that directs people to your site. For example,

- Space ad "A": http://www.yourcompany.com/a
- Space ad "B": http://www.yourcompany.com/b
- Space ad "C": http://www.yourcompany.com/c

☑ Upon keying this address, the visitor can be greeted with a thank you that is versioned for the publication of origin, such as "Thank you for your interest in our ad in magazine "A"! We hope you enjoy your next few minutes at our site." You can then send the visitor directly to your home page.

☑ But, if you're interested in knowing which Web directories are generating the most traffic for you, you must assign a different URL to your entire site for each directory. This is because some search engines index every page of a site, and you won't be able to control where a visitor enters your site.

☑ To keep one domain name but have a discretely different address for each Web directory, place the code immediately after your domain name on every page. For example:

- Web directory "A": http://www.yourcompanya.com

- Web directory "B": http://www.yourcompanyb.com

- Web directory "C": http://www.yourcompanyc.com

☑ You can code e-mail reply addresses. For example,

- JXL2@www.yourcompany.com
- JXL3@www.yourcompany.com
- JXL4@www.yourcompany.com

Jeff Laurie is a direct response and online marketing consultant based in Cambridge, Massachusetts. He specializes in magazine circulation promotion and affinity group marketing and customer retention programs.

12

THE ETHICS OF ADVERTISING

The following headline ran over a recent news article in the *Richmond Times-Dispatch*: "Girls to study ad techniques to resist wiles." The staff writer for the paper went on to describe a $164,205 federally financed project to teach seventh-grade girls "the subtleties of the advertising trade." The project's goal? To deter drinking and smoking. Its methods? Teaching marketing techniques to the girls. A supporter of the project is Bronwyn Blackwood, a health educator with the University of Virginia's Institute for Substance Abuse Studies. In her words, "We want them (the girls) to be able to look at advertising and tell exactly how it was put together, what group they're targeting and what message they're trying to convey. We want the girls to be able to fend it off."

This is the world we as direct marketers work in, and we ignore society's increasing savvy, skepticism, and strict standards at our peril. Distrust of advertising isn't new. Way back in 1758, Samuel Jackson wrote, "Advertisements are now so numerous that they are very negligently perused, and it is therefore become necessary to gain attention by magnificence of promises, and by eloquences sometimes sublime and sometimes pathetic."

One of the best defenses of advertising is John O'Toole's *The Trouble with Advertising*, published in 1981. In it, O'Toole, former chairman of the board of Foote, Cone, and Belding outlines a contract that he believes exists between advertisers and the American public. As you read that contract reprinted here, consider for yourself if you think it still applies in today's world:

> I'm an advertiser. You're a consumer. I'm going to communicate to you through advertising. Now, advertising, as we both know, is salesmanship functioning in the paid space and time of mass communications media. That's all it is. Like any salesman, its purpose is commercial. It's going to present products and services in their best light. It's not going to tell you what's good about the other guy's product or service. There are plenty of ways for you to find out about that (see my competitor's contract under separate cover). It's going to be corny at times; maybe there'll be a little too much of it now and then. We're all human.
>
> But I promise you this. My advertising won't lie to you, and it will not deliberately try to mislead you. It won't bore the hell out of you or treat you as though you were a fool or embarrass you or your family. But remember, it's a salesman. Its purpose is to persuade you to trade your hard-earned cash for my product or service.
>
> In return for your putting up with all this, I'm going to support those newspapers and magazines and radio stations and TV programs you like so much. I'm going to pay for music, situation comedies, news, stories, movies, variety shows, football games, cartoon shows and reportage on every aspect of life you may be interested in.
>
> In the process you'll get a lot of important information to help you make informed choices. And you'll get what those lawyers call "puffery." You'll get news about new products you'll like, and you'll be persuaded to try some you'll never buy again. That's the way it goes.
>
> What do you say? Is it a deal? Great. I'm glad we understand each other.

Whether targeting susceptible children or seniors or anyone, your single most important ethical responsibility in writing direct mail copy lies in telling the truth. Usually, you can do this and still put your product or service in a good light. If you can't, maybe you shouldn't be selling what you're trying to sell..

Here's what Dorothy Kerr, former chair of the Direct Marketing Association Committee on Ethical Business Practices and current director of database marketing and strategic information for Strong Funds, has to say about copywriting ethics in today's world:

> When I started out as a copywriter, I was told that the more I knew about my intended audience, the better I would be able to write.

Back then, whatever information we were given was processed only through our minds and imaginations. Using individual data in our copy—even if it had been available—was simply impractical for any kind of mass marketing.

But now things have changed. It's possible to cost-effectively store ever-increasing amounts of information about our prospects and customers. New technologies allow us to use that data not only for targeting purposes but also to create a seemingly infinite number of variations of our letters, based on different data elements.

With all that power available to us, it's tempting to use it, to create a tour de force filled with the display of our knowledge of the individual consumer. To the consumer, however, our efforts are likely to be regarded not as friendly one-on-one communications but rather a demonstration of invasion of privacy.

As writers, we need to keep in mind that what we can appropriately write to customers with whom we have established a relationship differs from what we can say to prospects. Customers have come to expect organizations with which they do business to know something about their preferences and buying patterns, and generally they are not bothered by such a reference in copy.

Prospects, however, are another matter. Quite often they are enraged when a letter mentions their birthdate, names of their children, make of car they drive, or similar information they consider private. It doesn't really matter whether they themselves made the information available. Even those who willingly filled out surveys that provided the data are not likely to remember a few months later.

Our challenge, as writers, is to use all of the data available as background to help us understand what will appeal to our target group and to help us develop the benefits most likely to sell. As a matter of fact, it comes right back to using our minds and imaginations to picture our prospects and to develop sales copy, just as the best copywriters have always done. Now, though, we also must take care to avoid the temptation of using personal information unwisely, just because the technology to do so exists.

In addition to responsible use of personal information, we need to avoid both deliberate deception and promising too much in our copy.

When he founded Time-Life Books, Jerry Hardy said: "Give the customer more value than he has a right to expect." Although as writers, we may not have much influence on the value offered to consumers, we can make sure that we are not guilty of setting the consumer up for disappointment through our copy. If a product or service has little appeal if described accurately, perhaps we should question whether we want to be involved.

Unfortunately, when it comes to deception, there are a few well-known copywriters who have taken the position that the ends justify the means. That's very shortsighted. Even though we may be able to increase response in the short term by using deceptive techniques, we need to think about longer-term effects. Is a slight lift in response worth the damage that is done to our industry by turning prospects into cynics? Or, even worse, into vocal critics of direct marketing?

Challenge yourself to find better creative solutions than government look-alike envelopes, or solicitations in the guise of an invoice, or phony checks. And take responsibility for helping clients understand the importance of ethical practices in direct marketing.

Why do we need to pay attention to consumer concerns? Not just because it's the right thing to do. Not just because it's good for business in the long run. As writers, we all need to operate ethically because if we don't, the pressure for government intervention could result in direct marketing as we know it being legislated out of business.

Come up with your own "rules of business." If you say you'll deliver a job by such-and-such a date, do it. Work for reputable companies. Treat the people with whom you work—clients, suppliers, colleagues and competitors—fairly. Avoid "questionable" formats and techniques like fake checks, illegal sweepstakes, luring readers to your Web site by showing a color photo of a bare-breasted woman like one real estate firm in the United Kingdom recently did. And tell the truth in every word of copy you write.

The Direct Marketing Association publishes *Guidelines for Ethical Business Practice*. This brochure describes principles of conduct like Article #1, Honesty:

All offers should be clear, honest, and complete so that the consumer may know the exact nature of what is being offered, the price, the terms of payment (including all extra charges), and the commitment involved in the placing of an order. Before publication of an offer, direct marketers should be prepared to substantiate any claims or offers made. Advertisements or specific claims which are untrue, misleading, deceptive, fraudulent, or unjustly disparaging of competitors should not be used.

Of the 42 other articles, 21 relate directly to honesty, covering topics like clarity, print size, actual conditions, identity of seller, solicitation in the guise of an invoice, and more. You can obtain a copy of this excellent handbook by writing the Direct Marketing Association's Ethics and Consumer Affairs Department at 1111 19th Street, NW, Suite 1100, Washington, D.C. 20036-3603. Or call them at 202-955-5030.

As direct response copywriters, our task can be an important one, for selling is a two-way human interaction. And if selling can be accomplished with honesty and dignity for both parties involved, that can pave the way for other human interactions to follow that pattern, too.

The only way we can enter our increasingly interactive future confidently is if we speak the truth and see with clear vision. If we remember that our direct marketing message is targeting neither a ZIP code, a database, nor a list, but a human being. And if we use words well to wend our way into that individual's head and heart, thereby enriching our targeted prospects, ourselves, and the entire direct response process.

Epilogue: The Copywriter's Toolbox

Words are what motivate. Words are what sell.

We have been stressing the importance of the tools that enable a copywriter to write on target: databases, mailing lists, marketing research, testing, and analyses. These are the tools that feed your words, that make them work as effective copy.

In the minds of most copywriters, however, copy—the word—is king. Without copy, you don't have an offer to present. Without copy, you can't speak to your target audience and you have no way to close the sale. Without copy, you are not just shooting from the hip, you're not firing anything at all.

But words are slippery things. There are times when nearly finished copy comes to a writer almost effortlessly; at other times, even the roughest draft can't be had at any price. The writer's struggle with the word, in fact, is nearly proverbial: not least because of the volumes of words that have been written on the subject! A search for the word "write" in the CD-ROM version of the *Columbia Dictionary of Quotations* will turn up more than 700 entries. By comparison, searches of "sex," "dies," and "eat" will turn up 289, 240, and 139 entries, respectively.

Just by the sheer weight of the quotations, the casual observer might suppose that writing is a well-understood process. After all, people have had more quotable things to say about it than they've had to say about eating, dying, and sex combined! But the quotations actually do very little to illuminate the process. They range from the fearsome: "To write is a humiliation" (author and critic Edward Dahlberg) to the tragic: "Often I think writing is a sheer paring away of oneself leaving always something thinner, barer, more meager" (novelist F. Scott Fitzgerald). Many of the 723 others are every bit as discouraging as these two.

Does that mean that the writing process is all pain and suffering? Not at all. The truth is, writing *can* be very difficult, but it doesn't have to be impossible. Writing is a craft, and, as is the case with any craft, there are techniques, "tricks." In this chapter, we're going to discuss the writing process itself—not what to write, but how to "prime the pump" and keep it flowing. Some of these techniques are true for writing generally, whereas others are specific to copywriting.

THE ABILITY TO MAKE IDEAS

To produce ideas when you need them, you need to understand something about creativity. Surprisingly, creativity is a fairly new concept. William James's classic text, *Psychology: The Briefer Course*, makes no mention of it. And it's only been during the last 20 to 30 years that techniques to enhance creativity have been commonly available. It's wordless thinking that generates ideas. You may find that you get most of your ideas when you're walking or swimming or running. Slow, repetitive, mindless action helps. Maybe you get your best ideas when you're taking a shower or right before you fall asleep at night. Whatever time is best for you, take note of it. Make an idea-generating activity a daily part of your life. In the midst of deadlines and pressure, only a clear head will be receptive to ideas.

Deadlines, moods, pressure. Sometimes it seems the world conspires to keep you from altering your perspective on it, which is what it takes to create ideas. But when you're stuck for an idea in a writing project, try laying aside the writing and do something else, something that forces you into wordless thinking. Something that puts the ever-vigilant critic in your head to sleep long enough for some ideas to come out.

There's a lot of theory behind the right-brain/left-brain duality that you don't need to understand in order to boost your creativity a little. What you do need to understand (and it's a point you'll see in all the creativity books) is that the way to get ideas is to suspend your judgement about them. If you want to make ideas, stop evaluating them. And this is what nearly all the creativity-building exercises come down to: suppressing the verbal, sequential, critical part of your mind that evaluates things. You can always evaluate your ideas later, after you have some.

Even ideas that seem bad can be valuable. They often lead to good ideas. Creativity is *not* a sequential process. The evaluative part of your mind wants to go step by step, but new ideas don't come from steps. If you've ever heard the story of Archimedes in his bath or Kekule's dream of snakes and the benzene ring, then you know the really grand ideas seem to come out of nowhere. They are not usually the result of sequential steps. In fact, trying to find them through sequential steps means they will always be hidden from you.

Sometimes you can work intensely on a letter for a day or so and you generate a lot of words and you do a lot of deep thinking, but the letter just doesn't seem to come together. Then you have to quit for the day and the letter comes together in your mind when you're in bed, or taking a shower, or riding the bus home. That's one way of getting ideas. Immerse yourself completely in the project and them change your scene and think about something else. *But immersion is the necessary first step.* If you try to simply change your scene without enough immersion beforehand, you're not giving yourself ideas, you're procrastinating!

What follows is a small catalog—by no means exhaustive—of resources you can tap to generate ideas and familiarize yourself with the product you'll be selling.

THE INFORMATION INVENTORY

Although you will need to generate ideas, writing does not mean creating information. For most writers, all the information they will ever need has already been created. Writing means arranging information. Outfit yourself with a reference library of a dozen well-chosen volumes, and then you will have an inventory of information to draw on. Go to your reference library, take out some information, and arrange it artfully in your own words. Bingo! You're writing.

What do you need in your information inventory? Here are half a dozen types of resources:

Quotations

Bartlett's Familiar Quotations is comprehensive and easy to use. Or try *The Columbia Dictionary of Quotations* (part of Microsoft Bookshelf) mentioned earlier. It's available on CD-ROM and offers a variety of information.

Sometimes you need a quotation because you simply require a sort of authoritative source for something you want to say, but that's only one use. Sometimes you can use a quotation book as a way of inspiring yourself. Sometimes you can even use it to find your theme. A quote from William Wordsworth graced the outer envelope of a package written for the American Psychiatric Association (APA) by expert Washington, D.C.-based copywriter Kate Petranech: "*Is* the child father of the man?" There was no mention of the APA on the outer envelope, only a street address. Inside, Wordsworth's familiar quote from "My Heart Leaps Up"—"The child is father of the man"—opens a flowing 4-page letter. The letter's opening paragraph again asks "Is he? That's what Freud believed, of course…claiming that 'neuroses are only acquired during early childhood.'" The letter goes on enticingly to offer a free copy of a major new study challenging this view as a trial introduction to *The American Journal of Psychiatry*.

Even if your initial quote isn't quite right for your intended audience, write it down and work with it for a little while, maybe something else can come of it. You should never be afraid to do this—most of writing, in fact, is *re*writing. Playing with words and ideas, moving them around in your head and on the paper until they fit together just so. Even if your first efforts aren't any good, they'll always lead to something else.

Dictionaries

An unabridged dictionary is also good to have in your personal library. *The Random House Dictionary of the English Language* is an excellent one, but almost any 12-pound dictionary is a good investment. An unabridged dictionary will not only give you a good solid definition for a word, but it will also explain the word's origins and usage.

You might also invest in an *Oxford English Dictionary* (*OED*), the definitive dictionary of English. It not only gives you a word's definition, but shows you how it has changed through time. There's also a CD-ROM edition of the *OED*.

The *American Heritage Electronic Dictionary* is a particularly good tool because it can help you retrieve a word from the tip of your tongue. If you can't remember what that broad-brimmed hat from the gangster era is called, you call up its search function and type in "hat AND brim." The dictionary will then give you a list of all the words that have those two words in their definitions, one of which is "fedora."

You can also get an unabridged *American Heritage* on CD-ROM as part of Microsoft Bookshelf, and this one has the ability to make your computer pronounce the words you look up. This is a dangerous dictionary to have, because you might end up playing with it when you should be writing. It doesn't matter if it is a paper or electronic version, an unabridged dictionary is absolutely essential if you're going to write seriously.

Encyclopedia

Almost any writing assignment can benefit from an encyclopedia. From a cruise through the Aegean Sea to membership in a zoological garden, almost anything you might be called on to promote, publicize, or market exists as an entry in an encyclopedia. The typical encyclopedia entry gives you a comprehensive introduction, and many of them include bibliographies if you want to go to the public library and get deeper into the topic.

The market has changed in the last decade. You no longer have to bankrupt yourself to own an encyclopedia. For one thing, there are lots of good single-volume desk encyclopedias, such as *The Random House Encyclopedia*, and you can get a CD-ROM–based encyclopedia (the equivalent of more than 20 volumes) for $100 or less. Two good CD-ROM–based encyclopedias are the *Grolier Multimedia Encyclopedia* and *Microsoft Encarta*. You might want to start your writing assignments by checking each one. They are computer software, so they help you look things up in ways you couldn't do with paper. If you have an assignment to sell hiking shoes, for example, you might want to mention some nice places to hike. If you looked up "hike" in the encyclopedia, it just tells how to do it. But when you tell one of these computer software programs to search all the articles for the words "hike" or "hiking," it comes back with a list of 50 entries, dozens of which are places you can hike.

If you don't have a CD-ROM drive or a CD-ROM–based encyclopedia, you can get access to one through an information service like CompuServe or America Online. These information services usually include access to an encyclopedia in the basic membership rate, and they usually have the kind of search capabilities just described.

Almost every writing assignment you will get requires getting a basic background in some topic very quickly. Whether you're doing a fund-raising letter to save grizzly bears or a subscription solicitation for a newsletter on stock funds, an encyclopedia is not a bad place to look in addition to all the client-provided material you'll get. Even if you're writing about your own product, and you think you know it inside and out, you may be surprised at the insights you gain by looking up some aspect of your business *or* your market in an encyclopedia.

Almanacs

Your personal library might also include a current almanac, something you can purchase each year for $12 or $13. One called *The Universal Almanac* has very well-organized statistics, but a number of others are on the market as well. All of them are filled with information on population, the economy, geography, and cultures. They usually have a summary of the current year's biggest news stories. They have a lot of information in a small space. Maybe for your assignment you need to know the population of Missouri or what movie received the Academy Award for Best Picture in 1973. An almanac is the fastest way to get that information.

Another title to include in this resource category is *The Statistical Abstract of the United States*, a book published by the U.S. Government Printing Office every year. You might want to get a new copy every 5 years or so. If you need to know average family size of rural Americans or the per capita ownership of washing machines, such facts are child's play for *The Statistical Abstract of the United States*. The book is almost nothing but numbers, but some of the numbers are fascinating, and the book has the additional virtue of being inexpensive.

Thesaurus

These days, most word-processing software packages have built-in thesauruses. The unabridged version of *Roget's International Thesaurus* is still one of the best tools around for finding the exact word you want.

Miscellaneous Reference Books

There are a number of other sources for you to consider keeping in your information inventory. A world atlas, a handbook of literature, a chronology of events, a grammar book, and other highly specialized reference books are all good possibilities.

USING THIS INFORMATION INVENTORY

You have an assignment. You're going to write a direct mail letter for a real estate agency that wants to build its listings. What do you do first? Get a little research under your belt. Ask the client for all the background information he or she can supply you with: brochures, catalogs, direct mail letters, annual reports, customer testimonials, agent records, anything you can get your hands on. You might even want to ask your client if you can interview some of the listing agents to ask them why they think their agency is best and what makes people list with certain firms.

After you've read the background material and done some interviews, consult your encyclopedia. Read what it says about homes, for instance. You'll be impressed. Then look in your quotation book under "home." Make some notes on this stuff while you're reading, because when you start writing, you'll remember some fact, but you won't remember it exactly, and if you haven't written it down, you'll have to page through everything to find it.

Prewriting research for a lead-generation effort to sell long-term care insurance from The Travelers for Net Plus Insurance Agency, Inc. (an account handled by Boston agency Berenson, Isham & Partners) led to nine pages of computer discoveries. These included a statistic from the *Universal Almanac* on the 44% chance people who reach age 65 have of spending some time in a nursing home,[*] and the fact from the *Grolier Multimedia Encyclopedia* that "Almost no private insurance plans pay for nursing home costs, and patients whose savings or income make them ineligible for Medicaid often face yearly nursing home bills of $50,000 or more."[†] Both were helpful in developing copy.

HOW TO AVOID PROCRASTINATING

While you're doing all your research, guard against procrastination. Reading stuff is almost always easier than writing it, so most of us will keep on reading long after we should have started writing. Don't fall into that trap. The reason research procrastination is especially bad is that it's real work, so you can sometimes do it without any pangs of conscience.

Most of us approach writing with a voice in our ear: "I don't feel like writing now. Maybe I should wait until I feel like writing."

Believe it or not, the surest way to feel like writing is to start writing. All writers know this, but we search continually for ways to start writing without actually putting words on paper. We create elaborate rituals and ceremonies to help us "slip into" the writing process: sharpening our pencils, rolling a fresh sheet of bond paper into the typewriter, cleaning up the files on our hard disk, putting on our writing slippers.

[*]*The Universal Almanac* 1995, edited by John W. Wright. Andrews and McMeel (Kansas City, MO: 1994) ISBN 0-8362-8032-6

[†]The 1995 *Grolier Multimedia Encyclopedia* (Macintosh Version 7.0) Grolier Electronic Publishing (Danbury, CT: 1995) ISBN 07172-3982-9

In general, any activity that doesn't involve putting words on paper is not a writing technique, it is a procrastination technique. That's not to say it's impossible to slip into the writing.

Roland Kuniholm, author of two excellent direct marketing books, *The Complete Book of Model Fundraising Letters* and *Maximum Gifts by Return Mail*, explains how he leaves research and begins to write:

> I have found that the greatest inhibitor to writing a good direct response letter is trying—in your first draft—to convey everything that your copy research has uncovered! It's important to do the research. And learn as much as you can about the offer/product, etc. Immerse yourself in the project. *Then put this information aside.* Temporarily. With too many facts and figures floating around in my mind as I start to write, the feeling part of me tends to get suppressed.
>
> So as I begin to write, I think primarily of how I want to sound to the prospect. What would an effective rhythm for this letter be? How can I achieve the right flair for attracting attention? What are my strongest feelings about this issue or product? When I interview fund-raising executives as background for a direct mail letter, I always like to ask this question: "What gets you mad about this issue?" With the emotional spigot turned on, I usually get the right stuff for a good letter. Strong emotions can make a seemingly dull subject come alive.
>
> After I get that first "rhythm/feeling" draft done, I go back over my copy with a more careful eye to incorporate all the necessary facts. Usually in my first draft, I find I haven't strayed too far afield anyway. Also in a second draft I edit to make sure that certain key principles are followed (e.g., highlighting the offer…asking for a response early and often…making sure I have a readable draft with short sentences and paragraphs, etc.)
>
> Lead with how you feel about a subject…then interweave all the necessary selling facts in your second draft. It works for me!

Top-notch copywriter Kate Petranech is president of her own successful direct marketing agency. She revs up for writing in this way:

> When I was in graduate school and having trouble getting started on a paper, I'd polish my shoes. By the time I was done, I'd be ready to write (as well as have the shiniest shoes in the English Department!) This might sound like a stall, but the gimmick—with variations—still works for me today. Here's how:
>
> Whenever I start a new direct mail package, I read all the resource materials, review my notes, and write a very rough draft of the order

card copy. It helps me focus on the offer. Then I move to the letter lead. If nothing happens after an hour, (i.e., no satisfactory lead), I shift to the outer envelope. Still nothing cooking?

I put everything aside and clean out old files, write overdue letters, pay my bills…whatever job's hanging around. During this time the package is unconsciously rattling around in my brain. Sometimes a headline or some teaser copy actually pops out. Mostly though, this little breather—which might last an hour or a couple of days—helps me break the ice and get comfortable with the job.

Three Ways to "Slip into" Writing

1. Make a List of Points You Want to Cover.

Listing points you want to make in your sales arguments can help you see more points. You can list points until you can't think of any more then re-arrange them in a persuasive order. Little remains of the writing assignment after that besides writing transitions between the points.

Here's a list made to start a letter about endangered species:

(Endangered species letter)

Wildlife sanctuaries slow the rate of extinctions(?)

600 species officially listed as endangered

3,800 species waiting to get on endangered list

Wildlife sanctuaries as libraries of wild creatures (?)

Earth loses 100 species a day

10% of bird species now considered to be endangered

You can make a list consisting of facts and ideas, all mixed up together, designating tentative ideas with a question mark.

Here's an instance of how listing points can help see more points: when we wrote down that the Earth loses 100 species a day, we wondered how many that worked out to per hour. Then we did some calculations and found a new and possibly even more powerful point: The Earth loses another species each and every 14 minutes. With a little word juggling, that point became a pretty attention-grabbing opening sentence for the letter.

Do you see how making a list gets your assignment started?

You may either love or resist using outlines. But after you start using outlining software on your computer, you may discover it can dramatically cut your writing time. Start up the program and list your points as fast as you can without worrying about their order. A good outliner will even let you "attach" stray thoughts to the points as they occur to you. After you've exhausted all your points, arrange them in the most effective order.

If you don't like the linear straitjacket of a list, try **cluster writing**, which is sort of free-form list making. On a clean sheet of paper, write the main topic in the center. Then, as fast as you can think of them, write around it the ideas that occur to you about the main topic. Draw lines to connect the ideas to show their relationships as you write them. Some ideas will generate ideas of their own, which you write around them, drawing lines to show the relationships.

Here is an initial cluster written when a computer company asked for a package inviting managers to attend a seminar on their new approach to creating information systems architectures:

Information Systems Cluster

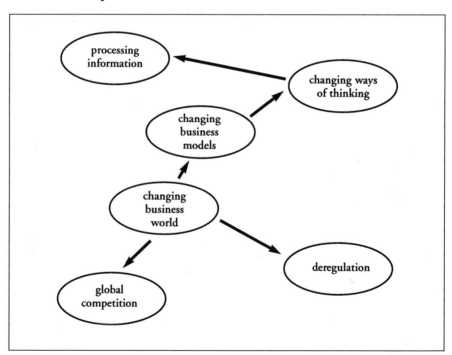

When you do cluster writing, just go as fast as you can. You can worry about getting the ideas in order later. The purpose of this exercise is to generate new ideas, and for a lot of people, it does. Because there doesn't have to be any order to the ideas, this technique helps to get you out of your linear, sequential, critical thinking mode. Getting out of that kind of thinking is essential to generating ideas.

2. Write a Letter to a Friend about the Project.

It's always easier to write something else than it is to write the current project. But if you have a writing assignment hanging over your head, and you can't make yourself work on it, write a letter to someone describing it. It will help if you know someone who's interested in what you're selling.

3. Look at Somebody Else's Work.

Go through the sample mailing pieces you're going to be collecting. You may find great ideas in advertising pieces completely unrelated to the particular product or service you're selling. But jot down any and all ideas—headlines, teasers, salutations. Then begin to improve on other people's work.

Do you notice some similarity in these three techniques? They all involve putting words on paper.

This is the great secret of writing: there is no substitute for getting the words on the paper. People who don't write share this fantasy that the writing exists before the writer sits down and does it. People somehow think there is ready-made copy inside the writer waiting to get out. Remember the story you probably learned in high school about Samuel Taylor Coleridge waking up from a laudanum-induced dream to dash out the mysterious poetic fragment, *Kubla Khan*, in a single sitting?

Whether your task is to write a sales letter, a brochure, or space ad, the words don't exist until you write them. And if you wait for those words to magically appear to you before you start writing, you're going to have to wait for a long, long time.

The act of writing, and nothing else, creates the writing. And the really interesting thing about writing is that doing *some* of it creates *more* of it. Up to a point (a point that's different for every piece of writing, by the way), the more you write about something, the more you have to say about it. The surest way to understand how you feel about an issue is to write about it. Perhaps you've had the experience of writing an essay for school in which your opinion about the issue changed as a result of writing about it. It happens to everybody. All the time. Writing is a generative process.

APPENDIX
Clubs and Associations

Compiled by Berenson, Isham and Partners

Mr. John R. Gustavson
President & CEO
Services
Canadian Direct Marketing Association
1 Concorde Gate
Ste 607
Don Mills, Ontario M3C 3N6
Canada
(416) 391-2362

Ms. Linda Kuschnir
Program Manager
Canadian Direct Marketing Association
1 Concorde Gate
Don Mills, Ontario M3C 3N6
Canada
(416) 391-2362

Ms. Bonnie Wasser
Program Manager
Canadian Direct Marketing Association
1 Concorde Gate
Don Mills, Ontario M3C 3N6
Canada
(416) 391-2362

Mr. James Church
Membership/Computer
Canadian Direct Marketing Association
1 Concorde Gate
Ste 607
Don Mills, Ontario M3C 3N6
Canada
(416) 391-2362

Mr. Scott McClellan
Communications Manager
Canadian Direct Marketing Association
1 Concorde Gate
Don Mills, Ontario M3C 3N6
Canada
(416) 391-2362

Arizona

Ms. Peggy Larson
Administrator
Phoenix Direct Marketing Club
Market Builders
831 North Alvaro Circle
Mesa, AZ 85205-5458
(602) 708-1901

Mr. Keith B. Lawson
President
Phoenix Direct Marketing Club
Market Builders
831 North Alvaro Circle
Mesa, AZ 85205-5458
(602) 641-1901

California

Mr. Robert J. Kweller
President
Direct Marketing Club of Southern
  California
NCM Direct
5037 Mammoth Avenue
Sherman Oaks, CA 91423
(818) 907-9464

Mr. James Elliott
President
San Diego Direct Marketing Club
Western Graphics
7614 Lemon Avenue
Lemon Grove, CA 92045
(619) 466-4157

Ms. Jessica Flavell
President
Northern California Catalog Club
Boudin Bakery
132 Hawthorne Street
San Francisco, CA 94107
(415) 882-1826

Mr. Mark Strockis
President
Direct Marketing Association of Orange
  County
DMA of Orange County
P.O. Box 8002
Newport Beach, CA 92658-8002
(800) 426-6026

Ms. Jan Nathan
Executive Director
Direct Marketing Club of Southern
  California
2401 Pacific Coast Highway
STE 102
Hermosa Beach, CA 90254
(310) 374-7499

Ms. Karen S. Stevens
Executive Director
San Diego Direct Marketing Club
Meeting Dynamics
9747 Business Park Avenue
San Diego, CA 92131
(619) 566-7857

Ms. Deborah Peck
Administrative Assistant
Northern California Catalog Club
365 Quail Run
Aptos, CA 95003
(418) 688-1812

Mr. Walter D. Abraham
President
Northern California Direct Marketing
 Club
Communicolor
500 Sutter Street
Ste 906
San Francisco, CA 94102-1121
(415) 434-1696

Colorado

Mr. David Ariss
President
Rocky Mountain Direct Marketing
 Association
G.A. Wright, Inc.
4010 Holly Street
Denver, CO 80216
(303) 333-4453

Ms. Marilee Yorchak
Executive Administrator
Rocky Mountain Direct Marketing
 Association
2459 South Ammons Street
Lakewood, CO 80227
(303) 986-7611

Connecticut

Mr. Neal Knofla
President
Direct Marketing Association of
 Connecticut
Newton Manufacturing Co.
176-2 Lincoln Street
Waterbury, CT 06710-1548
(203) 757-4404

District of Columbia

Ms. Sherryl M. Marshall
Executive Director
Direct Marketing Association of
 Washington
7702 Leesburg Pike, #400
Falls Church, VA 22043
(703) 821-3629

Ms. Patricia Silver
President
Direct Marketing Association of
 Washington
Silver Marketing Inc.
7910 Woodmont Avenue
Bethesda, MD 20814
(301) 951-3505

Ms. Anne Chalmers
President
Women's Direct Response Group of
 Washington
Chalmers Marketing Group
103 West Monroe Avenue
Alexandria, VA 22301-1921
(703) 548-6440

Florida

Mr. Robert Dunhill
President
Florida Direct Marketing Association
Dunhill International List Company, Inc.
1951 N.W. 19th Street
Boca Raton, FL 33431-7344
(800) 386-4455

Ms. Betty Kaufman
President
Gold Coast Chapter
Florida Direct Marketing Association
8851 N.W. 10th Place
Ste 102
Plantation, FL 33322
(305) 472-6374

Mr. Rod Smith
President
Suncoast Chapter
Instant Web
3235 San Bernardino Street
Clearwater, FL 34619
(813) 724-1624

Mr. Max Hinton
President
Central Florida Chapter
Data Management Associates
1260 Clearmont Street, NE
Palm Bay, FL 32905-4051
(407) 729-0573

Mr. Mitch Talenfeld
Chairman
Gold Coast Chapter
Kar Printing of Florida, Inc.
13930 N.W. 60th Avenue
Miami Lakes, FL 33014
(305) 557-4782

Ms. Colleen Shue
President
Southwest Chapter
Customers First
3521 Tassel Flower Court
Bonita Springs, FL 33923
(813) 495-8918

Georgia

Mr. W. Michael King
President
D.M. Interest Group of the Atlanta Amer.
 Marketing Assn.
King & More!, Inc.
90 West Wieuca Road
Ste 210
Atlanta, GA 30324
(404) 252-0841

Mr. Hub Hardeman
President
DM Group of the Atlanta
Ad Club
Pareto
1148 Franklin Road
Ste G
Marietta, GA 30067
(404) 644-1910

Ms. Sherree Meyers
Vice President
D.M. Interest Group of the Atlanta Amer.
 Marketing Assn.
National Direct Service
460 Englewood Ave., S.E.
Atlanta, GA 30315
(404) 624-5435

Hawaii

Mr. Chuck Fischer
President
Direct Response Advertising & Marketing
 Assn. of Hawaii
Val-Pak Hawaii
1833 Kalakaua Avenue
Ste 1010
Honolulu, HI 96815-1528
(808) 944-2000

Ms. Linda S. Kramer
Vice President
Direct Response Advertising & Marketing
  Assn. of Hawaii
Direct Marketing Managers of Hawaii
Div. of MVNP
700 Bishop Street
12th Fl
Honolulu, HI 96813
(808) 545-2122

Illinois

Mr. Sid Liebenson
President
Chicago Association of Direct Marketing
Draft Direct Worldwide
142 East Ontario Street
Chicago, IL 60611-2818
(312) 944-3500

Ms. Jean Nelson
Executive Director
Chicago Association of Direct Marketing
200 North Michigan
#300
Chicago, IL 60601
(312) 541-1272

Indiana

Ms. Janet I. Harris
President
Direct Marketing Association of
  Indianapolis
Harris Marketing, Inc.
6100 North Keystone Avenue
Ste 427
Indianapolis, IN 46220-2428
(317) 251-9729

Ms. Diana Sparks
President
Direct Marketing Association of
  Indianapolis
American Trucker
7355 North Woodland Drive
Indianapolis, IN 46278
(317) 297-5500

Kentucky

Stacy L. Hollowell
President
Louisville Direct Marketing Association
Electronic Systems USA, Inc.
9410 Bubsen Pkwy.
Louisville, KY 40220
(502) 495-6700

Massachusetts

Ms. Beth Drysdale
Associate Manager
New England Direct Marketing
  Association
6 Abbott Road
Wellesley, MA 02181
(617) 237-1366

Mr. Edward Lupo
President
New England Direct Marketing
  Association
Banta Direct Marketing Group
214 Prospect Street
Brockton, MA 02401
(508) 586-6157

Maryland

Ms. Holly Rich
President
Direct Marketing Association of Baltimore
Doner Direct
400 East Pratt Street
Baltimore, MD 21202
(410) 385-9347

Michigan

Ms. Ann Dixon
First Vice President
Direct Marketing Association of Detroit
Comerica Bank
P.O. Box 75000
Detroit, MI 48275-2325
(313) 222-7814

Ms. Nancy Leavy
President
Direct Marketing Association of Detroit
McCann Erickson Detroit
775 West Big Beaver
Troy, MI 48085
(810) 362-5693

Minnesota

Ms. Laura L. Burkholder
President
Midwest Direct Marketing Association
North American Outdoor Group, Inc.
12301 Whitewater Drive
P.O. Box 3401
Minnetonka, MN 55343
(612) 936-9333

Ms. Karen Wesloh
Executive Director
Midwest Direct Marketing Association
4248 Park Glen Road
Minneapolis, MN 55416
(612) 927-9220

Missouri

Ms. Pauline R. Battiste
President
Direct Marketing Association of St. Louis
ICS Diversified
2392 Gressom Street
St. Louis, MO 63141
(314) 997-1767

Ms. Olivia Golden
Executive Director
Kansas City Direct Marketing Association
638 West 39th Street
P.O. Box 419264
Kansas City, MO 64141-6264
(816) 561-5323

Ms. Sally Arn-O'Brien
Executive Director
Direct Marketing Association of St. Louis
12686 Lonsdale Drive
St. Louis, MO 63044
(314) 291-3144

Ms. Jennifer M. Super
President
Kansas City Direct Marketing Association
Wolferman's, Inc.
8900 Marshall Drive
Lenexa, KS 66215-5916
(913) 541-7803

New York

Mr. Jeffrey E. Danowitz
President
Direct Marketing Club of New York
Deaver-Danowitz
12 East 86th Street
New York, NY 10028
(212) 570-0991

Mr. Brian S. Snieder
First Vice President
Direct Marketing Club of New York
GRI Direct
PO Box 601
Norwalk, CT 06852-0601

Mr. Ron Moss
President
Direct Marketing Idea Exchange
The New York Times
1515 Broad Street
Bldg. B-2
Bloomfield, NJ 07003
(201) 338-8303

Mr. Hank Hoke
President
Long Island Direct Marketing Association
Direct Marketing Magazine
224 Seventh Street
Garden City, NY 11530
(516) 868-1732

Ms. Mary Bonaccio
Co-President
Upstate New York Direct Marketing
  Association
Catalyst Direct, Inc.
333 West Commercial Street
East Rochester, NY 14445
(716) 385-0104

Ms. Carol Rallo
President
Upstate New York Direct Marketing
  Association
Catalyst Direct, Inc.
333 West Commercial Street
East Rochester, NY 14445
(716) 383-6189

Ms. Gail Henry
Co-President
Hudson Valley Direct Marketing Club
Leon Henry Inc.
455 Central Avenue
Scarsdale, NY 10583
(914) 723-3176

Miss Michele Kestin
Secretary
Long Island Direct Marketing Association
Fala Direct Marketing, Inc.
70 Marcus Drive
Melville, NY 11747-4278
(516) 391-0264

Mr. James M. Dellavilla
Co-President
Upstate New York District Marketing
  Association
Chase Manhattan Bank, N.A.
One Chase Square
Rochester, NY 14643
(716) 258-4110

Ms. Danielle Brooks
President
Women in Direct Marketing International
The Polk Company
521 Fifth Avenue
11th Fl
New York, NY 10175-0105
(212) 856-8268

North Carolina

Mr. George Wehmann
President
The Carolinas Direct Marketing
  Association
Direct Marketing Resources Group, Inc.
2524 Birchford Ct.
Raleigh, NC 27604
(919) 990-1441

Ohio

Mr. John Dobbs
President
Cincinnati Direct Marketing Club
Hensley Segal
11590 Century Boulevard
Cincinnati, OH 45246
(513) 671-3811

Mr. Chris McGovern
President
Mid-Ohio Direct Marketing Association
CM Direct Response, Inc.
1973 Inchcliff Road
Columbus, OH 43221
(614) 486-1973

Ms. Jean Gianfagna
President
Northeast Ohio Direct Marketing
  Association
Gianfagna Marketing Communications
2680 Broadmore Lane
Cleveland, OH 44145-2958
(216) 892-4999

Mr. Keith Norris
President
Dayton Direct Marketing Club
Sterling Graphics
3201 N. Dixie Drive
Dayton, OH 45414
(513) 278-0641

Ms. Joyce Affeldt
Vice President-Membership
Northeast Ohio Direct Marketing
  Association
American Mail-Well Envelope
4500 Tiedeman Road
Cleveland, OH 44144
(216) 252-4100

Oklahoma

Mr. Monty Moeller
President
Direct Marketing Association of Tulsa
Moeller Ad Group
250 East First Street
Tulsa, OK 74103
(918) 588-1900

Oregon

Mr. Ronald Lebow
President
Mail/Advertising Service Association of
  America
Four Star Associates
1560 Fifth Avenue
Bay Shore, NY 11706
(516) 968-4100

Mr. Nick Verlotta
President
Oregon Direct Marketing Association
Lynx Communication
2901 Carriage Way
West Linn, OR 97068
(503) 239-8338

Pennsylvania

Mr. Robert Muma
President
Philadelphia Direct Marketing Association
Allen Envelope Corporation
1001 Cassatt Road
Berwyn, PA 19312
(610) 296-0500

Ms. Arlene Claffee
Executive Administrator
Philadelphia Direct Marketing Association
1781 Sentry Parkway West
Ste One
Blue Bell, PA 19422
(215) 540-2257

Texas

Ms. Beth Frysztak
President
Houston Direct Marketing Association
Database America Companies
100 Paragon Drive
Montvale, NJ 07645-0416
(201) 476-2000

Ms. Ellen Reagan
Executive Director
Dallas - Ft. Worth Direct Marketing
  Association
Direct Marketing Association of North
  Texas
4020 McEwen
Ste 105
Dallas, TX 75244-5019
(817) 640-7018

Mr. A.C. Oppermann
President
Dallas - Ft. Worth Direct Marketing
  Association
Personalized Graphics, Inc.
5050 Quorum Drive
Ste 700
Dallas, TX 75240
(214) 663-0588

Mr. Fred Tregaskis
Vice President (Programs)
Dallas - Ft. Worth Direct Marketing
  Association
Fred Tregaskis Consulting Services
267 Oak Hill Drive
Trophy Club, TX 76262
(817) 491-0932

Vermont

Mr. George Duncan
President
Vermont/New Hampshire Direct
  Marketing Group
Duncan Direct Associates
16 Elm Street
Peterborough, NH 03458
(603) 924-3121

Washington

Ms. Jill Eenigenburg
President
Seattle Direct Marketing Association
14504 S.E. 47th Place
Bellevue, WA 98006
(206) 649-0777

Wisconsin

Andrah Grothey
Vice President
Wisconsin Direct Marketing Association
Advent
Box 405 Leon Road
Menomone Falls, WI 53052
(414) 253-3176

Ms. Karen Hendrickson
Executive Director
Wisconsin Direct Marketing Association
2830 North 48th Street
Milwaukee, WI 53210
(414) 873-9362

INDEX